Peggy Tibbetts

Crazy Bitch: Living with Canine Compulsive Disorder

By Peggy Tibbetts

Sisterhood Publications

COPYRIGHT

Published digitally and traditionally by:
Sisterhood Publications
www.sisterhoodpublications.com

Print Edition:
ISBN-10:1-940016-01-0

ISBN-13: 978-1-940016-01-6

Cover design by NM Draney
Photograph by Peggy Tibbetts

Also by Peggy Tibbetts

The Road to Weird
Rumors of War
Letters to Juniper
PFC Liberty Stryker

"Tibbetts is a skilled and masterful writer. This is a book you will want to share with your children, your parents, and your friends."-Natalie R. Collins, author of *Wives and Sisters, Behind Closed Doors, The Fourth World, Sister Wife,* and *Twisted Sister*

Dedication

For Venus.
We will never forget you

Crazy Bitch

Introduction

Writers are animal people. When you read social media outlets like Facebook and Twitter, you hear comments like "my cat is sleeping on my keyboard," or "Finished my pages for today, now the dog needs a walk." We thrive on our furbabies. They offer unconditional love, curling up next to your side on a day when your editor ripped apart your manuscript, or you got yet another rejection letter. They are there, warm, and soft to the touch.

They are our alter egos, our psychologists, our friends.

My dog, Stormy, is an example. He's not the smartest of dogs. I say that with love in my heart, I promise. One time he got into a pack of chewing gum and ate every piece. Now, one would think chewing gum and dogs don't go together. But apparently, Stormy likes gum. But gum does not like him. After we discovered the empty wrappers (how he got them unwrapped without opposable thumbs is beyond me), we did a little research to ensure it wouldn't "gum up" his intestinal system. But it was worse than that. Xylitol, which is used in almost all gums, is deadly for dogs. So he got a trip to the emergency vet and an overnight stay, and I got a $500 bill.

Now people who don't like dogs would say that would be the end. Out you go. But we don't throw away our children, and let's face it: they make equally bad mistakes—if not worse.

So Peggy and her family adopted Venus, discovered she had canine compulsive disorder, and to add to it, was from a temperamental breed, Akbash, that was used primarily for protecting herds of sheep. Off to the pound with you—not. Because Venus was a dog with an irrepressible spirit. She was smart, amusing, and witty—when she wasn't crazy.

Mental illness is still a taboo subject in our society. No one likes to admit someone in their family is "crazy." What does one say when the crazy one is a dog? I know what most people would do. But Peggy Tibbetts is not "most people" and Venus was not just a dog.

She was family. They signed on for life, and they did their best.

When I got a call from Peggy one day, explaining to me the extent to which certain members of their community were going to drive Venus to bark, I told her to get a restraining order. It was that bad. She does not exaggerate this story. She was granted the restraining order, and those aren't easy to get.

These people, we can only assume, do not appreciate life the way we do. They are not prepared to give their all for the animals they bring into their home. I might have mentioned that both Peggy and

Venus are extraordinary.

And this is a story you will never forget. Prepare for a range of emotions you can't keep back. Prepare for anger, pain, and tears. You will cry. And you will wonder why some two-legged creatures are allowed to walk this earth.

Venus was unforgettable. This is her story, told in a way that is also unforgettable.

--Natalie R. Collins—author of the critically-acclaimed *Wives and Sisters, Behind Closed Doors,* and *Ties That Bind*

Chapter 1 - Dogland

Every small western town has a favorite watering hole, a place where locals hang out. Usually it's a bar. Silt has two liquor stores, three gas stations, two motels, three restaurants, and a beauty shop. But no bar. The tiny town is one of dozens of Colorado bedroom communities within driving distance of a ski resort, in this case Aspen. For truckers and travelers on I-70, it's just another pit stop between Denver and Salt Lake City.

Silt's watering hole is the local dog park. River Park is an island in the Colorado River. Two bridges on County Road 311 connect it to the rest of the world. For decades, maybe even centuries, the park has been enjoyed by rafters, fishermen, dog owners and their dogs.

My husband Tod and I nicknamed the park Dogland. It looks like something out of a dog's imagination. If you asked a group of active, intelligent dogs — any breed or mix — to come up with a plan for an amusement park, a Disneyland for dogs, they would invent Dogland. Dirt paths meander like dog tracks in fresh snow under a canopy of mostly cottonwood and elm trees, then wind through alpine currant and buffaloberry thickets, and end up on the riverside. Besides running off-leash and sniffing, dogs can choose from a variety of other activities. They can splash around in the triangle pond near the trailhead or swim across the irrigation ditch and explore the island's wild side. The cool river water is good for wading or fetching sticks.

Dogland's 27 acres are abundant with wildlife too numerous to mention. Okay — frogs, snakes, lizards, chipmunks, mice, deer, eagles, herons, hawks, owls — to name a few. Most people assume dogs and wildlife don't mix well. They're dead wrong. Dogland has taught us that when given the opportunity, and with adult supervision, dogs can learn to respect wildlife and share habitat.

On a cloudless mid-August morning, I leaned against the picnic table near the triangle pond while my dogs — Zeus, a black and white Alaskan Malamute, and Venus, a white Akbash Lab mix — goofed around with the other dogs. Jeanne was already tossing sticks into the pond for Trevor, her Black Lab.

Carol showed up with her Chocolate Lab, Buddha and Black Lab, Fannie.

"Where's Tommy?" I asked, referring to her infant son.

"He was up half the night so he's home napping. I left Daddy in charge," she said. "Me and the dogs made a break for it. How's that for freedom?"

We laughed.

Amanda arrived with her white Husky, Sasha. While the dogs played, we yakked, sort of a Dogland version of The View. We started out talking about babies and moved to politics. Then, as usual, we settled on a common theme—our dogs.

Of the four of us, Amanda was a relative newcomer to the park. I had seen her several times. We had introduced ourselves and our dogs but had never stopped to chat. That particular day she was curious about my dogs. "How old is Zeus?"

"He's seven. We've had him since he was eight weeks old."

Zeus's satellite dish ears perked up. His mouth opened in a wide grin and his fluffy tail waved at us as he pranced up to Amanda because she said his name. He nuzzled her hand. *Pet me.*

Leaning forward she held his gigantic head in her hands and scratched under his ears. "Look at his head. It's huge." She stuck her face in his. "You are such a teddy bear."

"He is," Carol chimed in. "Zeus is like, the perfect dog."

I laughed. "I don't think there's such a thing as the perfect dog."

"Oh come on," Carol said. "He's smart. He's mellow. And so well-trained."

"Did you take him to obedience school?" Jeanne asked. "Or use a trainer?"

I shook my head. "I never really had to train him. He just does what I want him to do."

"See what I mean? He's the perfect dog," Carol insisted.

"He's what I would call an easy dog." I glanced down at Fannie stretched out on the ground. She held her head erect with a pensive look in her eyes, hanging on our every word. "What about Fannie? Look at her show off what a perfect dog she is."

Zeus wandered over and sniffed Fannie up and down. His mouth opened in a wide grin. *She smells like the baby.*

Carol shook her head. "No way. We can't have a cat because of her. She hates cats. She has food issues with Buddha. And she definitely does not do what I want. She does what she damn well pleases."

Fannie glanced around looking as though she'd just swallowed a cat.

"Well, Zeus hates loud noises. Thunder, gunshots, fireworks, motorcycles — you name it."

"So does Sasha," Amanda said.

"And when he gets wet or in high humidity, he stinks like a dog. But he hates baths and hates being brushed. He also doesn't like it when I touch his feet, so trimming his nails is a real pain."

"Oh man," Amanda said. "You just described Sasha."

"Okay. You win." Carol tossed up her hands. "Zeus is not the perfect dog."

Buddha stood in pond water up to his knees and barked as Venus chased Trevor in circles in an effort to snatch the stick hanging from his mouth.

"What's your other dog's name?" Amanda asked.

"Venus," I said.

Jeanne shouted at Trevor in a feeble attempt to interrupt the chase. She looked at me. "Wow. That Venus has got some energy. How old is she?"

"She turned three in May. We adopted her when she was ten months. She's definitely not the perfect dog."

"Why do you say that?" Amanda asked.

"She was hard to train. As you can see she tries to dominate other dogs and she doesn't always listen very well. She's kind of a lady and a tramp. But she has matured into a good dog. She is much easier to handle now than when she was a pup."

Venus lost interest in the stick game and trotted toward Zeus, who sniffed around a brush pile nearby.

"She's a Yellow Lab, right?" Jeanne asked.

"She's part Lab," I said.

"And part Akbash," Carol added.

Amanda looked at her. "What's an Akbash?"

"They're those big, white dogs you see guarding the sheep up on the Cutoff Road," Carol said.

"Her previous owner told us she was part Great Pyrenees and part Lab, but Carol convinced us otherwise," I explained.

Venus wiggled over and pressed her 90 pound frame against my thigh. *Pet me.* I stroked her sleek, white fur tinged with golden highlights, which took on a pink hue in direct sunlight. Her soulful brown eyes peered up at me. "She is certainly the most beautiful dog we've ever had—and the most manipulative."

"Gabriel was totally manipulative." Carol looked at Amanda. "Richard and I had a purebred Akbash named Gabriel. Venus looks exactly like him. She even acts like him, except Gabriel was unpredictable. He couldn't play with other dogs like she does. He always got aggressive. We couldn't have another dog with him. He wouldn't allow it. Luckily Venus doesn't have that problem. She and Zeus get along great. They're good for each other."

Carol and I had been friends for more than two years. Even though I'm almost 20 years older than she is, Venus created an instant bond between us because of Gabriel.

When Tod and I adopted Venus, she wasn't leash trained. Her previous owners lived in an unincorporated village with no animal control officer. Venus had been allowed to roam the streets. When she returned she was the lady of the house and slept on the couch. In dogdom, she was a free spirit. In human terms, she was a tramp.

As a result, whenever we let her off-leash she bolted and we had to track her down. Before we could teach her to follow commands off-leash we had to train her on the leash. For the first couple months Venus went everywhere on a leash, including Dogland. Early on in our training, Carol and Richard confronted Tod and me at the park.

"Why do you keep her on leash?" Richard demanded.

"Because we're training her," Tod said.

"Seems kind of cruel when all the other dogs get to run around off-leash," Carol said.

"I realize she's big but she's not quite a year old. Still a pup. She was never leash trained. We had to start somewhere," I said.

"Why don't you just let her go and see what happens?" Richard suggested.

"We tried that on the BLM land," Tod said. "She ran away."

"We found her a half hour later herding a sheep," I said.

Carol laughed. "One sheep?"

"Yeah. Then it took us another half hour to find the rest of the herd," Tod said.

"Just trust us, you guys," I said. "We know what we're doing. This will work. You'll see."

Within two months Venus walked off-leash at Dogland with the rest of the dogs.

When Richard saw her he said, "I gotta hand it to you. The leash training worked. She's doing great."

"Thanks." I tossed a hefty stick in the river. Venus leaped in the air and splashed into the water after it.

"She doesn't always bring it back," Tod said. "But we figured out if we keep her busy chasing sticks, she doesn't run away."

"I should probably explain why we're so fixated on Venus," Carol said. "Just so you don't think we're rude—or crazy." She told us about Gabriel. "She looks so much like him it's spooky."

"He lived in a cabin with me up in the mountains above Aspen for a year," Richard said. "When we moved back to civilization he couldn't handle it. He turned aggressive."

"He killed our friend's cat. He fought with other dogs, growled at kids," Carol said. "He was no angel, let me tell you."

"He never adjusted to town life," Richard said. "But that's a big problem with Akbash dogs. They have a wild streak."

I was almost afraid to ask the question. "What happened to him?"

"He died from bloat when he was six," Carol said.

I shook my head. "How sad."

Venus had lost her stick so Tod found another and aimed close to the river's edge. She raced over and pawed at it like a grizzly catching salmon. She picked it up in her teeth, tossed it, and splashed in after it again.

"Gabriel had a lot of anxiety," Richard said. "We always said if you bred a Lab with an Akbash you'd have the perfect dog."

"Except the woman we got her from said she's part Great Pyrenees and part Lab," I explained.

Venus dropped the stick at our feet. *Throw it.*

Richard stroked her wet head. "When I look at Venus I see Akbash. I see Gabriel."

"I need to show you a photo of him," Carol said. "In the meantime, Google Akbash dogs."

But I didn't want any part of the trouble they described. So I dismissed their wacky theory.

On the short drive home, Tod said, "You know, I have noticed how much Venus looks like those dogs that live with the sheep up on the ranch. I just didn't know what they were called."

I ignored him. "I think Gabriel was one of those dogs that's hard to get over. And I think they're transferring a lot of that onto Venus. But she's not Gabriel."

Chapter 2 - Call of the Wild

Carol never swayed from her belief that Venus was part Akbash but she didn't pester me about it either, until one month before our Dogland conversation. We went to lunch at the local café. Over chef's salads with too much iceberg lettuce and weak iced tea, we caught up on our human news and talked about our dogs.

"We've been camping a lot," I told her. "We were up at Meadow Lake before the Fourth. We call it snack lake. It's like a scavenger hunt for dogs. They toss fish heads and scarf up fish guts. Totally disgusting. They love it."

Carol laughed. "Sounds like Buddha and Fannie's kind of fun. We'll have to go up there one of these days."

"Tod rides his mountain bike on the Jeep trails. He took Venus with him. She kept up. He said she was really into it."

"Just like Gabriel." She peeked at her five-month-old son Tommy as he snoozed in the stroller beside the table. "He used to love going on those back country bike rides with Richard."

I cleared my throat. "Carol, Venus isn't Gabriel."

"No but she is Akbash. Have you seen those dogs on the Cutoff Road?"

"Yes." I stabbed a pale tomato wedge with my fork and then released it. Too firm.

"They look exactly like her."

"Okay. You're right. They do."

"They're purebred Akbash. Richard stopped and asked the rancher one day."

"Oh." I took in a long, slow breath.

"Okay. Forget about Gabriel. When you go home Google Akbash images. I'm one hundred percent certain you'll see Venus staring back at you."

I exhaled. "Let's say you're right. What difference does it make?"

"It makes a big difference. Richard bought Gabriel from a guy when he was a puppy. A couple days later he saw an ad in the paper. This rancher wanted information on the guy who stole his Akbash puppies. Richard called him and offered to bring his puppy back but the rancher wanted the name of the guy who sold him the puppy. He didn't want the puppy."

"Why not?"

"He said he wasn't any good to him anymore because he'd been taken out of the wild. To make a long story short he warned Richard that he had his hands full with Gabriel. He said he'd never heard of an Akbash surviving domesticated life."

I raised my eyebrows. "Sounds ominous. What do you think he meant?"

"The problems we had with Gabriel. The aggression, the dominance, the food issues, and the anxiety. The rancher predicted all of it."

"Well Venus is three now and she's fine."

"You're right. Maybe it's the Lab in her that sort of balances things out."

"Or maybe she's not Akbash."

When I went home I Googled "Akbash." Akbash comes from the Turkish word "akbas" meaning "white head." The Akbash dog is a white livestock guardian breed native to the plains and mountains of western Turkey in the region known as the Akbash. The Akbash is an ancient breed of domestic dog and is thought to have derived from similar breeds in Italy and Hungary, but its exact ancestry is not clearly defined. The Akbash was originally bred by shepherds around 3,000 years ago to create a white dog that could guard their flock of sheep. It is widely believed that a white guard dog was wanted to ensure that it wasn't mistaken for a hungry gray wolf.

Americans David and Judy Nelson studied the dogs in Turkey beginning in the 1970s, and imported over forty Akbash dogs to the United States. These dogs became the foundation stock for the breed in the United States and Canada. In 1980, the U.S. Department of Agriculture introduced Akbash dogs to its Predator Control Program and the dogs performed successfully. The United Kennel Club recognized the Akbash dog on January 1, 1998. The American Kennel Club does not recognize the breed.

I clicked on the Akbash images and was stunned by the photos. One after another looked strikingly like our Venus. The almost black eyes against the pure white coat, the long legs, and curly tail were unmistakable.

Then I Googled "Great Pyrenees" and clicked on the images. Great Pyrenees have thick legs, square heads, and long, fluffy fur. Their tails don't even curl. The description of the Great Pyrenees' general demeanor as "quiet composure, both patient and tolerant" was definitely *not* our Venus.

I looked up Akbash temperament at the Dog Breed Info Center website:

"Because of its strong independent nature, it thinks twice upon receiving commands. Not recommended for first time dog owners, or people who do not wish to have a serious guard dog. Companion dog owners should be prepared to spend a fair amount of money on good fencing and a lot of time on socialization and maintaining the humans pack leader status over the dog. The Akbash dog needs a firm, but calm, confident, consistent owner."

It was a description of Venus.

Later I showed Tod the Google images. He stared at the Akbash photos. "Wow. Carol is right. Venus might even be purebred."

"She's not. She has webbed feet, like a Lab."

His eyes widened.

"I checked. Her head is smaller than the Akbash." I Googled "Yellow Lab" and pointed at the images on the computer screen. "Her sleek ears and pointed snout are Yellow Lab."

He peered at me. "You don't want her to be Akbash."

I sighed. "Carol and Richard had so many problems with Gabriel."

"And we've had our share of problems with Venus. Knowing who she is will help us understand her better." He studied the Yellow Lab images. "I think the Lab in her takes some of the edge off her Akbash nature."

"I think so, too. She's mellowed out a lot this past year."

On Friday that week we piled the dogs in our pickup camper and embarked on the long, winding road up to pristine Meadow Lake, which sat at an altitude of 9500 feet in the Flat Tops Wilderness. As our pickup descended from the ridge into the meadow, we saw a herd of about 200 sheep grazing on the hillside across from the campground.

The sign posted at the campground read:

- When approaching a band of sheep, allow time for the guard dogs to see you and determine you are not a threat. Remain calm. If you do not appear to be a threat, the dogs will often just watch you pass by.
- If you have a dog with you, it may appear to guard dogs as a threat if it gets too close to the band or tries to chase sheep. Keep your dog close to you and under control. Leash your dog for as long as you can see the sheep band.
- Try not to "split" the band by walking through it; instead travel around the sheep via the least disruptive route. Keep as much space as practical between you and the sheep band, especially if you have a dog with you. As you pass, keep line of sight between you, your pets and the guard dogs.
- Bicycle riders should dismount from their bikes and walk past the band with the bike between you and the livestock protection dog. Do not remount until you are well

past the sheep.

DO NOT:

- Chase or harass sheep or livestock protection dogs.
- Try to outrun livestock protection dogs. If a guard dog approaches you, tell it to "go back to the sheep," or tell it, "No!" in a firm voice. Do not attempt to hit or throw things at it.
- Attempt to befriend or feed livestock protection dogs. They are not pets. They are lean athletic working dogs, which are cared for by their owners.
- Allow your pets to run towards or harass sheep. They may be perceived as predators by the livestock protection dog and attacked.
- Mistake a livestock protection dog as lost and take it with you.

We spent the next couple days fascinated with the four Akbash dogs and their flock as we watched them through binoculars. Tod rode his bike on the Jeep trail below them to get a better look.

Meanwhile the dogs and I hiked around the lake. Every couple hundred feet they stopped and tossed their noses up as they listened to the "baahs." Then they looked at me. *Sheep.*

"Yes. Sheep," I said.

When Tod returned he said, "As I climbed the hill the two dogs closest to the road appeared to be sleeping. As I passed by the herd, they both stood up and watched me."

"They were sizing you up to determine whether you were a threat," I said.

"They let me pass so they must've decided I was okay." He shook his head in amazement. "They're really smart."

"Venus does that," I said. "Sizes people up."

He nodded.

For the first night and most of Saturday, the four Akbash were on their own with the sheep. We heard them bark at the coyotes after dark. If we weren't watching them, we watched Venus and Zeus. They were as curious as we were, especially Venus. She parked her butt where she had the best view of the hillside. Both dogs were religious nappers but they skipped a few that weekend.

Saturday evening brought more excitement when the sheepherder arrived in his old Ford pickup with a pop-up camper on the back. As he drove up the hillside, the sheep followed his truck. Then the Akbash dogs went to work. Sheep ranchers and Akbash experts insist they are not herding dogs because they are raised to live with the sheep and act as guardians. The four dogs we watched did not run around barking like the Border Collies at sheep dog trials depicted in the movie, *Babe.* They didn't bark at all. But they were busy while the sheep were on the move. They behaved more like a stealth Navy SEAL team as they silently spread out and patrolled the perimeters of the herd with precision timing drawn from some ancient instinct. When a sheep straggled, the dog used his body to nudge it back in line with the others. The truck stopped below the ridge crest. The sheep halted and started grazing while the Akbash assumed their positions for night watch.

Later as we sat by the campfire under brilliant starlight, the coyotes yipped and the Akbash barked.

"Do you hear that?" I asked. "Sounds just like Venus."

Head erect, ears perked up, Venus's eyes glowed in the firelight as she listened. Every now and then she let go a short "woof-woof" as though encouraging her brethren in the wild.

"Do you think Venus would like to be out there with them?" Tod asked.

"Only if they have a comfortable mattress for her to sleep on." The table in our camper converted into a bed which was where Venus always slept.

Tod laughed. "She is pampered."

Zeus stretched out in the dirt behind our camp chairs, his chin on his paws, eyes closed. The fire was too hot for his woolly body. His ears twitched with each distant yip and bark. *Some peace and quiet please. I need a nap.*

Venus and Zeus were aware of the activity up on the ridge. But they sensed everything so much differently than we humans. I thought about how they viewed the sheep, the Akbash, and the coyotes from their perspective as domesticated dogs. Zeus's thoughts had always been easy to read. *Guarding sheep looks like too much work.*

Tod stirred the fire and added more logs.

"It's been good for me to see the Akbash dogs in action. They're amazing," I said. "I can also see how our two dogs could not be more different."

"How so?"

"Zeus wouldn't run after you on your mountain bike if you offered grilled salmon every day for a month. But Venus loves it."

Tod shrugged. "Malamutes are lazy."

"I can't even imagine him guarding sheep." I laughed.

"He's more of a people dog."

"In the wild, Venus would probably look upon Zeus as a predator."

"Maybe so." He reached over and scratched her ears. "Luckily she doesn't live in the wild."

Venus licked his forearm. She was not so easy to read. I wondered what she was thinking.

Chapter 3 - A hint of madness

We headed up to Meadow Lake the next weekend in hopes of seeing the Akbash with the sheep again. Bow hunting begins around the first of September and muzzle loading starts soon after. Dogs and hunters don't mix so it was our last trip up there for the season. But the sheep had moved on to greener meadows. Venus and Zeus didn't care. Venus went on bike rides with Tod. They enjoyed barbequed chicken and baked beans. They swam in Meadow Lake and scoured the shoreline for fish parts.

Late Sunday morning as we packed up, I heard Venus snarl. I turned in the direction of the camper in time to see her snap at Zeus. He recoiled. Tod was right there and grabbed her collar.

"Calm down." He ushered her into the camper for a time out.

"What was that about?" I asked.

Tod scratched his head. "I'm not sure."

Two weeks later, we traveled to Wisconsin over Labor Day weekend to visit my family. Our daughter, Emily (who was pregnant at the time) and then six-year-old granddaughter, Kaley, came with us. The dogs rode in the camper. The journey took two days. We stayed for three. Living in a camper and going for leash walks several times a day was a drastic change from camping at Meadow Lake, but the dogs seemed to take it in stride, although Venus was more anxious than Zeus.

On the afternoon of our last day we visited my sister Marsha and her husband Don at their home on two wooded acres overlooking Tainter Lake. We had walked the dogs in the morning and planned to walk them on the lake trail near their property. They ran around and sniffed when we first arrived. We hadn't seen Marsha and Don for several years so we introduced them to our dogs.

"You remember Zeus," Tod said. "And this is Venus."

"She's part Akbash. We thought she was a Great Pyrenees Lab mix but she's not. We just figured out she's Akbash." It was how I began every conversation about Venus since we had learned her true identity. I said it almost like an apology, but I found it helped me accept the reality. Of course we had to explain "Akbash."

We humans hung out on the front porch and talked. Zeus parked himself at my feet, the center of attention. Venus chose a spot in the sun, between the woods and our human circle. Eventually the conversation turned to our dogs again. Marsha and Don still grieved over the loss of both their German Shepherd and Golden Retriever to cancer the previous winter.

"I don't think we'll get another dog," Marsha said.

I shook my head. "I couldn't live without a dog."

"They just break your heart," she said.

Don stood up and went in the house.

"He wants another dog," I said.

Marsha sighed. "Of course."

"Get a small dog," Emily suggested. "They live longer. Not as prone to cancer."

"I know." Marsha reached down and stroked Zeus's giant head. "But I love big dogs." She looked over at Venus. "And that Venus. Such a beautiful dog. How long have you had her?"

"Two years. She's three now."

"She's so mellow and well-behaved. They both are."

"She has grown up a lot this past year," I said. "She wasn't always so mellow. We've had our ups and downs."

The screen door opened and Don walked out holding a bowl of grapes. Zeus stood up and sniffed the bowl. A flash of white fur streaked in front of me. Venus grabbed Zeus by the neck. Zeus yelped. Venus clamped her jaws.

Tod, Emily, Marsha, and I tried to pry her off him but she had lockjaw. Don grabbed a pail of water nearby. I held her collar as he dumped it on her head. She released, snapping and snarling. We separated the dogs. Emily had a single bite on her arm that was bleeding. Zeus had a bite on his neck which was also bleeding. Tod put Zeus in the pickup. Emily headed for the bathroom.

"What the hell was that?" Don asked.

I put my hands on my hips and stared at Venus as she paced back and forth in front of us, panting. "So much for Miss Mellow."

"I think you scared her, Don," Marsha said. "She was sound asleep. She's in a strange place."

I shook my head. "That's no excuse."

"Maybe she was protecting Emily because she's pregnant," Don said. "I did walk toward her first."

"It's possible," Tod said. "This trip hasn't been easy for her. We've been camping a lot this summer. I don't think this is what she expected. She's just stressed out."

I nodded. "She's definitely wound up."

"I'm going to check on Emily's arm." Tod retreated indoors.

"Let's take her for a walk," Marsha said.

"Yeah. She needs to let off some steam." I exhaled. "Me too."

Venus calmed down during our walk. We watched her trot along behind Kaley and Julie, Marsha's seven-year-old granddaughter, wearing a wide grin.

"I still don't understand what happened," I said. "Did you see how fast she morphed from calm to aggressive? Like a split second."

"It was a shock. That's for sure," Marsha said. "But you know, dogs fight. God knows ours did. Usually over food. She probably woke up from a sound sleep and thought Don was giving Zeus a bowl of food. She didn't want to miss out."

"Venus doesn't even like grapes." We both laughed. Then I got serious. "I see it differently. I know Venus. I don't think she was sound asleep. She's constantly aware of her surroundings. She heard Don in the kitchen. She probably even smelled the grapes when he put them in the bowl. She heard him walk through the foyer and knew exactly when he opened the door."

Marsha shook her head. "No dog is that calculating."

"Venus is. That's Akbash. It's how they survive in the wild with the sheep."

"But she's not a wild dog," she said. "I think you're overreacting. Maybe she's just not a good traveler. You've been lucky with Zeus. He's such a perfect dog."

I laughed. "That's what everyone says."

"Seriously," she insisted. "He must outweigh her by 20 or 30 pounds. He could've killed her. Instead he acted like she hurt his feelings."

"She did." I didn't see the point in telling her Venus had been to California, Denver, Moab, and Lake Powell with us many times without any problems. Because of the incident at Meadow Lake two weeks earlier, I had brought along a homeopathic remedy for anxious dogs called Aggression Formula which contains scutellaria, chamomilla, belladonna, arsenicum album, and hepar sulph. I started dosing Venus with it and her behavior returned to normal.

We left Wisconsin for home the next morning. I kept Venus on Aggression Formula and she didn't show any further aggression toward Zeus on the two-day trip. However at a gas station in Denver, when a woman tried to pet her, she barked and lunged at her from the leash, which was not typical behavior. Emily was holding the leash. I thought maybe she was protecting her after all.

Tuesday evening after we arrived home, Tod munched on popcorn in the kitchen. He tossed some to Venus, then Zeus. *Pow!* Venus attacked Zeus again. She clamped down on his sore neck. As Tod lunged toward them, his forearm collided with Zeus's open mouth. His incisor snagged him. I dumped a bowl of water on Venus's head. She let go and Zeus fled downstairs. I put her outside.

Tod cleaned up the puncture wound on his arm. "She's just tired from the long drive and being cooped up in the camper."

"We need to stop making excuses for her behavior," I snapped.

The next day I ordered Pet Calm another homeopathic remedy

which contains scutellaria, passiflora, kali phos, and argentums nitricum to add to the Aggression Formula and made an appointment with our vet. We kept the dogs separated for two days. Venus pretended nothing had happened, though she hated being separated from Zeus.

By the time Venus and I got in to see Dr. Shari Price the following week, Venus was on Pet Calm and Aggression Formula and acted like her normal self. Dr. Price was new to Silt Animal Hospital so it was our first meeting. I reported on Venus's aggressive behavior. Dr. Price and I went over her entire history from the moment we adopted her, including our recent discovery that she was part Akbash, not Great Pyrenees.

Dr. Price raised her eyebrows. "Akbash are dominant, aggressive dogs. Has she shown any aggression in the past?"

"Just puppy stuff when she first came to live with us. She had some minor dominance issues with Zeus but nothing like what happened over Labor Day. That was different."

"What does she do for exercise?"

"She walks off-leash at Dogland for about forty minutes a day. We take the dogs with us when we go hiking, camping, and cross-country skiing."

"So she gets a lot of exercise off-leash," she said. "How does she do on a leash?"

I shrugged. "She's okay."

"Put her back on the leash and work on her behavior modification. Make sure she follows commands and doesn't get to run the show." She walked over deliberately and stroked Venus's head. Her tail thumped on the tile floor. "She seems fine with me and she doesn't even know me. She's calm. Good eye contact. No anxiety about being at the vet. Yeah, good girl." Venus licked her hand. "Keep her on those homeopathic remedies for now since they seem to be working. Let me know if anything changes."

Our leash re-training began at Dogland. We put her on the leash for the first 15 minutes until we felt certain she was calm and paying attention, then we let her go. We ran into Carol and Tommy with Buddha and Fannie one morning. Venus was on the leash.

"What's up with Venus?" Carol asked.

"She's been acting weird." I described the incidents.

"I don't understand why she would go after Zeus all of a sudden," Carol said. "I mean, she's crazy about him. She never lets him out of her sight."

"We don't get it either," I said.

"Do you think it has anything to do with Emily being pregnant?" she asked. "Maybe she's feeling overly protective. It is her nature, after all."

I shrugged. "I hope that's all it is."

In the meantime Zeus had his own health issues. The previous June, his thyroid had tested low. I had put him on natural raw thyroid over the summer, but it wasn't working. He tested low again at the end of September.

"I think it's time to treat him with Soloxine," Dr. Landers said.

I agreed. Zeus had been stressed out and grumpy since the Labor Day weekend scuffle. Within a week on Soloxine, he perked up. Venus was back to her happy-go-lucky self. The work we did with her on the leash reminded her who was in control. She and Zeus hung out together like normal dogs. Or so it seemed.

One morning in mid-October at Dogland, she and Zeus ran toward the pond. An older Black Lab mix stood off to the side next to a woman. He growled at Venus. She snarled and jumped on him.

Tod was right there and hollered, "Venus! Stop it!"

She backed off. He put her on the leash and apologized to the woman.

She shrugged. "My dog started it."

The next week I was alone with the dogs at the park. We were on the riverside trail. Amanda and Sasha walked out of the buffaloberry thicket.

I waved and said, "Good morning."

As we passed each other on the trail Venus snarled, jumped on Sasha, and knocked her down. I grabbed her collar and snapped the leash on it. Sasha wasn't injured, though she and Amanda were stunned.

Embarrassed I muttered, "I'm so sorry. I don't know why she did that."

"I think maybe we startled her," Amanda said.

I knew better and shook my head. "That's no excuse." I took Venus back to my Jeep and left her inside while Zeus and I finished our walk.

The incidents bothered me. While everyone around me made excuses for her behavior, I was the one who spent the most time with her. Her random aggressive outbursts made no sense to me. I had been dosing her with the homeopathic remedies twice a day. I upped it to three times a day.

The first week of November, all hell broke loose.

Chapter 4 - The dog bomb

While eating lunch at the kitchen counter one day in early November, I noticed Venus chewing on her leg. I examined the spot she was chewing. It looked red and irritated so I put some calendula ointment on it. I thought she had scratched it on a branch at Dogland.

After supper that evening, Tod headed out to go to a meeting. Our kitchen and living room are on the second floor of our home. The front door is at the bottom of the stairway, on the first floor. Zeus was standing at the top of the stairs. About two minutes after Tod left, Venus walked up to Zeus and sniffed his neck. Then she grabbed hold and knocked him down. I grabbed the bowl of dog water and threw it on her head. Zeus scrambled to his feet, but Venus struck again and pinned him against the wall.

Lucy, our 17-year-old senile Himalayan, appeared out of nowhere. Clueless, she wandered through the melee like Mr. Magoo. Venus ignored her. But I scooped her up and set her on the couch.

In the kitchen, I refilled the water bowl. Each snarl and growl tore me apart. Venus still had Zeus pinned down in the living room. With the bowl in one hand, I straddled her hind quarters and nudged her with my legs. I dumped the water on her head. Zeus slid out from underneath her. I grabbed her collar, but she snapped at me and got away. She lunged at Zeus and pushed him down 13 steps.

Alone, with 200 pounds of snarling dog bomb tumbling down the stairs, I panicked and screamed, “Help!” My scream echoed to the ceiling, mocking me.

I ran back to the kitchen, grabbed a plastic pitcher with a handle, and filled it with water. Zeus howled. *Halp!* Venus snarled. I figured she had Zeus pinned down again. I had no clue whether either of them had been injured in the fall.

As I took a deep breath to calm myself, I glanced across the kitchen counter at the knives. What if the third bowl of water didn’t work? Would I have to kill her?

I had the scene at the bottom of the stairs exactly right. Venus was on Zeus’s back with her teeth sunk into the fur on his neck. I straddled her again, grabbed her collar and pulled up as I dumped two quarts of water on her head. She gasped and let go of Zeus.

“Run, Zeus! Run!” I screamed.

He struggled to a stand and stumbled around the corner toward my office. I held Venus with both hands and both legs as she snapped and snarled. Slowly I nudged her toward the service door to the garage, 90 pounds of sheer madness beneath me fighting every inch of the way.

"Calm down. Calm down ...." I repeated like a mantra.

I needed one hand to open the door so I had to wait until she stopped snapping at me. She took a breath. I grabbed the door knob, opened the door, and used my whole body to shove her into the garage.

I shut the door and leaned against it, exhausted. Then I saw them. Pink puddles. Everywhere. Blood mixed with water.

Panicked again I ran into my office and knelt down to see how badly Zeus was injured. He leaned against the door, shaking. When I touched his neck to remove his collar he snapped at my hand. *Don't touch me.*

I lost it. I fell back on the carpet and wept. Venus was turning my gentle giant into a monster. My dogs were a mess. Eventually Zeus lay down next to me and shoved his nose in my neck. *Sorry.* I removed his collar and checked the wound underneath. It wasn't even bloody, just raw from being chewed. I doused it with colloidal silver. He stopped shaking.

"What're we gonna do about Venus?" I asked him.

He groaned. *That's your problem. I need a nap.*

So where did all that blood come from? Venus?

The dog door in the garage accesses the yard. From the yard the dogs can walk on the side porch and front porch, which is gated. I walked out the front door and opened the gate. Venus jumped up. I sat down calmly on the green wicker chair. She averted her glassy eyes from mine. She wouldn't—or couldn't — make eye contact. She bounced up and down, crying. Not a whiny whimper. More like a crazed wailing. She seemed confused. I had nothing to fear. She wasn't Cujo. She behaved more like a faulty electronic toy stuck in action mode. Not hooked up right. Blood was smeared on the right side of her head. I went back inside to get some baby wipes. (Helpful hint: Baby wipes work great for removing blood, dirt, even cow poop, from white dog fur.)

I wiped off the blood and found only a two-inch scratch on her nose. I observed her for a little while. Still anxious, she bounced around nervously, panting and whimpering. I thought maybe I could calm her down if I sat there silently. I couldn't shake the bizarre scene in my mind as she viciously attacked Zeus while Lucy calmly waltzed through the middle of it unharmed. She was so different from the Venus who played in the park with the other dogs in August.

My right foot felt wet against my flip-flop. I looked down and saw a trail of blood from my leg to my foot. I retreated inside to the bathroom and cleaned up. I had two teeth marks on my right leg, and a red paw print and two toenail holes on my left ankle. The paw print matched Zeus's back foot exactly. The teeth marks matched Venus. Even though they were only surface wounds, they had bled out a lot.

Venus's behavior baffled me. Her attack on Zeus was ferocious. Yet his wounds were minor. I figured that was somehow significant, but I didn't know why. She threw her weight around amid much teeth gnashing but she wasn't out to kill him, or me. She didn't know what she was doing. She went postal. She became a dog bomb.

Needless to say, we separated the dogs. Neither Tod nor I slept well that night. We shut Venus in the garage, so naturally she yelped and barked when she wasn't sleeping. Images of the attack haunted me. And the question. The one I didn't have an answer for. *What happened to Venus?*

Chapter 5 - Sick puppy

The next day I called Silt Animal Hospital and explained my emergency. The receptionist told me to bring her in right away. When I described Venus's meltdown to Dr. Price, she was as surprised and puzzled as I was. "When I see an aggressive dog—especially an aggressive *big* dog—the problem is usually with the owner," she said. "A big dog is so cute as a puppy but then it gets big. The owner becomes insecure and fearful of the dog. Or the dog is caged or tied up, and aggression develops."

"I've had big dogs most of my life," I said. "But I've never been through anything like this before."

"Yeah. Clearly you're not the problem here."

"It's not like I haven't wondered if I'm doing something wrong. But Zeus is so mellow. If it was my fault then he would have behavior problems, too."

She nodded. "Exactly. I've seen you with both dogs. Watching you handle Venus now, I can see you're in control. Look at you. Your legs have teeth and claw marks on them."

I had worn denim capris because long pants chafed the wounds. I shrugged. "Could've been worse."

She frowned. "You just described a horrific ordeal. You broke up a fight by yourself. Yet you don't show any fear of her."

I stroked Venus's head and blinked back tears, unable to speak.

"This is something else." She took a deep breath and let it out. "There have been studies about canine compulsive disorder. It can appear suddenly in three-year-old dogs—very often rescue dogs—as they progress into adulthood. Venus is three and you adopted her. CCD is similar to obsessive-compulsive disorder in humans. Dogs exhibit anxiety, obsessions, or even difficulty coping with certain situations."

"Is aggressive behavior also a symptom of CCD?"

She shook her head. "Not always. But in some cases anxiety gradually takes over the brain and one day the dog snaps. Because Venus was an adopted —or rescue—dog, we don't know what happened to her in the first ten months of her life. She may have been abused. Abused puppies very often develop anxiety or aggression issues as adult dogs."

After consulting with her boss, Dr. Landers, Dr. Price prescribed the antidepressant clomipramine. Treatment began with 50 mg twice a day. Dr. Price explained, "The dosing begins gradually. Don't expect the drug to take effect for up to two weeks. After two weeks we'll add another 25 milligrams to each dose for a total of 75 milligrams twice a day."

I have never been a big fan of pharmaceuticals. I prefer holistic, naturopathic treatment with vitamins, herbs, and homeopathic remedies. But we had been using those and they weren't working. We had no choice. We had to stop the violence.

"We will need to muzzle Venus," Dr. Price said. "I want to do a blood draw and run some tests to make sure we're not dealing with any other health issues."

Venus backed away at the sight of the soft nylon and Velcro muzzle. She tossed her head back. *No way.* But I was able to slip it on without too much fuss.

I pointed out the contrast in her behavior. "Look at how Venus is behaving right now. She's nervous about the muzzle but she's handling it okay."

"She trusts you," Dr. Price said.

"You cannot imagine the difference from last night. If I hadn't been right there in the middle of it, I never would've believed this dog was capable of exploding like that."

"I do understand what you're saying." She tied the rubber strap around Venus's foreleg. "That's why I'm so convinced this is a mental disorder." When she inserted the needle Venus winced and tossed her head wildly like a horse.

"Shh-shh." I held her firmly. Once the needle was out she exhaled and relaxed. The instant I separated the Velcro on the muzzle, she shook it off, sputtering and sneezing. *Yuck. That smells like dogs.*

"Good dog." Dr. Price patted her head and offered her a biscuit, which she devoured.

"See what I mean? Her behavior was so bizarre last night. She had every opportunity to attack me. I was in the fight. I was on top of both dogs." I told her about Lucy stumbling into the middle of it.

She raised her eyebrows. "That's actually a good sign. Dog specific aggression is just that. Dog specific. It doesn't transfer to humans."

I exhaled. "That's a relief. I babysit my granddaughter. Venus is quite attached to her. Kaley's never alone with the dogs. As a general rule I think kids and pets should be supervised."

"You and me both," she said. "I wish more people felt that way. Though you might want to watch how Venus behaves toward Zeus around your granddaughter. Do they compete for her attention?"

I laughed. "No. Zeus likes to watch Kaley from a safe distance. Preferably lying down. He's grateful Venus is willing to play with her so he doesn't have to."

She smiled. "I don't think you have anything to worry about."

She also recommended we see a dog behaviorist. "You could use some help. Rehabilitating Venus is going to take a lot of work. You can start by separating the dogs' food dishes."

"But they don't have food issues," I said.

She nodded. "They do. You just haven't seen it. It's subtle."

"She fought over popcorn a couple months ago," I recalled.

"Something was going on there," she said. "You need to learn how to look for triggers. Anxious dogs tend to fixate, then it escalates."

"Okay. That's interesting," I said. "Because during lunch yesterday before Venus attacked Zeus, I noticed she was chewing on her leg. I thought she had scratched it on a bush at the park. Maybe it was red and sore because she was chewing on it obsessively. Like a fixation."

"It could have been a trigger that her anxiety was escalating," she said. "A dog behaviorist can help you figure out what sets her off. The problem is the dog behaviorist I recommend doesn't live in the valley and she won't be back to see clients until mid-December."

My heart sank. What were supposed to do until December? I wrote down the information anyway.

Finally—and rather ominously—Dr. Price said, "The fact is you're leaving here with a dangerous dog. Until the medication takes effect that's how you need to handle her. But I trust you can do that. If anything changes you need to call me immediately. Otherwise I want to see her in four weeks."

I felt discouraged when I left. I didn't blame Dr. Price. It wasn't her fault. On the contrary, her diagnosis was a key part of the puzzle. She understood Venus's condition and she didn't sugar coat it for me. She had made it perfectly clear the drug was only a tool we would use as part of Venus's rehabilitation. I had never lived with an aggressive dog before. A "dangerous" dog.

Dr. Price called later to say Venus's blood work checked out fine. We kept the dogs separated. If Zeus came in the house, Venus went outside, and vice versa. If they both wanted to be outside, I tied Zeus in the front yard, which is not fenced. Our fenced yard has two interior gates and three exterior gates, which was helpful for separating the dogs, but also tricky. Sometimes an exterior gate was left ajar and Zeus or Venus wandered around the neighborhood until one of us realized our mistake. Sort of a like a Chinese fire drill with dogs. Organized chaos.

In the evenings we walked them around the neighborhood on leashes, so keeping them separated on those walks wasn't a problem. Zeus ignored Venus, and she fixated on him.

Indoors, a wooden gate at the top of the stairs made the separation slightly more manageable. We put a bowl of water and Venus's food bowl in the downstairs bathroom and kept the light on. She had come to us with an irrational fear of bathrooms. She wouldn't set foot in one. We assumed her previous owners had shut her in the bathroom while they were at work. Bad move.

"Maybe this will cure her bathroom phobia," I said.

Venus became the downstairs dog, and Zeus the upstairs dog. Sometimes they switched. Zeus wanted absolutely nothing to do with her. He ignored or avoided her. They weren't allowed near each other. I took Zeus to Dogland, then Tod took Venus to Dogland.

After three days I said, "We can't live like this." Venus was anxious and Zeus was stressed out.

We discussed all our options. We consulted and commiserated with Emily, Carol, and Richard.

"Should we try to find another home for her?" Tod asked.

"You mean one without other dogs? Or kids? Or people? That doesn't even make sense," I snapped.

"You're right. We adopted her. We have to do whatever we can to help her," he said.

"I think we're probably the only ones who *can* help her." But I was worried. The homeopathic remedies hadn't worked. What if the clomipramine didn't work either? What if her aggression continued? Would we have to put her down?

And what about Zeus? The only real danger she posed was to him. It didn't seem fair to make him live with the stress.

Tod has his own office five blocks away, and it's spacious. He decided to take Venus to the office with him and give Zeus a break. Since he walked back and forth, it gave him more opportunities to work with her on the leash and provided more exercise for her.

At home, every time I walked upstairs I flashed back to the trauma of her meltdown. With Venus out of the house I decided to get rid of the negative energy still lingering from the attack. I sat on the bottom step by the front door and burned sage, a smudging ceremony to cleanse the house of negative energy.

The orange embers and green smoke of the burning sage ignited my frustration and rage. I resented Venus. No. I hated what she did to Zeus. He was bigger than her. Why didn't he fight back? Maybe he would have been more seriously injured. Smart dog. Smarter than me. Tears seeped out.

I thought about the first night we brought Venus home. Leaving her previous family had been a jolt. She was so freaked out she rolled around until she twisted herself into a bundle of nerves. From that wriggling white mass of fur she'd grown into a beautiful dog with a big personality—and a mental disorder.

How could I fix her?

Even though Dr. Price had said we shouldn't expect the clomipramine to take effect right away, within a few days we saw a calmer, less anxious Venus. She even seemed a little less fixated on Zeus. She had begun slowly accepting her new limitations and life on the leash.

We felt more hopeful with each passing day. I read as much information on CCD as I could find, which did not amount to much. CCD was identified as an illness in 2000 by Andrew Luescher, director of the Purdue University Animal Behavior Clinic. Similar to OCD (obsessive-compulsive behavior) in humans, CCD involves obsessive, repetitive behavior of any kind. It's caused by prolonged frustration, anxiety, and/or stress. Because of the effectiveness of drugs known as serotonin re-uptake inhibitors, like clomipramine, in dogs with CCD, researchers believe there is evidence that serotonin levels in the dog's brain are involved in the condition, although to what degree is not well understood.

Researchers believe CCD could be a genetic disorder. There is no known cause since each dog is different and the symptoms vary. It is a progressive disease, therefore the onset is often difficult to determine. With Venus it may have developed gradually since birth or perhaps it had come on more suddenly, as appeared to be the case. Not all dogs with CCD display aggression. Some dogs lick or chew on themselves so badly they require medical attention, which is a form of self-aggression. The search for case studies was like trying to unearth secret government files. They were under lock and key at Purdue, not for public consumption. Not a good sign.

From my own research I learned that even with medication and rehabilitation it would take four to six months before we could assess Venus's progress. The daunting reality of her mental illness slowly settled in. Her meltdown played over and over in my head like a video loop. What, if anything, set her off? Why Zeus?

Learning about CCD helped me understand her aggression. It was simple really. She was sick. Seeing her meltdown as a malfunction in her brain took the violence out of it. Once I adjusted my own feelings about it, it became easier to forgive her.

I told Tod, "The thing is, Zeus is hypothyroid and will be on medication for the rest of his life. Venus could have cancer, or diabetes, or epilepsy, and we would deal with it."

"This is different," he said. "It's not physical. It's mental."

"We have to try to fix her," I said.

The problem was Zeus. He wouldn't even look at her. *Venus who?*

Chapter 6 - Torn between two dogs

With two dogs it's easy to slip into the two-headed dog syndrome, especially when they go everywhere and do everything together, which was how it had been with Zeus and Venus for more than two solid years.

After her meltdown, Zeus didn't want to have anything to do with the crazy bitch. Who could blame him? He was five years old when we adopted her. He had always been his own dog. By ignoring her, he declared his independence. Which was fine for him, but Tod and I could not sustain the Chinese-fire-drill-with-dogs lifestyle. We had to find a way to gradually bring them together, yet respect Zeus's demand for his own personal space.

"Maybe if we help him define his space, then Venus will respect it, too," I said.

After only four days on clomipramine, Venus had calmed down—a little. It was time to move forward—in baby steps. But how?

Dogland had always been a neutral zone for them. Since Venus had to be on the leash, she would be completely under control. Plus their neighborhood leash walks had been going well. We had a wire barrier for the back of the Jeep to separate the back seat from the rear section, but we hadn't used it in two years so it was stored away. Venus and Zeus had always ridden in the rear section together. We needed to make a change. Tod found the barrier and put it up. I laid a dog rug on the back seat for Venus. We loaded her first.

Next came Zeus. He sniffed around and checked out the new

arrangement. He knew we were headed to Dogland with Venus. He also knew the barrier would keep them apart. He signaled his approval by climbing up his dog ramp into the rear section. As we had hoped, Dogland was a walk in the park for them. The healing had begun.

We kept Venus on the leash because she was still anxious and unpredictable around other dogs. During those first few visits to the park, I noticed her anxiety around other dogs made me nervous. I needed to get over it.

A week after her meltdown, while on my own with the dogs at Dogland, it hit me. Why Venus made me nervous. It was her unpredictability; the way she could morph from happy-slappy dog into crazy bitch in a split second.

Venus stopped and sniffed a patch of weeds. Zeus walked over to her and sniffed, too. She sniffed his neck. I tensed up. Whenever she attacked Zeus, she always went for the same spot on his neck, behind his right ear. I pulled her away from him and kept moving. She maintained a slight lead on the leash. As I often did I rested my hand between Zeus's shoulders while he walked beside me off-leash. If only I could put body armor on him. Doggie Kevlar. Suddenly the image of a studded leather dog collar popped into my brain. I stopped in my tracks and looked at Zeus. "Did you just put that in my head?"

He raised his thick, white brows. *Cool, huh?*

Tod happened to be in Grand Junction that morning so I called him and told him about my vision. "Sounds like a good idea," he said. "I'll pick one up at the pet store."

When he came home for lunch with the extra-large spiked collar, I had to laugh. I showed Zeus. “Is this really what you want?”

He sniffed it. Then he stuck his nose through and slipped it on. He looked up at Tod. *Check this out.*

“If Venus tries to sink her teeth into that, she’s going to get a mouthful of metal,” Tod said.

I scratched behind Zeus’s ears. “We’ll have to call you Spike from now on.” I noticed the fur was matted where Venus had bitten him. I had been pouring colloidal silver onto the wound area but otherwise left it alone to heal. I took off the collar and gently removed the dead fur from his neck with a tweezers, which exposed a two-inch circle of bare skin. About a dozen tiny cuts remained. Not a single puncture wound. It looked as though Venus had chewed on his neck, much like she had chewed on her own leg. Likewise my wounds were healing and weren’t punctures either. Her teeth had only grazed my leg.

Out of sheer anxiety she had pinned Zeus down and chewed on his neck. More proof she didn’t want to kill him. Her aggression was a manifestation of her anxiety. She chewed up dog toys. She chewed on herself. She chewed on Zeus. Scattered puzzle pieces.

As word spread among our Dogland friends about Venus’s mental illness, reactions were mixed. Everyone was curious.

One day Bethany asked, “What’s with Zeus and the spiked collar?”

I told her about Venus. Bethany worked with healing crystals and offered to help. “I’ll come over this afternoon.”

She arrived with her suitcase full of powerful BioGenesis crystals. Zeus stayed outside. Indoors I played new age music on the stereo. Venus danced around Bethany and me.

“This little anxiety dance is typical behavior,” I said. “She doesn’t have control of the situation and she doesn’t know what’s going on. That makes her nervous. Let’s keep talking and ignore her.”

We sat on the carpet. Bethany spread out several small colored wheels and explained they represented progress, transformation, and regeneration. I tried to get Venus to sit down near them but she ignored me. She bounced like Tigger, demanding Bethany’s attention.

Bethany held up the Flame of Genesis, a crystal spear. “This supports healing from trauma.” She waved it around Venus several times. Within seconds, she slumped to the floor and lay on the wheels. She rolled over on her back between us as Bethany circled the flame crystal above her.

Venus sneezed—over and over. We couldn’t help but laugh. She must have sneezed a dozen times.

“I sense a release of negative energy in her sneezes,” Bethany said.

I nodded. “This is amazing. She is definitely letting go of

something."

Within ten minutes, Venus stretched out on her side, breathing deeply in a state of total relaxation. She had achieved serenity, an unusual state of being for her.

Zeus and Bethany already shared a bond. A year earlier, he and Venus were playing tag at Dogland. As he ran full speed down an embankment, Venus body checked him. His back legs splayed sideways. His right hip bounced hard on the dirt trail right in front of us. Tod and I attempted to get him to lie still but he jumped up and trotted away. His back grew increasingly stiff and sore over the ensuing weeks. Dr. Landers had prescribed prednisone but it didn't touch the pain. Zeus was miserable. Bethany had noticed him walking stiffly in the park. When I told her what had happened she brought over her crystals and directed healing energy into his back injury. After the treatment he was remarkably improved. Gradually the stiffness and soreness abated.

Therefore, Bethany and I weren't surprised to see him waiting eagerly at the gate when we ventured onto the porch after Venus fell asleep. Zeus pressed against Bethany's legs in a big-dog hug. *I love you.* He sniffed the flame crystal in her hand with anticipation, not suspicion. *I remember this.* As she waved it over him, he sat down and stretched his neck to absorb the healing energy.

Bethany laughed. "His energy seems just fine."

He nuzzled her free hand. *Do it again.*

She did. As she climbed in her car to leave she said, "Email me a recent photo of Venus and I'll keep it in the case to send her positive energy."

Venus seemed spent and slept a lot the rest of the day.

The next morning a big screw-up happened. As I finished pilling Venus, Tod said, "Wait. I already pilled her."

"Oops! Too late," I said. We had given her 100 mg of clomipramine instead of 50 mg. A double dose. I didn't know what to expect. "I'll call Dr. Price."

"Aren't we supposed to increase her dose to 75 milligrams next week?" Tod asked. "I don't think the double dose will kill her."

Four hours later at Dogland she was slow and lethargic.

"She slept all morning at the office," Tod said.

"It looks like 100 milligrams is too much drug," I said. "But I still think she has too much anxiety at 50 milligrams. Maybe 75 will be the magic number."

Another Dogland friend, Kathy, had advised me to get a can of pepper spray. "I've worked with aggressive rescue dogs at the shelter. It works to break up dog fights."

I bought a couple cans knowing full well that doing so was an admission I might have to use it. Sort of like expecting the worst.

But I didn't buy it for Venus. Nor did I buy the studded collar for Zeus. I bought them for myself. In order to help her, I had to stop feeling anxious about her unpredictability. In order to relax with her, I needed to feel in control. I looked upon the spiked collar and the pepper spray as tools to help me control the situation if she snapped again.

The rest of the week we saw the effects of the clomipramine and Bethany's crystal healing. When Venus played with dog toys she didn't destroy them like she usually did. When she played fetch she didn't clamp down on the toy and refuse to give it up. She let go on command and sat and waited for me to toss it. On walks, Venus used any excuse to get close to Zeus and check out the spiked collar. She sniffed and backed off respectfully.

We even relaxed the separation rules indoors. After dinner we opened the gate. The problem was when she came upstairs, Zeus went downstairs. If she walked in a room, Zeus left the room. If she went outside, he came inside. I took my signals from Zeus. *I don't trust her.*

So neither did we. Even though she behaved calmly at home, on walks her anxiety returned, especially with dogs she didn't know. We were relieved she had stopped attacking Zeus. But if we had not controlled her on the leash at Dogland she would have behaved aggressively toward other dogs. The bomb still ticked inside her.

I counted the days until we could increase the clomipramine from 50 mg to 75 mg. I still didn't have a handle on the type of behavior modification needed to rehabilitate her. Everything I had read recommended exercise for anxiety. Venus was up to four walks a day.

Obedience training was also recommended. But she was trained. When she wasn't feeling anxious, she was obedient. Whenever I tried to visualize her at obedience class she whipped herself into a frenzy and beat up another dog. Feeding her anxiety didn't seem like an effective strategy. Her issues were anxiety and aggression—not obedience.

On top of my worries about her rehabilitation, my greatest challenge was yet to come. Tod was scheduled to leave town. Every month he spent a week at company headquarters in Chicago. I had always handled the dogs just fine without him. It was never an issue. But it had only been two weeks since her meltdown. He was about to leave me alone with two dogs who didn't seem to like each other anymore.

Chapter 7 - The Dog Whisperer

The weekend before Tod left for Chicago, I saw Carol at Dogland.

"Venus seems a lot calmer," she said. "How are things going with her and Zeus?"

"Not well," I said. "They're fine here at the park. But Zeus doesn't really want anything to do with her at home. And who can blame him? I don't know if he will ever trust her again."

"That's so sad," she said. "What are you going to do?"

I shrugged. "I don't know. I don't have any answers. We just keep working with her."

"Don't give up on her," she said. "If anyone can save Venus, it's you guys. That's why she ended up here. With you. Cuz you'll figure out what to do."

I smiled. "Thanks. I needed to hear that."

I worked on my self-confidence. All my life, I have had a special connection with animals. I've raised dozens of Persians and Himalayans. I've bred, raised, and kept dozens of dogs. Point is, this wasn't my first time at the circus. I'm not a "dog trainer" but ever since I was a kid I trained my own dogs. I have always trusted my own instincts with animals and my own instincts had not failed me. My dad always said I had a "way with animals."

Several years ago, a neighbor and horse breeder, Karl Larson, told me his horses were calmer and friendlier around me than with anyone else. One summer he rescued an abused donkey named Virgil. "Be careful, he's a mean one," Karl warned. "Hates people. He bites and kicks."

I visited Virgil often and fed him carrots and apple slices while I talked to him and stroked his ears. He never bit me or kicked me. Gradually his fear and anger faded away.

Karl was able to place him in a new home by summer's end. "All because of you," he said. "You have that animal magic."

I believe there's something to all that. Some people have it, some people don't. Venus challenged everything I ever knew about animals. Why couldn't I work my animal magic with Venus?

She enjoyed spending mornings at Tod's office. The extra walks to and from, plus having the run of the office, was good for her. It gave her a job to do. But we were concerned that the combination of Tod's absence and taking away her new office routine would increase her anxiety at home. Emily also works at Tod's office so she offered to take Venus with her for at least three mornings.

Before Tod left on Monday afternoon, we made sure Venus had three short walks. Even so, she still bounced and whined at the door as he drove away.

I decided to calm her anxiety with meditation. I called her into the bedroom while I sat on the rug in a lotus position. "Sit." She ignored me and did her anxiety dance. I closed my eyes and began deep breathing. "A-um." *Bop.* She poked me in face with her nose. I kept my eyes closed and ignored her. "A-um." *Bop. Bop.* Again with the nose in the face. Again I ignored her. "A-um." *Bop. Bop. BOP.* She almost knocked me over. "Ouch!" I opened my eyes and pushed her away. "Go lie down."

She licked my face. More anxiety dance. Time out.

I let her out on the front porch. She ran around the back of the house, through the dog door into the garage, and barked at the service door. I took it as a sign. She wanted to be near me while I meditated even though she was being a pest. I let her back in. But I tried a different tactic. I stretched out on the carpet, face down and covered my face with my hands. She poked at me and pawed the carpet. I nearly suffocated trying not to laugh. Eventually she lay quietly beside me. I hung on to the moment as long as I could. We had accomplished something. What it was exactly, I had no clue.

I looked up "dog aggression" on the Internet which led me to the *Dog Whisperer* website and an announcement that the program would be returning to the National Geographic Channel beginning with a re-run of an older episode about dog aggression. What luck. I set the DVR to record.

I had watched a couple episodes of the *Dog Whisperer* before we adopted Venus but had not kept up with it. Cesar Millan seemed like a really good dog trainer and nice enough guy, but I thought the dog owners were idiots. There was a woman who was afraid of her own dog, and a couple who never walked their dog. Why do those people even have dogs?

I was supposed to increase Venus's clomipramine from 50 mg (two 25-mg tablets) twice a day to 75 mg (three 25-mg tablets) on Tuesday. I cheated and upped it on Monday night. It was my first evening alone in the house with those two mooks and I didn't want any trouble. Even though we had been opening the gate after dinner when Tod was home, I kept the gate closed and the dogs separated. They hadn't even started going out in the yard together. The only time they were together was during walks. I decided not to make any changes in their routine while Tod was away.

I assessed my "tools." In addition to the clomipramine I had the leashes, Zeus's studded collar, pepper spray, indoor and outdoor gates, and a ridiculous Chinese-fire-drill-with-dogs routine. How the hell had my life come to this?

The 75 mg dosage worked. Venus acted calmer right away. By Wednesday I felt certain we could get through the week without any problems.

Then I sat down and watched the *Dog Whisperer* episode I had recorded. Two Pit Bulls, Isis and Tina, fought constantly. Their aggression threatened to break up their owners' relationship. Isis and Tina hated each other. Cesar trained the owners how to work with the dogs to build a positive, healthy relationship. I was blown away. Zeus and Venus weren't anywhere near as bad as Isis and Tina, which meant there was hope we could repair what Venus had broken.

Call it a revelation—or divine intervention—or canine intervention. I knew I had found my answer. A guru. His name was Cesar Millan.

I watched the episode twice and picked up several tips on how to train Venus right away, starting with the leash. We were giving her way too much control. I reined her in. I also made her sit until she calmed down when she acted too aggressively toward other dogs. By the end of the week Venus and I had made good progress. I couldn't wait to show Tod the episode and how we had applied what I learned.

When he got home Friday night he noticed immediately how much calmer Venus behaved and how much more control I had gained over her anxiety. Cesar's trademark, "Shhh-t-t-t!" and finger snaps worked like a charm. Distraction. We watched the episode and Tod saw how Cesar's dog psychology and people training worked.

"What this means is that in order to rehabilitate Venus, we have to start all over again with her training," I said. "It's a huge challenge but at least now we have a resource to help us get through this."

I set the DVR to record the upcoming *Dog Whisperer* marathon on Thanksgiving weekend. We continued working with Venus. No fixating. No dominance. No anxiety. We opened the gate in the house and we let the dogs out in the yard together with supervision. Zeus didn't always stay in the same room with her. And he didn't always stay in the yard with her. But sometimes he did, though he kept his distance.

Thanksgiving Day went smoothly. The dogs were calm and well behaved, even around all the food—which usually made Venus anxious, then Zeus would get all grumpy. But that didn't happen. We watched several *Dog Whisperer* episodes and learned more tips and tricks to work on with Venus.

On Saturday, we took the dogs up to the West Elk trails. It was our first cross-country ski outing for the season. We had trained them to do skijoring.

Skijoring is a winter sport that combines cross-country skiing with dog power. The skier is attached to her dog with a belt and towline and is pulled by the dog across the snow. More than one dog can be used but usually no more than three. Skijoring has been around for hundreds of years. Scandinavians transported goods in sleds and pulks (similar to toboggans). For control they pulled the sled as they skied. For draft power they hitched themselves to horses or reindeer, similar to how Tod and the dogs pulled Kaley's sled.

These days skijoring is a team sport for humans to enjoy with their dogs. It's easy for dogs to learn and creates a strong bond. Plus it's a hell of a lot of fun. When the dog gets into the rhythm of his gait, the sensation is like skimming across the snow.

As a young dog, Zeus was the best. He kept a steady pace and never strayed off the trail. However it is strenuous exercise, so for that reason he wasn't into it as much as he got older. Venus loved it, but she tended to lose her focus and required more supervision than Zeus. If she spotted a critter as small as a mouse skittering across the snow she bounded off the *piste* with skier in tow.

That day Zeus was hooked up to my towline and Venus pulled Tod. We stopped at Dorothy's View to gaze upon Mt. Sopris and drink in the crisp, clean air.

"Remember last year?" I asked. "We hooked the dogs together as a team and they pulled Kaley's sled. We trained Venus to do that. What the hell went wrong?"

Tod shrugged. "She wasn't crazy back then."

We skied off toward the intersection of Kay's Loop and Eric's Loop where we let the dogs loose from their towlines. As we continued on, something wonderful happened. Zeus and Venus walked together side by side, flanks touching. They sniffed together. They played together. She didn't fixate on him. He didn't ignore her. It was like old times. Zeus seemed to remember what it was he used to love about Venus—her companionship. Tears streamed down my face as I skied.

We devoured *Dog Whisperer* episodes as quickly as they appeared in the DVR queue. We liked Cesar's holistic approach to dog rehabilitation. The way he considered the dog's breed, energy level, training—or not—living conditions, and what sort of pack leadership—or not—comes from the humans around the dog.

Using Cesar's criteria we evaluated our situation. Tod and I were pretty good pack leaders. We didn't "humanize" our dogs. We gave them plenty of exercise, discipline, and affection. I had always been on top of the discipline but I needed to be more patient with Venus. When her anxiety level rose and I had to tell her to sit ten times and she refused, I tended to lose my cool and yell, "Sit dammit!" Just the opposite, Tod needed to be less permissive and more consistent. He cut her way too much slack. Too often he rewarded her anxiety with the affection she craved.

The first thing we needed to do was help Venus control her anxiety. We learned about triggers—situations that activated her anxiety—and how to identify them. Zeus got a lot of exercise for his age, so he tired more easily than her. When he was tired he didn't like to be messed with. As I pointed out, Venus was a nose bopper, which annoyed him and he grumbled at her. That was a trigger. When he grumbled, she became anxious. We worked on training Venus to leave Zeus alone when he was tired.

Family members coming and going was another trigger. Or

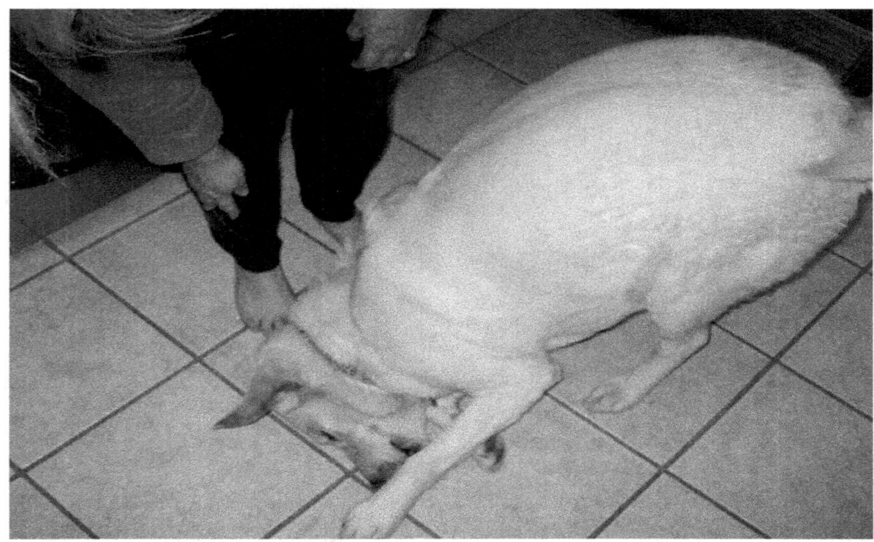

people coming to the door. Any activity at the front door gave her anxiety, a common issue Cesar addressed often. We worked on distracting her during those situations by making her sit until she calmed down.

We learned how to recognize when Venus exhibited dominant behavior, because aggression usually followed. Even though she weighed 90 pounds, she had a habit of walking across the back of the couch. We used to think she was funny like a clown, until we realized she was displaying dominant behavior. We made her stop. In fact much of her attention-seeking, clownish behavior—which had once made us laugh—ceased being funny because we saw through it. She used the spotlight to control situations and gain dominance. As cute as she was, the cuteness led to bad behaviors. Even though we corrected her dominant behaviors, she didn't lose her comical spirit. When told to sit, she liked to put her head on the floor and stick her big butt in the air. We called her "upside down dog."

She also rolled on her back, and grinned upside down. We called it her "wide evil grin." She still tossed her dog toys, but she wasn't allowed to smack Zeus with them. Another favorite pastime of hers was to sit on the chair at the kitchen counter and watch me cook because she wasn't allowed in the kitchen. Even with the drugs and the discipline she kept her fabulousness.

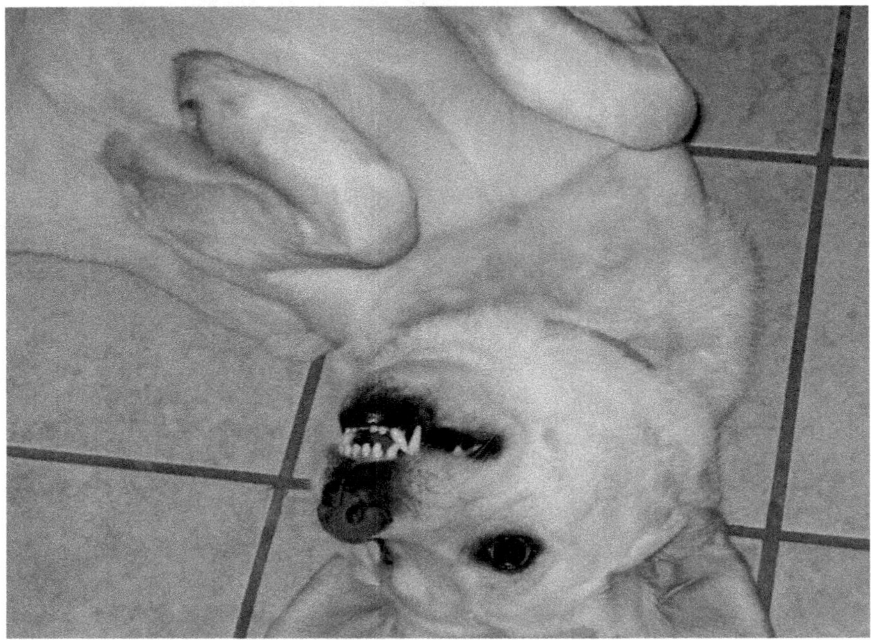

From Cesar's methods, we gained expert advice for dealing with all types of dog anxiety and/or aggression. He usually recommended ten minutes a day on the treadmill. We didn't own a treadmill so we decided our four walks a day were just as effective. The idea was to drain her energy.

With severe "red zone" aggression cases, Cesar usually took the dogs to live with his stable pack for several weeks. Since we don't live near LA, that was never an option. Venus had to mingle with other dogs at the park, so we worked on her social skills there. She had adopted a territorial attitude at the park that she hadn't displayed before her meltdown. We had good days and bad days. What mattered most was we were making steady progress with her.

Yet so much about Venus haunted me. Why did she go crazy? Perhaps she was genetically pre-disposed to mental illness. Veterinary medical researchers suggest an imbalance of serotonin in the brain can cause CCD in dogs. Researchers also recommend taking other factors into consideration, including the dog's breed, plus the levels of "stress, frustration, and/or conflict" in the dog's life, which was exactly how Cesar evaluated each dog.

The clomipramine combined with dog psychology were just the beginning of Venus's rehabilitation. Our next step was to look into her past to find more of the missing puzzle pieces.

Chapter 8 - Panicky pup

In my daydreams I imagined playing doggie psychologist. Venus lay upside down on the couch, as she loved to do, and told me what was really bugging her. She was never one to wear her heart on her paw like Zeus did. I almost always knew what he was thinking. Communicating with Venus involved a deeper intuition. From the *Dog Whisperer* episodes we learned how to recognize subtle signals of anxiety and dominance in her behaviors and how to re-direct her. Change her focus, change her mind.

The first week of December, Venus was scheduled for her four-week checkup. The night before, Tod and I discussed keeping her clomipramine dosage at 75 mg twice a day. The day we accidentally double dosed her she acted sluggish. At 75 mg she was still Venus, yet calmer and more amenable to training. She had responded so quickly to the techniques we'd learned from Cesar, we almost felt like we were cheating with the drug. Almost.

Dr. Price was impressed with how well Venus was doing. She explained the next dosage level would be 100 mg, then up to a maximum 125 mg twice a day according to Venus's weight.

"We've decided we'd like to keep her at her current dosage," I told her. "We're addicted to the *Dog Whisperer.* We're using his dog psychology method on her, and it's working well for us."

Dr. Price seemed surprised but she confessed she loved the show, too. "You're right. It's obviously working. Venus is so calm today. Let's keep her on 75 milligrams. If you change your minds at any point just call me."

"The only problem she has with the pills is sometimes she gags," I said.

"How do you pill her?" she asked.

"I just stick it down her throat."

"Clomipramine can cause dry mouth. It probably gets stuck and dissolves in her throat. It's pretty bitter. Try putting it in a spoonful of peanut butter."

The peanut butter trick led to a comical illustration of the difference between Zeus and Venus. Zeus took Soloxine twice a day for hypothyroidism. So we pilled them at the same time. I tried the peanut butter that evening. Venus loved it. Zeus wrinkled his nose but ate it anyway. The next morning he was ready for me. I stuck the spoonful of peanut butter, with the pill hidden inside, on the roof of his mouth. He rolled his tongue and the wad of peanut butter shot across the room.

Cracked me up. It was news to me he didn't like peanut butter. Or else he preferred my finger down his throat. Weird dog.

Finding the magic dosage coupled with Cesar's rehabilitation method gave us a whole new level of confidence with Venus. Even though her progress was slow and gradual, we continued to see improvement. Training her to control her behavior was only half the battle. We needed to understand the psychological factors that led to her meltdown. When rehabilitating a dog, Cesar always took into consideration the dog's history and breed. Likewise we evaluated Venus. There must have been some signs we missed along the way.

I even considered her birth sign. She was born on May 31, a Gemini dog with dual personalities. As a Gemini myself, I thought I should have been able to help her overcome her evil twin.

Venus was 10 months old when we adopted her from a family. Her name was Shiloh. We brought Zeus with us because we wanted to be sure they liked each other before we took her home. "Shiloh" wasn't the least bit territorial. The two dogs pranced around and played like normal dogs. It looked like love at first sight.

Nancy, the mom, said they had to give her up because she and her husband (we never met him) were working long hours and their two kids were in school so they didn't have time to spend with her. "She climbs over the fence all the time and runs with the other dogs in the neighborhood. But then she makes a mess when we leave her inside. She opens cupboards and eats the food."

We stood in the narrow strip of yard and watched the high energy white pup tear around with Zeus.

"Her favorite thing to do is sit on the couch and watch TV with me," Nancy said, which struck me as odd. The dog didn't act like the couch potato type.

Nancy also claimed she was part Great Pyrenees and part Lab. We knew a lot about both breeds. Labs are good-natured, high energy dogs and Great Pyrenees are mellow, low energy. Seemed like a good mix. So we decided to take her home.

Our decision set off an outburst of frustration and regret about giving her up from Nancy and the kids. The kids cried and "Shiloh" balked when it came time to get in the pickup with us. The scene was emotionally draining for everyone.

Once we got her settled at home we quickly discovered why Zeus was so delighted with her. She was in heat. Even neutered males respond to female hormones so I made an appointment the next day for spay surgery. During the first week it became obvious she'd had little, if any, training. She had a "do as I please" attitude and didn't respond well to simple commands. She never came to the name Shiloh, so I tried several different sounds to see which one caught her attention. I called out different names at her and she responded to Vicky. She liked the "V" sound. I wanted a name to go with Zeus so the choice was easy. Venus.

In place of discipline, she had evidently been punished. When told to "sit and stay" she cowered then tried to flee, and often did. Her behavior told us that most likely someone had smacked her in the sit and stay position. "Sit and stay" is, of course, the cornerstone of any dog obedience regimen. Building trust was a challenge.

The first blush on the white rose faded. Zeus took his time adjusting to Venus. Every time Emily stopped by, he acted overeager around her and seemed to push Venus off on her. Then after she left, he acted sullen and ignored Venus.

"I think he wants Emily to take Venus home with her," I told Tod. "Whenever she brings her dogs over, eventually they go back home. He's trying to get rid of Venus."

Maybe he knew something we didn't.

When Venus recovered from the spay surgery, more behavior problems arose. Twice she climbed over the front gate and escaped. We installed an electric wire around the perimeter of our fence. After one low voltage buzz at the gate she never tried to escape again.

Zeus had always trusted us and accepted Tod and I as his pack leaders. Because he was the older, more stable dog, we assumed Venus would be submissive toward him and learn from his behavior. For the most part she did, yet sometimes she rebelled against her place in our pack. As a one-year-old pup Venus weighed 70 pounds. Zeus weighed 140. It was crazy for her to take on a dog twice her size. But she tried.

One morning while they played tag in the yard Venus grabbed Zeus by his collar. Somehow her lower jaw got tangled. She panicked and began snapping and snarling. Luckily I was home and managed to unhook his collar before she strangled him. Zeus and I were both bitten in the process. I kept Zeus's collar off for a couple weeks. I played with them daily to show Venus how to play fair. It worked and we eventually put Zeus's collar back on, though I loosened it to slip off more easily. When she nipped at his collar during play we corrected her.

At the end of her first month with us, we took the dogs camping in Utah. There was an incident the first night. Venus started eating the food in Zeus's dish. He walked over and growled at her. She lunged at him. He pinned her on the ground. We pulled them apart. The fight amounted to no more than teeth gnashing and gobs of saliva, and there were no injuries. Zeus handled the incident perfectly. He put Venus in her place. Nothing more needed to be done. We thought Venus was crazy to take him on and she'd learned her lesson.

At the time it seemed logical that her anxious, dominant behavior was related to having her spayed while she was in heat, which could have caused a sudden decrease in estrogen, along with a surge in testosterone. We put her on the homeopathic remedy Aggression Formula.

In the early days of their relationship, Venus occasionally showed jealousy toward Zeus. She acted like she was starved for affection and didn't want us to pay attention to him at all. One morning I stood on the porch and talked to Zeus while I scratched his ears. Venus walked over and nose bopped him. Zeus gave a low growl, a warning to back off. She snapped at him. I grabbed her collar to pull her away and she bit my arm. It could also be said that my arm was in the way when she snapped at Zeus and I got bit. True—but it was no excuse. Biting me was unacceptable.

The way we handled her jealousy was the same way we had handled it with our other dog pairs in the past. We played with them. With Venus and Zeus we used Jolly Balls, ten-inch polyethylene balls with handles. Horse people and big dog people prefer them because they are virtually indestructible. The handle makes them really easy to toss and easy for dogs and horses to pick up. Venus had a red ball. Zeus had a purple one. Each dog could chase his own ball, but not the other dog's ball. In early childhood parenting circles the practice is known as parallel play. In dogdom, it's a game without competition to teach the dogs to play side-by-side, while enjoying the attention of their humans.

On a camping trip to the Flat Tops in mid-July, Venus dug up an elk bone and teased Zeus with it. I ordered her to stop. We tried to get the bone away from her which delighted her even more. Zeus stepped in and growled at her. She dropped the bone and lunged at him. Because we were right in the middle of it, we separated them before a fight broke out. Tod grabbed her and I snatched the bone. He put her in the camper for a time out and gave her some Aggression Formula. Meanwhile I hid the bone in the pickup. She calmed down and that was the end of it.

We kept Venus on the Aggression Formula for about six months. There were no more incidents. She seemed happier and more stable. Venus and Zeus became good buddies. She accepted Tod's and my roles as pack leaders. She played well with the other dogs at Dogland. If another dog challenged her she stood her ground but didn't fight, which was normal dog behavior. She adored Kaley and never snapped at her. From the moment she met them, Venus loved our cats and treated them like they were her little lambs.

As we gained a better understanding of dog psychology, we recognized some things we could have done better back then. In retrospect, we didn't fully understand her anxiety.

Most of our dogs had been Golden Retrievers. Zeus was our

second Malamute. No dog is easy to train and they all had their quirks. But my dogs had always respected me as the boss, or pack leader. Venus was different. When I looked back on our first year with her I recognized something. With a big dog, it's important for the human to establish physical dominance. In other words, the dog must always think the human is bigger than him. I had that power over Zeus from puppyhood. Venus weighed 70 pounds when we adopted her. No small dog. Whenever I had tried to bring her down to the ground, to surrender, she fought back. When I couldn't control her physically I yelled at her. With practice I figured out that when I raised my voice she didn't listen. When I lowered my voice to almost a whisper she had to strain her ears to hear. The softer my voice, the more she listened.

We came to the conclusion the bad behaviors during her first six months with us were rooted in separation anxiety. As I mentioned, she showed signs that she had been punished and shut in the bathroom when she was a puppy. She probably wasn't beaten. It seemed more likely the punishment and confinement had caused her to develop anxiety, but not necessarily aggression. The snapping, snarling, even biting she engaged in when we first adopted her amounted to an undisciplined puppy testing the pack. The aggression witnessed in her as a mature three-year-old was something else.

A few puzzle pieces fell into place. We had the anxiety thing figured out. But we still had obsession and aggression staring us in the face.

Medical researchers and Cesar Millan have pointed to breed as a factor. Knowing she was Akbash was only part of the puzzle. There was so much more about the Akbash dog breed we did not yet understand.

Chapter 9 - The grizzly bear and the elephant

Psychoanalyzing obsessive dog behavior can lead to— well—obsession. It's a matter of perspective. It was easy to get caught up in the psychology and forget we were dealing with dogs. Dogs do think. But they think like dogs. Not like humans. Therefore, understanding breed characteristics was crucial. It kept us focused on dog behavior. Breed is all about genetics and temperament. We had only begun to understand the Akbash in Venus.

When Venus's mental problems gradually emerged in the months before her meltdown, Carol and Richard had shared their Gabriel stories with us. After her meltdown, they encouraged us to stick with her. Because of her experience with Gabriel, Carol became my lifeline. Besides, Venus had known Buddha and Fannie since we adopted her. Together at the park, our dogs made a stable pack which was essential to her rehabilitation. She was always calm with them. The two Labs together brought out the Lab in her. Sometimes I just needed to hear Carol say, "Venus is doing so well. Gabriel could never play with other dogs like she does."

Once we understood what she was, we had to figure out what it meant. The Akbash dog is a low energy guardian dog. Their protective nature makes them territorial. The Labrador Retriever is a high energy hunting dog. Both are working dog breeds, but the territorial nature mixed with high energy seemed like a recipe for obsession. Yet obsession is what makes the Akbash dog a perfect guardian for a herd of sheep. The dog must simultaneously keep track of the sheep while looking out for predators. In order for the dog to become good at his job he must be obsessed with guarding his sheep.

While observing the Akbash at Meadow Lake, we had noticed that a dog could be lying in the grass, looking as though he was sound asleep, and suddenly jump to his feet barking ferociously. We had seen the same behavior in Venus.

A working dog needs a job to do. The new going-to-the-office routine had been working out well for her. It gave her another job to do—guard the office—and added variety to her routine so she wasn't bored.

Learning about the Akbash breed and watching Venus, we figured out she was a checker—a "rain dog." When she came in the house, she checked on Zeus, she checked on the cats, she checked her food dish. Then she settled down. When she went outside, if Zeus was out, she checked on him first.

"She probably has a whole other checking ritual she does around the yard," I said.

"If obsession is the nature of her breed, it makes sense we have to allow some of that," Tod said.

I agreed. "Her rain dog routine seems harmless."

However obsession can lead to controlling behaviors, which meant we couldn't allow her to take it to the next level.

Several breed descriptions stressed the Akbash are guardian dogs, not herding dogs. However when we observed the dogs at work with the sheep we saw them make every effort to keep the herd together. If a sheep wandered, a dog nipped at it to nudge it back toward the herd. We translated that behavior to Venus and Zeus. When she nose-bopped him, nipped at him, pawed him, or threw toys at him, she was trying to control him. But he didn't like it. So we taught her to leave him alone. She could look but not touch. "Leave it," was the command.

Zeus was not a sheep. He was a purebred Alaskan Malamute. Malamute temperament is not as easily describable as other breeds. Each individual dog's temperament is a reflection of the environment in which he's raised. A neglected or abused Malamute, because of its size alone, can become a huge problem. Even though they are not considered guardian dogs, a Malamute will protect his owner—if he trusts him. Above all else, Malamutes are fiercely loyal to their pack.

In general Malamutes are intelligent, social, good-natured, and communicative. At times they are high energy working dogs. Other times they are low energy companion dogs. They are highly adaptable, yet they thrive on routine. Most Malamutes adopt rituals over simple acts. Zeus picked up his food dish with his teeth and banged it on the floor while he ate. He circled three times before lying down. Our previous Malamute, Apollo, also had rituals. We have a saying, "If you do something twice with a Malamute, it's a ritual."

Therefore ritual behavior was a characteristic of both Akbash and Malamutes. Other than the fact they are both dog breeds, they shared little else in common. Combining an Akbash and a Malamute seemed like pairing a grizzly bear with an elephant. A really bad marriage.

Analyzing the breeds was less comforting than we'd hoped. The question wasn't so much whether Venus could be rehabilitated. The question was whether the two dogs could live together under the same roof. What it boiled down to was how Zeus responded to Venus. His behavior was fascinating.

Zeus was a keen observer, a thinker. When we started watching the *Dog Whisperer,* he couldn't help but notice our walks had turned into training sessions. He also noticed we were training Venus to leave him alone. About a month after her meltdown, he started watching the *Dog Whisperer,* too. I know it might seem bizarre to anyone who has never witnessed it, but some dogs do watch TV. In one particular episode a one-year-old female Pit Bull named Justice was undisciplined and out of control. She had begun to act aggressively toward the family's six-year-old male Golden Retriever mix, Percy. Cesar expressed enormous empathy toward Percy for having to put up with the "crazy bitch." Zeus perked up his ears and looked at the TV. *He feels my pain.* Cesar showed the owners how the older, more stable dog could be encouraged to train the younger dog.

After the episode, Zeus paid more attention and participated in Venus's training. He showed her by example how to walk properly on the leash. When we approached other dogs or strangers he tossed his head in the air. *Watch me.* Then he walked on, ignoring the distraction. We encouraged him. We made a special point to watch episodes that included using the energy of the calm, stable older dog to get the younger, messed-up dog to follow commands.

When we told Venus to sit, Zeus sat and then looked at her. *See? Like this.* At Dogland we started letting her off-leash if no one else was around, or if there were dogs she knew well. Zeus showed her how to greet other dogs in a friendly way, instead of charging up to them. If she charged anyway, Zeus ran interference and blocked her. *Not so fast. Let's do this together.* When she wandered off, Zeus found her and brought her back to us. We never instructed him to do any of those things. He learned from watching the *Dog Whisperer.*

In another episode, Cesar showed how one dog will discipline another dog with a growl or nip (or bite), or a combination of both. That is not dominance or aggression. It is one dog telling the other one to stop the bad behavior. Right after we saw the episode, Zeus tried it out on Venus when he didn't know I was looking. The dogs were in the yard and another dog walked by. They always got excited when a dog walked by, which was normal. With Venus it could become obsessive. That day her bark turned ferocious as she dashed madly up and down the fence line. Zeus blocked her and did a combination growl with a nip. *Settle down, bitch.* I held my breath. A month earlier she would have snarled, jumped on him, and pinned him down. She looked startled for a second. *How dare you!* Then she lowered her head and backed away, and eventually lay down.

It was a pivotal moment. I felt the impact. It was amazing to see Zeus actually change her mind. As we trained her, he must have seen how much control we had gained by distracting her from bad behaviors, which gave him the confidence to participate without fear of being attacked.

His can-do attitude was a perfect example of Malamute behavior. Like Cesar has said, "dogs don't rationalize," but Malamutes do think their way through obstacles. They handle challenges with intelligence, patience, and perseverance. Sometimes Malamutes think too much. When Zeus kept his distance and ignored Venus he was overthinking and dwelling on the problem. He was feeling sorry for himself. We encouraged the Malamute in Zeus to be the calm, stable example to Venus—the teacher.

Christmas Eve brought the birth of our grandson, Henry. Our lives were filled with all the fun and chaos of a new baby. Kaley and Venus were already close. Venus followed her everywhere. Whenever Emily brought baby Henry into the house, Venus lay quietly nearby, watching him, protecting him like a newborn lamb.

We also noticed the beginnings of a healthier, more trusting relationship between Venus and Zeus. We gave them each a pink blanket for Christmas. Pink represents balanced energy. We had learned her obsessive nature was an Akbash breed characteristic, which was intensified because of her high energy, Lab mix. We were still analyzing what caused her anxiety. Was it too much confinement and/or punishment as a puppy? Or was it something else?

Chapter 10 - Obsession

Dog psychology was powerful stuff. I began thinking like a dog. I sensed energies in people and dogs more easily. I psychoanalyzed them. The brown Pit Bull mix down the street ran the fence line and barked at my dogs when we walked past because he was jealous. He wanted to go for a walk, too. Trevor didn't listen to Jeanne because she shouted at him too much. Sasha was timid and fearful because Amanda was over-protective and treated her like a child. I was obsessed.

No matter how much we learned from the *Dog Whisperer,* we knew we weren't just dealing with behavioral issues with Venus. Even though we saw gradual progress, in some respects Venus seemed untrainable. She often repeated bad behaviors, no matter how many times we corrected her. A sure sign of mental illness.

We didn't even know if her progress was normal. I desperately wanted a prognosis. I felt like I was blindfolded, riding backwards on a horse. I had to let the horse lead the way, or in my case, the dog. Venus was my case study.

Tod and I walked the dogs together as much as possible with our odd schedules. It was often our only opportunity to discuss Venus. I was perfectly capable of walking them by myself. I used my skijoring equipment, a waist belt and towline, for Zeus because he didn't pull, and a flexi-leash for Venus. She was good on the leash—most of the time. She had her quirks. A big one was middle-school-age boys. Whenever we met up with young boys she barked and lunged. If the boys were willing, we asked them to stand still. Or, as Cesar would say, "No touch, no talk, no eye contact."

But whenever we tried that line their reply was always, "Huh?"

Instead we said, "Don't touch Venus. Don't talk to her. Don't look at her."

We assured them she wouldn't bite. Then we let her sniff them and eventually she let them pet her and play with her. No matter how many times we put her through the drill, she still barked and lunged at young boys, even the ones she had met.

One evening in January after meeting up with three young boys, Tod said, "I'm not sure what the deal is with young boys."

"It's fear. She's afraid of them," I said. "But I don't know why."

"It's like she perceives them as a threat for some reason," he said. "It doesn't seem to matter how many times we correct her. So it's not just the fear and anxiety. It's obsession, too."

"Anxiety, obsession, aggression. They're all connected," I said. "I don't think we can fully understand her aggression until we understand her obsession."

In spite of our higher learning and our psychological approach, sometimes our life with dogs was reduced to animal carcasses and vomit. In February, some health issues cropped up in both dogs over President's Day weekend. Venus liked to track down and dig up dead animals at Dogland, and especially along the West Elk trail. She could sniff out an elk carcass buried in the snow from a hundred yards away. She was enjoying a productive winter. So many elk bones, so little time. Unfortunately her nasty habit had resulted in sores on top of red, swollen skin around her mouth. Dr. Price called it a "localized scleroderma" and prescribed antibiotics.

"I know it's hard to keep her from finding dead stuff but try to keep her from chewing on it," Dr. Price said.

Which meant from then on I would have to "own" the smelly dead things in order to get them away from her. Lucky me.

Zeus had been puking yellow bile during exercise for a few days. As with most large breed dogs, Malamutes and Akbash are at risk for bloat, especially as they age. The infamous Gabriel had died from bloat. So did my niece's German Shepherd. We fed our dogs grain-free dry dog food. Zeus ate once a day, in the evening. Dr. Price said he didn't show any signs of bloat but he probably had gastritis from exercising on an empty stomach.

"How much exercise does he get?" she asked.

"A half-hour walk in the morning. 20 minutes in the evening. And ten minutes before bed," I said. "On weekends we ski for two hours and he keeps up."

She raised her eyebrows. "Wow. That's a lot of exercise for an eight-year-old Malamute. I'd say that's about the max for him. And you need to make sure he eats something in the morning at least an hour before he exercises."

Malamutes have a tendency to be fussy eaters. Zeus had raised fussy eating to the level of performance art. We considered the options. He refused to eat dry food in the morning. Period. I didn't want to climb that hill. He had turned up his nose at canned food in the past. Cooked turkey burger would be a good protein source and he liked it. But it would add too much fat to his diet. And what if he decided he'd rather eat turkey burger than dog food? There was that whole ritual thing.

Zeus liked scrambled egg, a good protein and easy to fix. No need to worry about his cholesterol because he got plenty of exercise. So I fed him a scrambled egg in the morning and he stopped puking.

My visit with Dr. Price gave me another angle to consider. We had been so focused on Venus's behavior and mental health, we forgot to factor in Zeus's health and how that affected her.

Zeus's thyroid level had tested low six months before her meltdown. Dr. Landers told me Zeus was 20 pounds overweight and hypothyroid. I flashed back to the reason why we adopted Venus. We thought Zeus was bored and lonely. We attributed human emotions to his weight gain and sluggishness. More than likely he was hypothyroid. We hadn't even considered a health problem.

When a dog senses weakness in another dog she will try to dominate him and/or become aggressive. In the wild, dogs will attack and kill an injured or sick dog. Rollie was a Rottweiler/Lab mix who had lost his left front leg in a collision with a bus. At Dogland, Venus bullied him mercilessly. *Hey three legs!* She knocked him down. *Because I can.* Then she rolled him over. *See how easy this is?* Every encounter with Rollie was an exercise in teaching her to "leave it."

Was Venus's aggression toward Zeus related to his hypothyroidism? Was she bullying him? In order to answer those questions, I had to figure out how she perceived his condition. Dogs sense energy, so there was no doubt in my mind she sensed his weakness. Rollie was missing a leg. His weakness was external. She wasn't vicious toward him. She knocked him down and rolled him over because it amused her, no matter how much it annoyed the rest of us, Rollie in particular.

Zeus's weakness was an internal imbalance. To understand how Venus handled it, I looked for clues in her history with our cats. When we adopted her we had six Himalayans. Five-year-old Moby was the youngest. She obsessed over him from day one. She sniffed him. She licked him. She tracked him. She slept near him. We thought she really, really liked Moby. Three months later he suffered a stroke and died. The necropsy showed his liver had grown around his heart. The vet said if he had only known, he could have fixed the problem surgically. If we had better understood Venus's obsessive behavior back then we would have understood she sensed something was wrong with Moby. She didn't have x-ray vision. She must have sensed his health problem in his energy.

The January after Venus's meltdown, Lucy died. She was "Mr. Magoo," the cat who stumbled into the dog fight. She had been in fragile health for about seven months. Venus had doted on her, too. Lucy never tolerated the sniffing and licking. But Venus always checked on her. Lucy had slept on the loveseat in the afternoon, with Venus nearby. Because of our experience with Moby, we knew why she obsessed about Lucy. She sensed her frail energy. Her death bothered Venus. She became anxious and obsessive about the other four cats. She wasn't aggressive, yet obsessive enough that we considered increasing the clomipramine. But we decided to wait. We reassured her. We kept an eye on her around the cats. Within a couple weeks she seemed satisfied the kitties were fine.

When I looked back on her sensitivity to Moby's and Lucy's failing health, it seemed like I had stumbled onto something. She sensed the imbalance in their energies and obsessed over them, but she didn't attack them.

With Zeus, her reaction was a little more complicated. His hypothyroidism didn't occur overnight. He gradually slowed down and gained weight over a three-year period. He probably had the beginnings of hypothyroidism when he met Venus. She had always obsessed over him. During the month prior to her meltdown, Zeus's health improved on Soloxine. He lost weight and gained energy. His mood lightened. If anything, Venus seemed less obsessed with him as he felt better. In the same time period, there were also the two instances where she attacked other dogs at the park. Those dogs weren't sick.

It didn't add up. I couldn't make the connection between Venus's aggression toward Zeus and his hypothyroidism. I believe his condition contributed to her obsession with him, but not the aggression. She obsessed over Rollie's missing leg but she didn't attack him. When she obsessed over Moby and Lucy she was never aggressive. Obnoxious maybe, but not aggressive.

Venus was sensitive to the energy around her. The sixth sense. All animals have it. The guardian Akbash in Venus made her genetically predisposed to react to her sixth sense. All dogs sense vibrational energy—positive, negative, unbalanced. What about Zeus? Did he sense Moby and Lucy's failing health? I'm sure he did, though he responded like a Malamute. He accepted it the same way he accepted three-legged Rollie. Venus reacted like an Akbash/Lab mix. She obsessed about it.

Another puzzle piece locked into place. Venus was more sensitive than normal to unbalanced energy. She was hypersensitive, which caused her anxiety and obsession.

Hypersensitivity. Anxiety. Obsession. Aggression. Venus had a lot going on in her brain—for a dog. Most experts in the dog world understand how stress, frustration, and/or conflict in the dog's life can trigger aggression. In every *Dog Whisperer* episode about aggression Cesar Millan insisted that the dog's ability to sense unbalanced or negative energy in humans or other animals could turn an anxious dog into an aggressive dog. In other words, show Cesar an aggressive dog and he looks for the source of unbalanced energy in the dog's life. We just needed to identify the source of the unbalanced energy in Venus's life.

Chapter 11 - No bad dogs, only bad people

"There is no such thing as a problem breed. However, there is no shortage of 'problem owners....'"

Cesar Millan's famous credo gave me plenty of sleepless nights. Even though Dr. Price, Tod, and Emily had assured me I had not caused Venus's aggression. Even though I knew she was mentally ill, in my darker moments I agonized over all the things I should have done differently from the moment we adopted her.

But then at the crack of dawn Zeus was always there with a wink and a nudge. *You know what they say. I'm the perfect dog.* Living proof I could raise a calm, stable beast. He wasn't to blame for Venus's aggression either. Even though he bore the brunt, he was never the target. She adored him. She was obsessed with him. He was her punching bag. Zeus was the battered spouse.

In dogdom it's called "redirected aggression." When a human or other animal taunts or arouses a dog into aggressive behavior, and the dog can't reach the taunter, she will turn her aggression toward someone else. For example, two dogs behind a fence might turn on each other as they bark at a dog passing by. Venus had never attacked Zeus under those circumstances, only because he didn't get over excited along with her. However when Venus did attack Zeus, she definitely took out her frustration on him.

What was the source of her frustration?

The more we understood dog psychology, the more we understood Venus. The more we understood Venus, the more sharply our own lives came into focus. The answer was right in front of us. Her frustration was the same as our frustration—the neighbors from hell. We knew we had a problem there. We didn't realize how much it had affected Venus.

Daryl and Margie Harrison, with first one son, then a second, have lived across the street since we moved to Silt in the mid-90s. They were here first. She was a stay-at-home mom when her boys were little. When they went off to school, she went with them and worked at every school they attended. Daryl was a truck mechanic. From the beginning we had very little in common so we never really hit it off.

We often compare life in Silt to the 90s TV show *Northern Exposure,* only we call it "Southwestern Exposure." Like Cicely, the fictional Alaskan village, Silt is a melting pot of ordinary, unique, and eccentric people. Before Silt, we had lived in the Minnesota north woods, a mile from Lake Superior. We had no close neighbors and kept to ourselves. When we sold our home, our nearest neighbor left a note in our mailbox: "Even though we didn't know each other very well, you were always good neighbors. Never any trouble. Sad to see you go."

Upon our arrival in Silt, we fell into the category of ordinary people with unique talents. Tod is an IT geek and I'm a writer. We were ill-prepared for small town life in a fish bowl. We're not exactly Welcome Wagon, block-party people. Tod's travel schedule doesn't allow much time for a social life. As a writer, I tend to be reclusive. To our new neighbors we must have seemed like mole people.

Margie and Daryl came across as hyper-vigilant from the get-go. Most of our conversations with them involved us listening to their gossip and complaints about the other neighbors. In their eyes everyone was getting away with something.

"If they feel that way about the other neighbors, they must think the same way about us," I told Tod.

He agreed. "They definitely have an opinion about everyone."

A few complaints surfaced during our first year via the police department. A couple months after we moved in we were told by Chief Suttle there had been a complaint about our Malamute, Apollo, being off-leash in our yard and allegedly scaring little kids. Sometimes he did run around off-leash but he never went after little kids.

"Just make sure you keep him on a leash when you walk him," Suttle said.

In those days, Tod's office was in our home. Within six months Chief Suttle showed up again to ask about his "home business." There had been a complaint about daily FedEx deliveries and truck traffic.

"We heard you're running a wholesale lumber business," Suttle said.

Tod explained that he was the IT manager for a wholesale lumber company and he wasn't operating the business out of our home. "Yes, FedEx does make deliveries a couple times a week. But I don't have anything to do with the truck traffic in this neighborhood."

"What about your wife? Is she running any sort of business?" Suttle asked.

"She's a writer," Tod said. "Why all the questions?"

"Like I said, we had a complaint. I'm just here to check it out," he said.

We suspected the Harrisons had complained about Apollo and Tod's home office. We never understood why they called the police rather than talk to us directly. More than anything, it was a rude awakening. Never before in our lives did we have neighbors and cops all up in our business. We each reacted in our own unique and eccentric ways. Tod decided to raise his profile in the community. He applied for a seat on the town planning and zoning commission and was accepted with open arms. I withdrew into my work and kept my distance from people. I admit I'm a lousy neighbor. I never have time for coffee and I think people should mind their own business.

But the Harrisons were also unique and eccentric in their own way. Minding their own business wasn't their style. The complaints didn't stop and were always delivered by cops. One holiday season Tod strung miniature white lights along our fence. A cop stopped by and said a neighbor complained our lights were too bright. Tod thought he was joking and laughed.

He wasn't joking. "Just be sure to turn them off by 9:00 p.m."

There wasn't a barrage of complaints during those early years, just petty grievances maybe once or twice a year. With Chief Suttle in charge, all the cops ever did was to inform us of the complaint and, in typical cop fashion, they made suggestions. We weren't warned or ticketed for any violations because we weren't breaking any laws. A gradual awareness set in that our neighbors, particularly the Harrisons, paid more attention to us than we did to them.

Seven years after we moved in we added a wrap-around porch and stucco-sided our house. What should have been a 90-day construction project dragged on five months. On top of coping with workers and trucks and noise all day long, I had to put up with the neighbors' complaints about the workers and trucks and noise. Everyone blamed us because it took so long—especially the Harrisons. The cops showed up a couple times, once about a complaint that we didn't have a permit. We did. Another complaint was about the noisy jackhammer. The cop pissed off Wiley, the contractor, so he left for the day— one of many such delays.

When the Harrisons couldn't get any satisfaction out of complaining to the cops, Margie came at me head on, something she had never done before. One morning before Wiley showed up, she marched over and complained about his loud radio and that he brought his dog with him.

I shrugged. "If you have a problem with Wiley, then you should talk to him."

"I'm telling *you,*" Margie snapped. "He works for you."

I laughed. "No. He doesn't. He's a self-employed contractor. He does what he wants when he wants."

Besides, I didn't think his radio was too loud and his dog Yogi (a Shepherd mix) was well-behaved. Zeus was an energetic two-year-old at the time. He and Yogi played in the yard until they passed out. The only problem was sometimes Wiley left one of the gates open and Zeus and Yogi wandered around the neighborhood (scaring little kids!). Eventually I did have to tell Wiley to make sure to shut the gates so the dogs didn't get out.

"So what?" He shrugged. "They get a little exercise."

"Well, the neighbors have already complained to the cops," I said. "So if the dogs get caught we'll both get fined a couple hundred bucks."

That pissed off Wiley and he left for the day.

The morning they poured concrete for the sidewalks and patio, the cement truck was parked in front of our house. The minute I walked out the door to check on all the action, Margie stomped toward me. There was no point in saying "good morning." I could tell she was mad.

She pointed at the truck and shouted over the engine, "That truck has to move. It's blocking my driveway."

"No it isn't," I shouted. "You can back out easily."

"But once I back out I can't get past the truck," she argued.

"Then go the other way!"

"You can't block the street like that!"

Fed up, I shot back, "You wanna make a bet? See that permit?" I pointed to the building permit posted in the window. "We paid to block this fucking street!" I walked away.

Things were never the same between us after that. Perhaps I should have gone the extra mile to foster better neighbor relations back then. Maybe I shouldn't have been such a bitch. My own failure at diplomacy made me partially to blame for the bad blood between us. My problem was, I wasn't interested in fostering their friendship.

People reveal a lot about their character by the way they treat their pets. The Harrisons had a female Black Lab named Cherokee, a trained hunting dog. She died a year after we adopted Venus. For most of her 11 years Cherokee lived in a four-by-six kennel with a dog house. She was seldom allowed indoors. They fed her and gave her water and, except for the occasional hunting trip, she was deprived of the human companionship all dogs crave. In the early days, Tod had asked Daryl about her living conditions.

"She's a trained hunting dog," he said. "Not a house pet."

But we had known a man in Minnesota who kept three or four trained hunting dogs at a time. Their living conditions were far superior to Cherokee's. Tod pointed out her living conditions to a cop once.

He shrugged. "The dog has food and shelter. It's not abused."

Zeus was very much aware of Cherokee's presence across the street. He saw her. He heard her bark. Dogs know things. They communicate with their energy. Zeus was very friendly. "The Wal-Mart greeter," we called him. He liked all dogs and most people. He went out of his way to greet other neighbors. But he always avoided the Harrisons. He didn't like the way they treated Cherokee.

Through several decades of marriage, Tod and I have lived many different places. We've had dozens of neighbors. Some real characters. I could write a book. But none quite like the Harrisons. In the interest of maintaining peace, we adopted a non-confrontational approach and stuck with it. In short, we ignored them.

Until the Harrisons found a scapegoat for their hostility. Her name was Venus.

Five months after we adopted Venus, we left the dogs over Labor Day weekend. Tracy, the pet sitter, came in twice a day. When we returned home, Tracy said Daryl had complained Venus "barked all night" while we were gone. We were surprised because she had often spent nights outside and hadn't barked unless she wanted in.

"Maybe she had separation anxiety because we were gone," I said.

Whatever the case, we took Daryl at his word. I sent flowers with a note of apology. The whole family arrived on my doorstep to thank me. Venus stood on the front porch behind the gate barking her fool head off. She would not calm down. I handed them treats to give her but she refused and growled at them. I had never seen her act that way. Even Zeus refused the treats and walked away.

"We didn't know you had another dog," Daryl said.

I raised my eyebrows.

"Until we heard her barking last week," he added.

I laughed. "How did you not notice this big, white dog hanging around our place all summer?" I suspected he was lying, even though it made no sense.

"We've never heard her barking before last weekend," he said. "You must keep her inside all the time."

"No. She's outside most of the time. Even at night." I looked him in the eye but he avoided me.

By then Venus's barking had become so out of control it was impossible to talk. I opened the gate thinking she would calm down and accept the treats. Instead she bolted down the sidewalk and ran away. While I walked down the street and coaxed her to come back, Daryl followed and lectured me about the perils of adopting a rescue dog.

"You can't train them," he said. "They have bad habits and you can't break 'em. She doesn't even come when she's called."

"She has never behaved this way before," I said.

When she finally returned she trotted a wide circle around the Harrison family. She wouldn't go near any of them. Venus told me a different story. She definitely knew the Harrisons and she did not like them. She feared them. Afterward I told Tod about the strange meeting.

"The whole thing gave me a bad feeling," I said. "I'm telling you Venus knows Daryl and she doesn't like him. She was afraid of him. And she wouldn't go anywhere near their boys."

"Something must have happened while we were gone," he said. "We just don't know what."

I asked our other neighbor, Irma Nossie, whether Venus barked all night while we were gone.

"No dear, we didn't hear a thing," she said. "If she was barking, we certainly didn't hear it."

"Did you hear her bark any time while we were gone?" I asked.

She shrugged. "Oh, once or twice. I don't remember. It wasn't anything out of the ordinary."

However, on full disclosure, Irma and Joe Nossie are an elderly couple and might not have heard Venus barking.

A couple months passed and then the weekend before Thanksgiving Daryl showed up while we were cleaning leaves off the front porch.

He stood with his arms folded across his chest. "I think you guys need to know your white Lab barks all the time when you're gone."

He seemed real uptight so I tried to humor him. "Oh come on now. You can't expect us to send flowers every time Venus barks."

"This is not a joke," he snapped. "I'm dead serious."

"Okay fine," I said. "A couple months ago you said you didn't want her to bark during the night. So we've been keeping her inside at night."

"I said she barks when you're gone."

"That's interesting," I said. "No one else has complained."

"Well I'm complaining," he said.

"Oh come on. It can't be that bad," I said. "We hardly ever leave the dogs."

"I'm telling you now. I want it to stop. Don't make me get the police involved," he warned as he stomped away.

Tod and I looked at each other. His attitude seemed way over the top. We have neighbors all around us. No one else had complained about Venus's barking. I saw Irma almost every day. If Venus had been barking a lot, she would've told me.

By that point in time, Tod had raised his profile to town trustee. Coincidentally a week later at the town board meeting, he was singled out when our dogs were accused of being out of control at Dogland. Madeleine Hatter addressed the board and complained that our dogs had roughed up her Scottish Terriers at the park on the Sunday before Thanksgiving.

Tod said, "I was with my dogs that day. They walked up to your dogs and sniffed them. Otherwise I didn't observe them doing anything to your dogs."

"I was afraid they would step on my dogs," she said.

"Mrs. Hatter, my dogs are not in the habit of stepping on other dogs," he said.

"They frightened my dogs," she insisted.

"My wife and I were right there. Your dogs didn't bark or act fearful. If our dogs were a problem you should have said something to us. But you didn't," Tod said. "Though I did notice you were talking to Mayor Minnifield in the parking lot as we were leaving."

Madeleine tossed her head. "I told him I thought the park was a mess. People don't pick up after their dogs. And dogs should be on a leash. Especially big dogs like your Huskies. I'm afraid of big dogs and I know other people are, too. So we stay away from that park. But it should be for everyone."

"Did the mayor ask you to come here and complain about my dogs?" Tod asked.

Mayor Minnifield objected.

"Yes he did," Madeleine said. "But I want to revise my complaint. It's not fair for my dogs to be on a leash with Tod's big, giant Huskies running around. We have a leash law in this town. It should be enforced at the park."

In response, the other board members decided they would impose a leash law at Dogland. Since Madeleine Hatter's complaint and Daryl Harrison's complaint seemed to rise out of thin air at the same time we wondered if they were somehow connected. As is typical with small town politics, it was no secret some of the other board members, including Mayor Minnifield, did not like Tod. We had good reason to be suspicious.

Nonetheless, I attended the next board meeting to defend myself and my dogs. Several other dog owners showed up at the meeting to protest the leash law and the trustees backed down. Afterward I stood outside the town hall talking to other dog owners. The park had never been officially designated as an off-leash dog park by ordinance. Dog owners had simply adopted it over the years. We decided it was time to make it official with a citizens' petition.

Venus and Zeus had been home in the yard for a little over an hour. The town hall is about three blocks as the crow flies from our house. I didn't hear any dogs barking while I stood outside or when I walked home. When I was a block away Venus barked excitedly. As I walked in the door I heard a voice on the answering machine. It was Margie Harrison complaining about the barking. She said Venus had been barking "for hours"—a lie.

A month later in early January, we went out to the annual town employee appreciation dinner. We were gone two hours and returned home to a message on our answering machine from Daryl. He swore at us about Venus's barking. He even played a recording of loud dog barking. It sounded like the dog was barking into a microphone.

"Wait a minute." I replayed the message. "If he was close enough to our fence to record her barking, then he provoked her."

The Harrisons were lying. But we had no way to prove she was not barking excessively when we were not at home.

"We need to get a bark collar," Tod said.

"No way," I argued. "Pay attention. Every complaint happened when we were doing something related to the town. Madeleine Hatter admitted the mayor encouraged her to complain about our dogs. Maybe he got to Daryl, too."

"You may be right," he said. "So if we use a bark collar it will put an end to Daryl's complaints."

I hated the whole idea but he bought one anyway.

Tod approached Daryl and told him about the bark collar. "Since you're the only one who has complained about her barking, it would help if you let us know whether the collar is working."

"Bark collars don't work," he said. "Besides it's no big deal. I don't really pay that much attention to your dog."

"I couldn't believe he said that," Tod told me afterward. "But I didn't want to argue with him. So I shook my head and walked away."

In the middle of winter I circulated a petition to designate River Park— aka Dogland—as an off-leash dog park. Most of the board members opposed my petition. If it was successful the board could not reject it, they could only approve it or send the matter to a special election. I only needed 62 signatures. Collecting signatures gave me the opportunity to ask all the neighbors around us if Venus barked a lot when we weren't home. They all said no.

One Saturday I used the petition as an excuse to pay a visit to the Harrisons. They signed the petition. I asked them how Venus was doing with the new bark collar. "Has she been barking when we're gone?"

Margie avoided my gaze. "I don't know." She glanced over at Daryl. "Have you noticed?"

He shrugged. "I don't pay much attention to your dogs."

"How does Kaley like kindergarten?" Margie changed the subject.

The very next day we returned home from a day of downhill skiing to two agitated dogs. We had left them in the yard. Venus was wearing the bark collar and she was hoarse. I took it off her. A warning ticket was attached to our front door. We noticed fresh tire tracks in the snow in our driveway and figured she had been barking because someone was on our property. Tod called Officer Dolittle, who had issued the warning ticket. He said he had received a complaint so he had pulled into our driveway and stayed there for 10 minutes and she had barked the whole time.

Tod was furious. "You had no right to park in our driveway and provoke our dogs."

"Well you didn't get a citation, just a warning," Dolittle said.

"That's not the point and you know it."

We were stunned. Officer Dolittle came to our house, parked in our driveway, and provoked Venus until she barked herself hoarse through the bark collar.

"This is animal cruelty on top of entrapment," I said.

The following week I talked to Irma and our other neighbor, Betty Paxton, and apologized for Venus's barking. They both said they had not heard her barking until they saw a police car in our driveway and assumed that was the reason for her barking.

A few weeks later, I turned in the dog park petition with 20 more signatures than I needed. We arrived home after an evening out to a message on the answering machine from Officer Dolittle again. He asked Tod to call him about our dog barking.

So he did. Dolittle told him there had been another complaint about our dogs. He said he had driven by but they weren't barking.

"That's because Venus was wearing a bark collar," Tod told him.

Dolittle said the caller had also complained that we neglected our dogs. The caller had alleged that we left them outside in the cold for hours without any food, water, or shelter. The temperature was 20 degrees that night and we had been gone for three hours.

Tod couldn't help but laugh. "That's ridiculous. The dogs have shelter and dog beds on the porch and they have a dog door into the garage. We keep their water pail in there. We don't feed them outside. I invite you to come over any time and see how my dogs are treated."

"A garage isn't warm enough," Dolittle said. "You should have doghouses or keep your dogs inside when it's cold."

They went round and round about the fact that we had two dogs but no dog houses. At one point Tod asked, "Could you please quote the ordinance that says if I don't have a heated garage I must provide a dog house?" He knew there was no such ordinance—and so did Dolittle.

"I'm just asking, why don't you have dog houses for your dogs?" Dolittle persisted.

"Because they don't live outdoors," Tod said. Finally he asked, "So were my dogs barking or not?"

Dolittle replied that he hadn't heard the dogs barking but someone had definitely complained about them. Of course we knew it was Daryl. We also knew at that moment his 11-year-old Cherokee was outdoors, huddled in her dog house, struggling to keep her old bones warm, while he complained that we left our dogs out in the cold. Maddening.

The conversation with Dolittle had insulted Tod. He talked about it with Police Chief Whittle. He also told him about the day Dolittle parked in our driveway and provoked the dogs to bark. "It looks to us like our dogs are being used to harass us," Tod said.

Chief Whittle said he would investigate the incidents, but he never did.

In April, my petition was grudgingly approved by the town board and River Park was officially designated an off-leash dog park. None of the board members, except Tod, thanked me for my efforts. But the dog owners in town were thrilled.

During the spring, political strife stirred up our little fish bowl. The town administrator, Tony Alexander and his wife Paulette, the planning director, plus the town treasurer, all resigned amid allegations Mayor Minnifield and Trustee Fellspar were harassing them at work, and interfering with their jobs. The news of the allegations wasn't a surprise, but the resignations came as a shock. We hadn't realized how stressful the situation had become for the staff. We wondered about our own situation. We already knew the mayor had encouraged Madeleine Hatter to complain about our dogs. Was Fellspar in on it, too? Perhaps he and the mayor had urged Daryl Harrison to complain and then demanded that Officer Dolittle respond.

There was also a shake-up in the police department. Chief Whittle had stepped down for health reasons, but he remained on the force. Officer Dolittle was fired, though we never found out why. The new police chief, Horace Bickle, was hired by the town board. The decision wasn't unanimous. Tod voted for the other applicant and Bickle knew it.

A couple months passed with no complaints from the Harrisons or the cops. Venus wore the bark collar when we left the dogs at home. One evening in July, Tod and I met with Tony and Paulette Alexander at their home to discuss forming a recall committee against Mayor Minnifield and Trustee Fellspar. In real life the mayor was a developer and Fellspar worked for a local lumber company. We had evidence of private meetings where they were offered kickbacks from another developer if they approved his re-zoning request. While the four of us talked outside on the Alexanders' deck, I noticed Officer Piddle drive by slowly.

Our meeting lasted about two hours. When we returned home both dogs were extremely agitated. Even Zeus was barking and he rarely barked. Venus was wearing the bark collar. She was whining and hoarse. A warning ticket hung from our front door handle. On the answering machine was a profanity-riddled message from Daryl. However the time of his call was after the time on the warning ticket. So we knew he wasn't the one who called the cops.

In the days afterward we conducted our own investigation into what happened that night. What we learned confirmed our suspicions. Fellspar had called in a complaint about our dogs barking to Officer Piddle. Fellspar didn't live anywhere near our house but he did live near the Alexanders' house. Officer Piddle knew we were meeting there because he drove by and saw our pickup. When Piddle delivered the warning ticket, the dogs barked at him, which prompted the message on our machine from Daryl. Piddle also happened to be working his final shift that night, as in leaving the department.

But we couldn't prove anything. The person who gave us the information was a cop. He wouldn't back us up because he was afraid of losing his job. He told Tod, "It was a political prank. Forget about it."

Easy for him to say. We knew Mayor Minnifield and Trustee Fellspar were influence peddling with developers all over the county. And because we knew, they retaliated by encouraging our neighbors and the cops to lie about our dogs. Their misconduct in office was serious enough, but they had personalized it by using our dogs to intimidate us. We refused to be intimidated. At the end of July, our committee filed petitions to recall Fellspar and Minnifield. Fellspar resigned immediately, but not Minnifield. He was outraged.

We were concerned about the dogs' safety during the petition drive so we kept them indoors while we were gone. Venus and Zeus were always well-behaved in the house. We didn't crate them. It was curious that Venus's previous owner Nancy had said she behaved so badly indoors. Venus never opened a cupboard or made a mess in our house. She and Zeus hung out and ate and slept. We usually left the radio tuned to new age music.

In August, we accused Mayor Minnifield of violating town ordinances. He had built a fence without a permit and most of it was on a neighboring property. His construction equipment was parked in the middle of a street in his subdivision, also without a permit. The mayor didn't think the rules applied to him. I posted photographs on my blog of the fence and the bulldozer blocking the street. The following Saturday we went for an hour-long bike ride and left the dogs out. Margie left a message on the machine and said Venus had been barking all day long. A lie.

In September we turned in our petition to recall Mayor Minnifield with more than enough signatures. Two days later we left the dogs out while we were gone for a few hours. A half hour after we left, Margie left a message complaining that Venus had barked all morning. Another lie.

A pattern had emerged. Every time I posted the mayor's violations on my blog, the Harrisons complained about Venus. I had already received hate emails from Minnifield's son and his friends.

It was obvious to Tod and me and everyone around us that it was all connected to the recall campaign.

Chapter 12 - Harassment

The recall campaign happened the year before Venus's meltdown. During that time we didn't notice whether the harassment was having a negative effect on Venus and Zeus. The signs were there, I'm sure. We weren't paying attention. Certainly they must have sensed the bad energy and felt stressed. It's the constant drip, drip, drip over time that does real psychological damage.

Even though our petition was successful, the mayoral recall had to go before the voters in the town election, which was scheduled for the following spring. We had a five-month long campaign ahead of us.

In November we flew to Hawaii for a week, leaving Emily to watch over our home and pets. We hadn't had any complaints in two months, though we hardly ever left the dogs at home and when we did Venus wore the bark collar. Coincidently, I hadn't posted anything about the mayor's misdeeds on my blog.

We left on a Saturday. Emily kept Venus at her house. She didn't want to leave Zeus alone so she brought Koho, her blind Husky, to stay with him. Koho and Zeus grew up together. As older dogs by then, they slept a lot and didn't bark. Koho had spent many nights with us. Our house was simply an extension of his house. Emily checked in twice a day, fed them, and walked them. She thought everything was fine until Wednesday morning. She found a warning ticket from Officer Tuttle on the front door. It was dated the previous day.

She took the ticket to the police station and explained to Chief Bickle and Officer Tuttle that she was taking care of our dogs while were out of town.

"We're well aware your parents are in Hawaii," Chief Bickle said.

"Oh really," Emily said. "That's interesting."

"Daryl Harrison filed a complaint yesterday about the Yellow Lab barking on Monday night," Bickle said. The cops always referred to Venus as the "Yellow Lab," same as Daryl. He showed her the complaint which stated: "Tod and Peggy Tibbetts' Yellow Lab began barking constantly at about 7:20 p.m."

"He's lying," Emily said. "Venus has been at my house since Saturday morning. My dog Koho was there with Zeus and they don't bark unless they're provoked."

"When I parked in the driveway yesterday both dogs were barking," Officer Tuttle said.

Emily couldn't believe it had happened again. "My Husky's blind. So when you parked in the driveway you obviously freaked him out and he barked." She glared at Chief Bickle. "This is harassment pure and simple. You're picking on my parents because of the recall."

He didn't take kindly to her accusation and she wound up with a citation. She took Koho and Zeus to her house.

On Saturday she came to our house and played her car stereo while she washed her SUV in the driveway.

Daryl strode across the street and shouted at her to turn off the music and leave. "You tried to trick me by switching dogs but I showed you. You got a ticket."

Furious, Emily chased him off our property. He threatened to call the cops. She's the one who should have called the cops but she didn't trust them. They were part of the problem.

When we arrived home Sunday she told us about the whole fiasco.

I shook my head. "Wow. They even harass us while we're on vacation."

By dragging Emily into it, they succeeded in proving her point. Harassment was our punishment for the recall. Daryl admitted he knew she switched dogs, which meant he filed a false complaint.

Tod noticed the date of the barking complaint on the citation didn't match the date on Daryl's complaint form. "This is bogus. Take it to court," he said.

There were no complaints in December. As usual we hardly ever left the dogs and when we did Venus wore the bark collar. I didn't post anything on my blog about the mayor either.

Tod went to court with Emily in January. Before going in front of the judge, they met with the town's attorney at the time, Wendy Grayson. Emily pointed out the different dates on the citation and the complaint form.

"We now have two different police officers who have admitted they parked in our driveway and sat there while the dogs barked," Tod said.

Grayson was well aware of town politics. "Do you think this is related to the recall?" she asked. "Some sort of retaliation?"

"Sure looks that way to me," he said.

She dismissed the citation.

The next day at around 5:30 p.m., I was home alone. Dogs barked outside. I headed for the door but the phone rang. The caller ID flashed Harrisons' number. I answered. Daryl hung up. I reacted like Pavlov's dog and plodded downstairs to bring the dogs inside. I found them both sprawled out on the carpet in my office. They weren't barking. They weren't even outside. I assumed Daryl found out the citation was dismissed. The hang-up call was meant to harass me, which was totally creepy, and a criminal offense.

On Sunday we went downhill skiing and left the dogs outside. It was 32 degrees and snowing. Midday Emily got a phone call from Officer Whittle. He told her to go over to our house and put the dogs inside because Daryl had complained again. When Emily arrived at our house she discovered fresh boot tracks in the snow. A man had been walking back and forth in front of our fence several times.

She tracked down Officer Whittle and told him about the boot tracks. "Did you walk in front of the fence?" she asked.

He said they weren't his tracks and added, "It could've been anybody."

"It's obvious Daryl provoked the dogs until they barked," she said.

Later when she told us what happened she added, "I know Whittle believed me but I could tell he didn't want to deal with it."

We checked out the boot tracks. She was right. Someone had been walking back and forth in front of our fence.

Several weeks passed. We only left the dogs outside when we went downhill skiing, which was only on Sundays, and not every Sunday. Eight hours was too long to leave them indoors. Luckily I worked at home and the Harrisons were gone all day during the week, taking their hostility with them. However when they came home, the dogs wanted in. They were indoors so much they didn't grow winter coats. Their whole routine had changed. The winter was colder than normal. Zeus was lethargic and grumpy. His beautiful fur coat looked dull and ratty. His thyroid level was probably low back then, we just didn't know it. He barked more. We thought he was stressed out. Veterinary researchers don't know what causes canine hypothyroidism. However it is an autoimmune response—stress turned inward.

Venus handled the stress differently. She became anxious and territorial. She barked at Daryl and his middle school-age boys when they were outside. She was trying to tell us something. She developed a mistrust of all middle school-age boys. When we combined her behavior with the boot tracks in the snow it was obvious Daryl, and probably his boys, were provoking the dogs.

We took them cross-country skiing with us every Saturday and walked them more during the week, hoping the activity would ease their stress.

The recall campaign was in full swing. Tony Alexander, the ex-town-administrator was running for mayor. We were consumed with phone calls, emails, signs, flyers, and newspaper reporters. Most of my blog posts were about town election information and encouraging people to register and vote.

Six weeks before the election, I posted a list of Mayor Minnifield's misdeeds in office. Four days later we went downhill skiing.

The weather forecast was sunny and mild, so we left the dogs outside. Venus wore the bark collar. We came home to an all too familiar scene. The dogs were agitated. Zeus was barking. Venus was hoarse and whining.

Ten minutes later a cop car pulled up. Another new cop, Officer Muddle, came to the door and asked Tod for his driver's license. "I had a complaint about your dogs barking. I'll have to issue a citation."

Tod held up the collar. "She was wearing a bark collar."

"I parked in front of your house for 10 minutes and both dogs were barking," Muddle said.

"So you provoked them," Tod said. "And it's not the first time the police have provoked my dogs. As far as I'm concerned this is harassment." He refused to hand over his license.

Muddle returned to his vehicle to write out the citation. Daryl charged out of his house and into the street. He shook his finger and yelled at Muddle, "You better be writing them a ticket, goddammit. Nothing has ever been done about this!"

If Tod or I had assaulted a cop that way, we would have been arrested. But not Daryl. Officer Muddle made his day.

The timing of my blog post and the citation was no coincidence. Everyone knew Mayor Minnifield had it in for us. Connecting the dots between him and the police was easy. We knew he owned a scanner so he could monitor police calls. We assumed whenever he heard a complaint about our dogs, he pressured the officers to do something about it, even if it meant sitting in our driveway to provoke them.

While I was collecting signatures for the recall petition, one of the mayor's neighbors said he had told her, "If you want to be safe in this town, don't sign that petition. I have the police department in my pocket."

Except for the fact that everybody seemed to know everybody in Silt, we didn't see any connection between the mayor and Daryl. We figured someone else was encouraging him. Fellspar, the ex-trustee who had resigned, was mad at us for filing the recall petition against him so he was a possible suspect. There was another trustee, Marybeth Christianson. She didn't like us either, especially me and my blog. She lived in our neighborhood. She definitely knew the Harrisons. In fact, during the recall petition drive we had seen her talking to Daryl in front his house several times. It wasn't a big stretch to imagine she had encouraged him to keep an eye on us, and make sure we abided by the law. Her trustee seat was not up for re-election that year so she had elevated herself above the rest of us. Publicly she condemned the recall campaign. In private conversations, she derided the mayor. She fit the profile of our suspect. Someone who appeared detached from the situation while sneaking around behind the scenes causing trouble.

Maybe we had it all figured out. Maybe we didn't. It didn't matter because we couldn't prove anything. We assumed once the election was over, things would calm down. We failed to understand what all the negative energy directed at us and our dogs was doing to them–especially Venus. We protected them from physical harm but we couldn't shield them from psychological harm.

Besides, we were swept up in the campaign which was going better than we had expected. We were having way too much fun to dwell on the negative stuff. Actual campaigning was easy. Mayor Minnifield was so unpopular we didn't have to twist any arms to convince voters. Along with my blog, we had attracted local media attention. Victory seemed all but certain. For us it not only meant a change for the better in our town government but also an end to the harassment.

Four trustee positions were up for grabs but only three people were running. I thought it would make things even more interesting if I ran for trustee. Everyone on the recall committee urged me to run. I had no problem getting 25 signatures for my nomination petition. A week later I made it official and turned in my paperwork.

Two days later, on a Sunday, Tod let the dogs out at 6:30 a.m. I was in the shower. Venus barked a couple times then stopped. The phone rang. It was Daryl. He hung up when Tod answered. She barked again. The phone rang again.

By then I was out of the shower. "What's going on?" I yelled. I picked up the phone. It was Daryl—again. He hung up.

We left the dogs inside while we went skiing that day.

On Monday, after Tod told Emily about the hang-up calls, she called me. "I'm really worried that Daryl is going to hurt the dogs, Mom. To be honest he scared the crap out of me that day he came over and yelled at me. Those hang-up calls are illegal. He's harassing you. You have to file a complaint."

I knew she was right. "I'm just concerned it'll make things worse."

"Things are pretty bad already," she said. "How much worse can it get?"

"Oh, it can get a whole lot worse. Believe me," I said.

But I filed a complaint the next day. I met with Chief Bickle. He read over my complaint. "This is about the barking dog citation you got last week," he said, referring to the incident with Officer Muddle.

"No. It's about Daryl Harrison making hang-up calls," I said.

"And he is upset about your dogs barking," he said.

"Daryl provoked the dogs that day," I said referring to the citation. "And so did the officer."

His face flushed with anger. "What do mean by that?"

"The officer admitted he parked in front of our house. He provoked our dogs," I said.

But he turned it around on me. "Dog owners have a responsibility. People have the right to complain."

We argued. I remembered what had happened to Emily. I didn't want another citation.

"Talk to Officer Whittle," I said. "He knows what's been going on. There should be an investigation. We believe the Harrisons and certain police officers are being encouraged to use our dogs to harass us."

Chief Bickle rolled his eyes. "If there's any harassment involved, that's a matter for the courts, not the police department," he said dismissively.

"What about the hang-up calls?" I asked.

"That's a statutory criminal offense," he replied. "You have two choices. You can press charges and the matter goes to court. But there's also the matter of the citation, which makes it look like you're retaliating, so it's—"

"No," I interrupted. "It looks like harassment, because that's what it is."

He gritted his teeth and glared at me. "Or we can schedule a mediation session. It's up to you."

Some choices. He had me backed into a corner. I tossed up my hands. "This is an impossible situation. We've never been through anything like this before. We have cops parked in our driveway when we're gone. We're concerned about the safety of our dogs. Our own safety. Daryl Harrison has a serious anger management problem. We just want the harassment to stop."

"Then I think we should give mediation a try," he said.

I reluctantly agreed. We had to start somewhere. We scheduled it for the first week in March.

Tod reacted positively to the news. "It will give us a chance to tell our side of the story. This isn't just about the Harrisons. I have a few things to say to Chief Bickle, too."

We should have pressed charges instead.

Chapter 13 - Dog fight

In preparation for the mediation session we visited three of our closest neighbors, the Nossies, the Paxtons, and Randy Flinch. We told them about the Harrisons' complaints about Venus's barking. They were sympathetic and supportive.

Irma Nossie said, "She's a good dog."

Joe Nossie nodded. "She barks for a reason, then she quiets down."

Betty Paxton said, "Venus is a good watch dog. We don't really hear her barking that much."

"So that's why the cops are at your house all the time," Art Paxton grumbled. "Is it against the law now to have a watch dog?"

"Apparently so," I said. "At least in our case."

They all agreed to sign a brief statement which said they did not think our dogs barked excessively, or created a nuisance.

Randy Flinch, the Harrisons' next-door neighbor, was our last stop. Our little chat with him was enlightening. "Venus barks sometimes." He laughed nervously. "A lot of dogs bark on this end of town. It's kinda hard to tell which one is barking. I think my dog barks more than she does. But I don't want him to complain about Baby." With a sigh of resignation he tossed up his hands. "Look, it's no secret how much he hates you guys. He told me more than once I better choose sides."

"Choose sides?" Tod asked.

"I don't know." He backed away. "I just don't want the guy mad at me. Okay?"

In spite of his fear of Daryl's wrath, Flinch signed the statement. "Because it's true," he said. "Besides if I say your dogs are a nuisance then you might come back and say Baby is a nuisance."

I rolled my eyes. "Look, we're not interested in fighting with anyone about anything. We're not petty and ornery like the Harrisons."

Tod rushed me out the door. As we walked home he said, "Did you hear that? Daryl told him to choose sides. Like it's a war. The guy is nuts."

"Who? Daryl or Flinch?"

The weekend before the mediation Venus pulled off a stunt worthy of "Stupid Pet Tricks." On Friday, Kaley (who was six at the time) came over and played her favorite Easter game — hide the plastic Easter eggs. It was my job to find them. Venus followed her as she placed the eggs around the house and then wiggled with delight each time I found an egg. Afterward I set the wire basket of plastic eggs on the end table in the living room.

We went downhill skiing on Sunday and left the dogs inside. When we returned, Venus and Zeus greeted us at the front door. I found a pink plastic egg on the bottom step. There was a blue egg in the mitten basket. At the top of the stairs I found a yellow egg. Venus pranced around excitedly. I checked the basket on the end table. It was empty. She had "hidden" all the eggs.

I clued Tod in to the game. Each time we found an egg Venus grinned and wagged her tail. *Good job. Now find the next one.* She followed us happily as we found all one dozen plastic eggs. They weren't exactly hidden, more like scattered around in the bedroom and living room. There was no doubt Venus had done it. Zeus hadn't played the game with Kaley and me. Venus, the clever clown dog, not only remembered the game, she mimicked it to entertain herself when she was bored.

She licked my hand as I dropped the eggs back in the basket. *That was fun.* I giggled. "Can you just imagine her picking each egg out of the basket with her mouth, then dropping it in a different spot?"

Tod laughed. "I wonder. Was this like a project she did all at once? Or did she pick up an egg and drop it every so often during the day until the basket was empty?"

"Well?" I patted her sleek head. "What do you say?" She grinned. *That's my little secret.*

Three days later we met at the town hall for the mediation session. Daryl and Margie Harrison were lying in wait, seated at the table with Chief Bickle.

Daryl pounced on us as we walked in the door. "Why do you hate us?"

"We don't hate you," Tod said. "Why are you harassing us?"

We sat down at the table, across from them. Chief Bickle was seated at the end, to my left.

Margie said, "Your dog barking constantly is harassing *us.*" Then she launched into a tirade about how Venus's barking kept them awake at night and disturbed the peace and quiet in the neighborhood. "Your dog has ruined our lives." It was quite the display of histrionics in front of Chief Bickle.

"Is this about just the one dog?" he asked. "Or both dogs?"

"Just the Yellow Lab," Daryl said. "We don't have a problem with the other dog."

I held up the complaint from the previous November. "This says both dogs."

"You heard what I said," Daryl snapped. "If you came here to argue with us, we're leaving."

"Okay, so we've established that your Yellow Lab named Venus is the problem," Bickle said. "Let's move on."

"I've logged all the incidents right here." Daryl handed over a spiral notebook.

Bickle looked it over. "None of these constitutes excessive barking." He showed Daryl a copy of the barking dog ordinance.

He pushed it away. "So you're holding them to the letter of the law and not the spirit of the law."

"What's that supposed to mean?" I asked.

Margie piped up. "Look at that smirk on your face. If you're going to be snide and sarcastic, we're leaving."

We got the message. They were looking for any excuse to walk out.

Daryl said, "Tod is a town trustee. I think he should be held to a higher standard."

"I have been held to a higher standard," Tod said. "You said nothing has been done about Venus's barking. But that's not true." He described all the efforts we had made to appease them, from the bark collar to keeping the dogs indoors.

"We keep them inside so much they don't even have winter coats," I said.

"That's *your* problem." Whenever Daryl looked at me he glared as though he wanted to reach across the table and strangle me.

I glanced at Bickle knowing he could see the hatred. Their hostility filled the room. Yet he made no mention of it.

I displayed the statements from the neighbors on the table. "I have brief statements from three close neighbors. They all said Venus does not bark excessively and they don't have any problems with our dogs." I turned to Bickle. "They also said you could contact them to discuss our dogs."

Daryl checked to see who the neighbors were then shoved the papers back at me. "These don't mean anything. We *do* have a problem with your dogs. That's why we're here."

"I'm sorry. I'm confused. Is it dog or dogs?" I quipped. "And actually we're here because of your hang-up calls."

"The problem is, no matter what we've done it's never enough," Tod said. "And now you're harassing us with hang-up calls."

"I had every right to make those calls," Daryl said. "You were letting her bark on purpose."

"That's not true," I said.

"According to state statute, placing hang-up calls does constitute harassment." Chief Bickle placed a copy of the statute in front of Daryl.

He pushed it away. "They weren't hang-up calls. They just didn't answer the phone. I could see through the window. They weren't anywhere near the phone."

My eyes almost popped out of my head. "How could you see inside a second story window from across the street?" I asked.

Daryl sneered at me and raised his eyebrows. Our house is a two-story with the living room, dining room, and kitchen on the second floor. The Harrison house is a single story. How could he see through our second-story window? How did he know where we kept the phone? Did he pick the lock and enter our house when no one was home?

I looked at Bickle. "Did you hear what he said? He admitted to spying on us."

He shrugged it off. "Let's get back to why we're here tonight. We need to find a way to resolve this. The Harrisons feel you're letting Venus bark to annoy them."

I rolled my eyes. "Let me explain something. I'm hearing impaired. I don't let Venus bark. Sometimes I can't hear her barking."

"What do you mean you're hearing impaired?" Daryl demanded.

"I'm deaf in my left ear," I said. "If I'm on the phone, or the TV is on I can't hear her bark."

"Huh!" Daryl snorted. "Likely excuse. Why are we just finding out about this now?"

"Cuz it's none of your business, that's why," I muttered.

"See what I mean?" Daryl looked at Bickle. "I don't have to put up with her attitude."

"The point is, Mrs. Tibbetts can't always hear the dog barking," he said.

"Venus isn't the only dog in the neighborhood that barks," Tod said. "Other dogs bark all the time. There's another dog that sounds just like her. In fact I've reacted to it, thinking it was Venus, only to find her in the house."

Daryl glared at him. "We're not talking about other dogs. We're talking about *your* dog."

"We've already established that," Bickle said.

Tod brought up the boot tracks in the snow outside the fence a few weeks earlier. Chief Bickle looked at Daryl.

He tossed up his hands. "The dog's barking was driving us crazy. So I went over to see if I could get it to shut up."

"That's not the best way to deal with a barking dog. It only makes the situation worse," Bickle said. "Besides, you need to keep off the Tibbetts' property when they're not home."

Tod looked at him. "What about the police? They provoked our dogs, too."

"I'm aware of those incidents and I'll put a stop to that," he said. "We have other ways of determining whether your dogs are barking. Let's get back to finding a way to resolve this. I'm open for suggestions."

"It's very simple," Daryl said. "We don't want their dogs to bark. At all."

"Well that's not possible," Bickle said. "Dogs bark."

Margie pulled a sheet of paper from her folder. “We figured you’d say that. So we’ve made a schedule. Their dogs can’t be outside from 8:00 p.m. to 6:45 a.m.”

I laughed. “You can’t be serious. And what part of your lives do we get to control?”

Margie leaned forward. I thought she might slap me. “You already control our lives by letting your dogs bark constantly.”

“This is ridiculous!” I wailed.

A shouting match erupted.

“Everybody calm down,” Bickle said. “You can’t expect the Tibbetts to keep the dogs inside that long. They have to relieve themselves.”

“Then they will have to have to go outside with them and keep them quiet,” Margie said.

Chief Bickle looked at Tod and me. “Are you willing to do that?”

I noticed they were back to talking about the dogs—not the dog—again. I sensed the confusion was deliberate and nothing would be gained by pointing it out one more time. Daryl would probably bite my head off again. I kept silent.

“Do we have any choice?” Tod asked.

“Do we have any choice whether your dog barks?” Margie snapped.

“Ignore it,” Tod said.

She and Tod argued. From then on it was a train wreck.

“Okay. Let’s make a deal,” Tod said. “In return for following your schedule, we get to leave the dogs out when we’re gone one night a week and on Sundays. And we’ll put the bark collar on Venus.”

“As long as you’re home by 8:00 and the dogs don’t bark,” Margie said.

I groaned. “Unbelievable.”

They both glared at me. Daryl added, “And you have to get a citronella bark collar because the shock collar doesn’t work.” He even insisted we hire a dog trainer to train Venus not to bark.

“I’ve trained quite a few dogs myself,” Chief Bickle said. “You can’t train a dog not to bark.”

“You can train a dog to do anything,” Daryl said.

Because we apparently hadn’t endured enough abuse, Chief Bickle said we had to meet again in three weeks to check on our progress. He said to the Harrisons, “If you have any complaints, do not call the Tibbetts. You have my cell number. Call me instead.” He looked at Tod and me. “Is there anything else you’d like to say?”

We responded with stunned silence. I stared at the clock. I wanted that hour of my life back. Daryl’s own logs proved Venus wasn’t barking “constantly.” She wasn’t a nuisance. Bickle should have told him to back off, quit filing false complaints, and stop harassing the Tibbettses. Instead he went along with their insane dog curfew as though we had committed a crime. We were dismissed.

On the walk home Tod said, "That was some mediation session. We proved he's harassing us. They attack us and we get slapped with a curfew. Pretty outrageous."

I un-gritted my teeth. "Well, we know one thing for certain. This isn't about Venus barking. It never was. This is all about us. They really do hate us."

"I don't understand why Bickle let them take control," Tod said. "He had Daryl on the hang-up calls. Then he turned it around on us. I think he believed them when they said we let her bark on purpose."

I shrugged. "I think he hates us, too."

When we walked in the door, Tod picked up the bark collar, removed the battery and threw it away. Daryl had admitted those were his boot tracks in the snow outside the fence. He had provoked Venus and Zeus. And so did the police.

Dogs don't rationalize. They react to conditioning. Almost every time we drove off in the pickup and left them outside, someone—the police, or Daryl, or one of his boys—provoked them until they barked. To complicate matters for our already anxious and obsessive Venus, she had been wearing a shock collar and getting buzzed every time she barked. By any definition that is torture. Animal cruelty. No wonder she became increasingly territorial. From that day forward the bark collar was just for show. I was right. Tod was wrong. The bark collar was a big mistake. We will always regret we tortured her that way. We learned our lesson.

The next day I ordered privacy shades to replace the blinds on our windows. Daryl had admitted to looking in our windows. He must've used binoculars. We were totally creeped out.

Mediation was a waste of time. We should have pressed charges.

Chapter 14 - No quarter asked, no quarter given

The curfew was absurd. It begged the question: Who was monitoring our behavior? The Harrisons? By going along with it Chief Bickle had, in essence, granted them permission to harass us. There was no other way to view the situation.

We loosely followed the 8:00 p.m. to 6:45 a.m. curfew with Venus. We let Zeus do as he damn well pleased. We left the dogs out only when we were gone on Sundays. Venus wore the bark collar *sans* battery, just for show.

"If Daryl sees her without the bark collar, he'll call the cops for sure," Tod said.

We had no time to dwell on absurdity. We had an election coming up. Because it was by mail, ballots trickled in to the town hall over a two-week period. The town clerk counted them as they arrived. On the Friday before the Tuesday election deadline, the recall was ahead by ten votes. When all the ballots were counted four days later, we lost. The recall lost. Our mayoral candidate lost. I lost my bid for trustee. Everyone was shocked. We knew it would be close but we were certain we would win.

One of the election judges confided to a recall committee member that the day before the election, 70 ballots were left in the ballot drop box outside the town hall. They were not mailed. The sudden, last-minute arrival of 13% of the total ballots received was highly unusual during a mail election. Even more suspicious, the 70 ballots were signed by newly registered voters. Oddly enough Mayor Minnifield won by 60 votes, after being behind by 10. Did the mayor pay special visits to newly registered voters to help them fill out their ballots? We'll never know. The town clerk didn't investigate.

The election judge also said the mayor dropped off two ballots signed by him but the town clerk allowed him to correct his "mistake." While I consoled my comrades on the committee I was quietly relieved. At least it was over. Maybe the nasty emails would stop. Maybe the Harrisons and the cops would stop harassing us.

We brought a professional mediator, Jack Morgan, with us to the next mediation session, which happened the day after the election. On full disclosure, Jack and Tod were both members of the same trails organization. So he was also a friend. When Tod told him about the first mediation session, Jack said we shouldn't go back without a mediator and offered to sit in.

Of course Daryl and Margie objected. But he convinced them as a professional he would be objective.

Chief Bickle asked the Harrisons if things had gotten any better, as though we were a couple of naughty teens. Daryl shrugged and begrudgingly said they hadn't had any problems with us since the last session.

Margie added, "But eventually they'll go back to letting Venus bark again. That's the way it always works. It gets better for a little while then it just gets worse again."

"Then what are we doing here?" Tod asked.

"We're here because you're a trustee and you get special treatment," Daryl said.

"Yeah," Margie said. "I'd like to know why this meeting had to wait until after the election."

I pushed my chair away from the table. "I thought we were here to talk about our dog barking."

"That's exactly why we're here," Bickle said. "So let's move on."

Jack spoke up then. "The Tibbetts are here because they are eager to resolve this problem. From my understanding of the circumstances that brought us here, they have responded and are responding to your complaints about their dog barking. I can assure you, the fact that they're here is all the evidence you need they are not being shown any favoritism or special treatment. They are not required by law to be here. And it's my understanding they haven't violated any laws."

"If you're just going to take their side, we're leaving," Margie snapped.

Jack encouraged Margie to speak her mind and assured her we'd all listen.

She lashed out at Tod. "It's obvious they don't want to be here. Look at Tod." She glared at him. "He's seething."

Jack asked Tod for his response.

He looked Margie in the eye. "After everything we've done to appease you, you still have the nerve to say we'll just let Venus bark again, like we're making her bark just to piss you off."

"Well aren't you?" Margie asked.

"Sure looks like that to us," Daryl sniped.

Jack held up his hands. "This isn't going to resolve anything. Mrs. Tibbetts hasn't had the chance to say anything. I think it's her turn."

I said, "I find it interesting that they say things have gotten better lately. Because nothing has changed. We're not doing anything differently."

"Did you get the citronella collar?" Bickle asked.

"Nope," I said. "You said his logs showed that Venus's barking did not violate the ordinance. I did a little research and the citronella collar is less effective than the shock collar."

"What about the dog trainer then?" Bickle asked.

"No again," I said. "You said yourself you can't train a dog not to bark. Venus is trained. I train my own dogs."

Daryl sneered. "And you failed miserably."

I answered back with my own attitude. "Thank you."

Tod spoke up. "Look, we've done everything we can to resolve this situation. By your own logs, her barking didn't violate the ordinance. I don't know what more we can do."

"You could always get rid of her," Daryl said.

A shouting match erupted.

Jack intervened. "Obviously the Tibbetts are not going to get rid of their dog. Tod said they've done everything they can to resolve this. I think that's been well documented. Going forward, does anyone have any other thoughts as to how we can resolve this situation?"

Daryl said, "Well, for one thing, I'd just like the Tibbetts to stop being so hostile toward us. They don't speak to us. They don't even wave anymore. With Tod being on the board and all, they set a bad example for our boys."

Jack looked at us. "Well how about it? Do you think you can ease the tension and restore a more friendly atmosphere?"

"No," Tod and I said in unison.

Jack asked if we cared to elaborate on our feelings.

Tod shook his head. "No thanks."

I leaned forward. "Let me get this straight. We're being forced to live by your rules, even though we have not violated any laws. You are the ones who violated the law. You made false complaints. You admitted to harassing us and our dogs. The police have harassed us and our dogs. But we are being treated like criminals. Now we have this hammer hanging over our heads and if we screw up. Bang!" I slammed my fist on the table. "And you want us to be nice to you?" I leaned back in my chair. "I don't think so."

I was so over it by then, but the session went on for another excruciating 15 minutes. Chief Bickle said the Harrisons were too focused on Venus's barking. He advised using white noise to mask other sounds. Daryl and Margie sat stoic and silent.

Jack talked about other neighbor disputes he had mediated and how they were resolved. "The best way to resolve these types of neighborhood disputes is if both sides agree to give a little." He looked at Daryl and Margie. "The Tibbetts have done everything you asked them to do. What are you willing to do?"

But they wouldn't give an inch.

As he wrapped up the session, Bickle told us, "From now on

when you're going to be out of town you will need to kennel your dogs instead of leaving them in your daughter's care. She clearly can't handle them."

"You mean we aren't allowed to have our dogs protecting our property while we're gone? Like any other citizen?" Tod asked.

"If you contact the police department before you leave town, we'll make sure your house is on the patrol roster." Bickle looked at Daryl. "We do that for all citizens, not just trustees."

"I have a question," I said. "Why are you putting all these rules and regulations on us? It's like we're on probation or something. But we haven't broken any law."

Bickle looked insulted. "These aren't rules and regulations. They're merely suggestions. Strictly voluntary. You're the ones who said you wanted to resolve this situation. You can do that by being more cooperative."

I stood up and walked out.

Afterward we lingered outside the town hall with Jack. He shook his head. "Wow. You are so right. This is not about Venus. Those people absolutely hate you. My wife and I had neighbors like them once. We eventually had to move. I don't see how you can ever resolve this. And I'm the professional." He laughed. "You're right about having made all the concessions."

"And they will hold this over our heads," I said.

He rolled his eyes. "There's no doubt about that. This whole matter was never handled properly by the police department from the beginning. If there's no evidence your dog's barking violated the law, it never should have come to this ...." Jack's voice trailed off. He looked past me while Bickle and the Harrisons filed out of the building and into their vehicles. As they drove off Jack raised his eyebrows. "I wonder what they were discussing behind closed doors after we left." He glanced around. "Here we are, out in the open where anyone can hear us."

I had been holding my breath since the three of them walked out. I finally exhaled. "Look, it's a relief to have one more sane person witness the hostility and harassment—not just from the Harrisons but Bickle, too."

Jack peered at Tod. "You haven't said much. Penny for your thoughts?"

He shrugged. "I don't know. This whole thing is bizarre."

"Yes. It is," Jack said. "You guys are being held to a much higher standard and clearly that has to do with your position on the board, Tod."

"They brought up the fact that I'm a trustee at both sessions," he said.

Jack frowned. "I noticed that tonight. What is so infuriating is these people basically admitted making false complaints, phone harassment, and provoking your dogs while Bickle just sat there. It was blatant. He's allowing the harassment."

"The cops have harassed us, too," Tod said.

"And I think that's likely related to politics and the recall." He signed. "We all have to hope, as I'm sure you do, now that the election is over this will all just fade away."

Friedrich Nietzsche said, "Hope is the worst of evils, for it prolongs the torments of man." To which I would add, "And dog."

The election was over. That much was true. But the hate emails did not stop. Most of them taunted me for losing the election, as if it mattered. One emailer said we were being watched, like that was news. I even got an email from Daryl with nasty comments about my blog and questioning my worth as a person.

The harassment took on a new twist. At a board meeting in May, the other board members and the new town attorney, Paul Wiesel (who was handpicked by the mayor), made a big stink about my blog. They said my opinions were interpreted as Tod's opinions and affected his ability to make objective decisions about issues before the board, and furthermore showed he had a vendetta against the mayor. They said he should not be allowed to vote on issues I had written about on my blog. We hired an attorney.

Meanwhile we had blown off the curfew. I stuffed the evil bark collar in a drawer. After ski season ended, we only left the dogs on Sunday mornings for four or five hours while we went to the Hot Springs Pool and ran errands in nearby Glenwood Springs. We left them indoors whenever we were gone during the evening. On weekdays, while the Harrisons were away at work and school, the dogs stayed outside all day. We even took them camping in Utah.

We hadn't heard a thing from the police department. It was our understanding Chief Bickle would call us if there were any complaints.

One Saturday afternoon we went for a bike ride. We had left the dogs outside. Tod took a longer route, so I headed home first. I had only been gone an hour. When I was two blocks from our house I saw a man walk out from the back side of our fence along the irrigation ditch. At first I thought Tod beat me home. But the man was taller. He walked around toward the front of the fence. Daryl.

I peddled madly like the Wicked Witch of the West. He turned and saw me. As our bad luck would have it, our neighborhood mailboxes are at the end of our property, about 15 feet from the end of our fence. Immediately Daryl trotted toward the mailboxes and crossed the street. He wasn't holding any mail in his hands.

Venus wasn't barking. I knew if I confronted him he would say he was checking his mail. When Tod got home we talked about calling the police and filing a complaint. But we knew Daryl would claim he was checking his mail.

"It will be your word against his," Tod said. "The cops won't do anything."

"I find it interesting that two months have gone by since the mediation without any problems or complaints," I said. "Now we're in the middle of a legal scuffle over my blog and Daryl is over here harassing our dogs."

"I think I know who's egging him on," Tod said. "I found out Marybeth Christianson has been conducting a behind-the-scenes campaign against your blog."

"What do you mean?"

"She's been talking to other board members and town staff." He laughed. "There's even talk about making an ordinance against board members and staff and their spouses having blogs."

"They can't do that."

"Of course they can't. But they can talk about it all they want."

"So you think Marybeth told Daryl to stir up some trouble with our dogs."

He shrugged. "We've seen this pattern before. Marybeth has always complained about your blog. And she's been acting real strange since the election. She won't even speak to me."

To settle the matter of my blog with the town board, our attorney wrote a letter and pointed out Tod and I are two different people and reminded them about the whole First Amendment, free speech thing. The matter fizzled and died like a soggy firecracker.

In the meantime, Tod had a trails meeting with Jack Morgan in his office one morning. When they were finished with trails business, Tod brought Jack up-to-date on the latest drama. I walked in at the tail end of their conversation.

Jack shook his head. "Look you guys, I'm concerned. Have you considered moving?"

Tod laughed.

"I'm serious," Jack said. "This is getting vicious."

"Okay." Tod tossed up his hands. "We've talked about moving. But you know as well as I do, houses don't sell overnight."

"There's a lot to consider," I spoke up. "Emily lives right down the street. I babysit Kaley. It's easier to be close by. Plus Tod travels so much. That kind of upheaval would be a huge burden on him. On all of us really."

Jack sighed. "I see what you mean."

Tod frowned. "Why should we be forced to turn our lives upside down because of some assholes? As far as I'm concerned the issue over

Venus's barking has been resolved. Daryl and the cops provoked the dogs. He filed false complaints. Case closed. Time to move on with our lives."

"Agreed." Jack nodded. "So have you thought about resigning from the board?"

"Yes," Tod said. "I just haven't made up my mind yet."

"Oh. I see." Jack scratched his head. "They've stripped you of any power you had on the board. They went after your wife, your daughter, and your dogs. And you're not fed up yet?"

Tod held up his hands. "Let me put it this way. I'm not convinced my resignation will stop the harassment."

"Well I'm convinced it won't stop if you remain on the board," Jack said.

"Exactly," I said. "We're damned if he does and damned if he doesn't. So we should do what's best for us. We should stand our ground."

"As long as you know what you're up against here. Things could get a whole lot worse," Jack warned.

We both nodded.

"Okay." He exhaled. "I know you know this but it bears repeating. Stay above the fray. So far you haven't jumped in the mosh pit with these idiots. You haven't retaliated against the Harrisons. You haven't punched a cop— which I have to say is admirable—not so sure I could have refrained under the circumstances. But anyway you haven't broken the law or been arrested. So keep it that way. No matter how much they piss you off." He looked at me.

We all laughed.

Talking to Jack was like a therapy session. Of all the people who knew what we were going through, Jack had actually witnessed the hostility from the Harrisons and the complicity from Bickle.

Lucky for us we had a confidante, a professional who had personal experience with a situation like ours. But our dogs didn't. How could we tell a dog like Venus to "stay above the fray?" We had no clue what was going on inside her brain.

Chapter 15 - Cause and effect

The summer after the recall was pivotal. It was the same summer Carol convinced us Venus was part Akbash, and months before Venus's meltdown. Zeus had started taking natural raw thyroid. He lost five pounds and had more energy on walks. I knew it could take up to three months for the natural treatment to work so we stuck with it. By all outward appearances, in spite of the stress we had all endured, Venus and Zeus behaved like normal, happy dogs.

Margie and the boys were home on weekdays because of summer break. The best thing for our dogs was to remove them from their hostile energy whenever possible. They spent weekdays in the yard, but we kept them inside in the evenings. On weekends we loaded up the camper and headed for the mountains, or the desert. The dogs lived for those weekends. So did we.

In mid-July, the Harrisons left town for a couple weeks. It was a blissful time.

Irma Nossie called one morning. "Did you do something to Venus?"

"No. She's fine. She's right here," I said. "Why do you ask?"

"Well we haven't heard her bark at all lately and we were afraid they made you have her vocal chords cut," she said.

I gasped. "Oh my God. That's horrible. We would never do anything like that. It's cruelty."

"Oh good," she said. "She's such a nice dog. But we were worried about her. She's been so quiet."

"That's because the Harrisons are gone," I said.

"Oh now, now," she said. "I'm sure that's not the reason."

"I'm sure it is," I said. "They provoke her."

While the Harrisons were away we let the dogs stay outside as much as they wanted, even during the night. We left them outside when we were gone. We even stayed home from camping one weekend so we could all feel what it was like to live without constantly being watched.

The Harrisons returned around the first of August. Venus and Zeus were back in the habit of staying outside while we were gone for a few hours and they liked it that way. At the time it seemed like the right thing to do instead of going on the defensive and shutting them indoors again. We suffered from a persistent optimism that things would get better.

In hindsight, there were signs of trouble during those first two weeks of August. Zeus gradually slowed down. All he did was sleep and eat. Venus was the opposite. She sped up. Several times I saw her attack the fence when other dogs walked by. At the time I didn't know her anxiety was escalating into territorial behavior.

As sensitive as Venus and Zeus were, it must have been a jolt to go from the peace and tranquility during the Harrisons' absence to the return of their hostile energy overnight. Not until after her meltdown, as we pieced together the events leading up to it, did we begin to see the correlation. We knew the dogs were being used to harass us. What we failed to grasp was that Venus and Zeus were being harassed, too. It affected them differently than it affected us. While we rationalized, they reacted—especially Venus.

In mid-August, when Venus snapped at Zeus while we were camping at Meadow Lake, she had an anxiety attack. The two incidents over Labor Day weekend were anxiety attacks that escalated into aggression. Then in October at Dogland she was aggressive toward Sasha and the other dog she didn't know. While she was unraveling something else was going on at the same time.

On October 15, we left the dogs outside during the evening while we were gone, as we had done since July. When we returned, the dogs were agitated about something but there was no ticket on the door or message on the machine.

On October 20, Tod sent an email to the other board members which included a newspaper article featuring Mayor Minnifield promoting his proposed new townhouse development. Except he neglected to identify himself as the owner of said development. Instead, he commented as the mayor about what an asset the development would be for the town. In his email, Tod pointed out that he had been held responsible for my opinions on my blog, therefore the mayor should be held responsible for what he actually said in the newspaper.

The next day, at 5:30 p.m., Tod received a call from Chief Bickle summoning him to the police station.

"Here we go again," I said. "You dared to challenge the mayor."

Tod rolled his eyes and headed for the police station where Chief Bickle informed him that moments earlier, Daryl had filed a complaint about Venus barking back on October 15, which was the same night we had noticed the dogs were agitated when we came home. According to Bickle, since the mediation sessions the Harrisons had indeed called the police and complained several times about our dogs barking. But the police had found another way to check on our dogs. They had parked in the street on the other side of the irrigation ditch. In other words, they staked out our house. Bickle said when officers responded to all complaints the dogs had not been barking, including October 15. It was a bogus complaint. And Bickle knew it.

"There's nothing I can do," he told Tod. "Daryl filed a written complaint. You'll have to take it to court." He handed over a citation.

Tod was stunned. "Why didn't you tell us about the previous complaints?"

"Because the dogs weren't barking," he said.

"You should have informed me that Daryl was still making false complaints and that you staked out our house," Tod said.

"I just did," Bickle said.

"There was no point in arguing with him. You know what he's like," Tod told me later. "He might as well have said 'talk to the hand'."

"I don't buy his excuse that there's nothing he can do because Daryl filed a written complaint. Is that Bickle's law?"

He rolled his eyes. "If that was true then I could file a written complaint that Daryl beats his wife and Bickle would have to arrest him."

"Exactly. So why doesn't he call bullshit on Daryl?"

He shrugged. "He hasn't before. Why start now?"

"Are you going to take it to court?"

"I don't know yet. First I'm going to have a little chat with the town attorney."

"Wiesel's no friend of yours after the whole flap over my blog." I picked at the chicken and asparagus on my plate.

"I don't plan to ask him for any favors. I just have a few questions. I wanted to talk to him about the mayor's comments in the paper anyway."

Venus's soulful brown eyes bored a hole through me. *Are you going to eat that chicken?* I ignored her and looked at Tod. "Okay. Let's review. Yesterday you sent out an email about the mayor promoting his development in the newspaper. Today Daryl files a bogus barking dog complaint—from a week ago. And even though Bickle knows it was bogus he gives you the citation anyway. It's like they want to make sure we know we're being harassed."

"I wonder who called Daryl and told him to file a written complaint."

"My money's on Bickle," I said.

"What about the mayor?"

"Minnifield has a scanner. Remember? He probably heard the call last week when Daryl complained about the dogs. Then you took him to task in your email and pissed him off. So he called up Bickle and told him to make damn sure you got a citation."

He let out a long, slow breath. "I see what you mean. They're sending me a message."

I stared at the cold clump of chicken on my plate. Venus stared at me with intense anticipation. *Let me clean off that plate for you.* I set it on the floor. She paused and glared defensively at Zeus who sat next to his food dish. She licked the plate clean. I should not have set my plate on the floor. Nothing happened—except the look she gave him—which said it all. What I didn't know then, but soon learned, was that Venus and Zeus had food issues.

Tod talked to Wiesel the next day. He told me about it afterward. "He said if I plead 'not guilty' then the town will have to hire a special prosecutor for the trial because I'm a trustee. So I paid the fine."

"You did what?" I asked.

"It'll cost the town a couple thousand to hire a special prosecutor," he said.

"So what?" I snapped. "It's the town's fault we're being harassed. Did you tell him Bickle admitted it was a false complaint?"

He nodded. "I laid it all out for him. He didn't have much to say. I think he's worried we'll sue the town."

"Maybe we should," I muttered.

"If it makes you feel any better I did talk to him about revising the barking dog ordinance. I told him they should require at least two complaints from two unrelated people. Then there should be a warning provision specifically outlined, plus some sort of defense for the owner if the dog was provoked."

"What did he say?"

"He wrote it down. But it takes months to change an ordinance."

I sighed. "So the way things stand, if the Harrisons complain about Venus barking, it doesn't matter if she's not barking, you get a citation. And because you're a trustee, you're automatically guilty and you have to pay the fine."

"Looks that way."

"I think you should resign from the board."

He nodded. "I'm thinking about it."

Two weeks later Venus exploded and attacked Zeus. While we thought everything was okay, Daryl and/or his boys must have been provoking her when we weren't home. Venus probably didn't bark every time. She likely didn't bark at all. Bickle confirmed as much. She didn't the day I saw him in our yard and she wasn't barking on October 15. But for Venus, who had recently discovered her inner Akbash, the torment of being stuck behind a fence while Daryl and his kids provoked her fed all her demons.

We didn't fully understand territorial aggression combined with redirected aggression until we studied dog psychology after her meltdown. In order to figure out why Venus became aggressive, all we needed to do was look at her behavior. During the three months prior to her meltdown, her normal territorial behavior progressed into territorial aggression.

Territorial (or protective) aggression is often exhibited when humans or animals approach the dog's property. Something about the sight, sound, or actions of the intruder causes anxiety and defensiveness in the dog. The dog feels fearful. Most of the time a dog will show territorial aggression on her own property. However, dogs with territorial aggression very often take the behavior with them wherever they go. Eventually Venus took her territorial aggression with her wherever she went, to Meadow Lake, then to Wisconsin.

The more the intruder invades the dog's territory, the more aggressive the dog becomes. The dog wants the intruder to leave. If the dog is behind a fence, her frustration and anxiety increase. When the dog is constantly exposed to repeated anxiety and frustration, she becomes even more fearful of the intruder. When the intruder leaves, the dog is convinced her ferocity has scared the intruder away.

Repeated harassment of the dog conditions her to be anxious, frustrated, and fearful. By the time Venus had her meltdown she had become anxious, frustrated, and fearful. Because Daryl and his kids provoked her, her territorial behavior gradually escalated into aggression.

The aggression she exhibited toward Zeus and other dogs was redirected aggression, which is a common side effect of territorial aggression. When Venus was harassed inside the fence while we weren't home, she could not rationalize that the threat was limited to our yard or those specific times. She had no concept of the limitations or severity of the threat.

Venus was intelligent and extremely sensitive. She hid plastic eggs around the house to amuse herself and us. She sensed Moby and Lucy's declining health. Because she was part Akbash, she possessed a strong guardian instinct. She had always sensed the Harrisons' hostility toward us. Her instincts told her they represented a constant threat. Whenever Daryl and his kids approached the fence she wasn't defending herself, she was protecting us. From her perspective, we were her sheep and a pack of coyotes lived across the street.

The final pieces fell into place. The night of her meltdown, Tod drove away in the pickup. Minutes later she brutally attacked Zeus. The pickup was a significant piece of the puzzle. Whenever she heard the pickup leave her brain had been conditioned to expect an intruder, a threat to her territory, because that's when Daryl or his kids showed up. She felt fearful. Zeus was the closest target. She redirected her fear into aggression toward him. His minor wounds indicated she wasn't trying to kill him. She was overcome with fear and anxiety because she had been conditioned to expect trouble when the pickup drove away. Perhaps

Daryl walked outside at the same time Tod backed out of the driveway. We'll never know. Dogs sense things beyond our human capabilities.

We had always thought the thrill for Daryl was siccing the cops on us. Therefore we assumed when he couldn't get a reaction out of the cops anymore, the thrill was gone. But what if he actually got a kick out of harassing our dogs? In the first mediation session he had said, "You can train a dog to do anything." A dog can be trained—or conditioned—to be aggressive. Certainly he knew that.

Chapter 16 - Watching the watchdogs

Understanding the connection between the harassment and Venus's mental illness was a significant breakthrough. The harassment didn't cause her mental illness. Most likely she was genetically predisposed to CCD. Her breed characteristics—territorial, protective Akbash combined with obsessive Lab — created the perfect conditions for her mental illness to bloom.

However the harassment did cause her aggression, which was a complication and not a symptom of CCD. Her Akbash nature combined with her mental illness made her prone to react aggressively when she felt fearful or threatened. In the immediate aftermath of her meltdown, we assumed the harassment was connected. We didn't know how until we understood dog psychology.

Even though clomipramine calmed her down enough to live in harmony with Zeus, she couldn't handle the sight of Daryl or his kids. She barked and lunged, displaying her fear and distrust. She didn't like cops either. As part of her rehabilitation we limited her exposure to the neighbors. From November through February, when we left the dogs at home, Venus stayed inside and Zeus stayed outside. Gradually her brain let go of her fixation on the intruder threat.

To help her overcome her fearfulness we addressed her self-esteem issues. We learned simple things from Cesar Millan, like how stroking a dog under the chin builds self-esteem, especially if the dog was smacked around in a previous life. Venus responded much better to chin stroking than head patting. The look of fear and anxiety in her dark eyes faded into warm, brown trust.

Part of helping her cope with her anxiety meant working on play. The oxymoron says it all. Venus worked too hard at play. As her anxiety level increased, she played too rough. She needed to lighten up. A game of fetch or tag with another dog could trigger her territorial behavior and bring on aggression. Our job was to make sure that didn't happen. Those issues were still new to us. Prior to her breakdown she was able to control her anxiety while playing with other dogs.

I made a special effort to meet up with Jeanne and Trevor at Dogland. Trevor was an extremely energetic Black Lab. Venus liked him. He reminded her how to chill out and play again. She even played tag again, her favorite game. In the process we learned how to read her signals so we could calm her down before she spun out of control.

Meanwhile Zeus was sending out his own signals. Before

Venus's meltdown, both dogs had slept on the floor in our bedroom at night. After her meltdown, Zeus slept downstairs on the rug in my office in front of the door, like he had an evacuation plan. One night in late January, Zeus walked into our bedroom and plopped down on the rug at the foot of the bed. Venus curled up on her spot next to the bed. I awakened in the middle of the night and found them sleeping nearly nose-to-nose. He trusted her again.

Neither of them trusted Daryl or his boys. The sight of them unnerved both dogs. One afternoon I left on a walk with the dogs at the same time Margie arrived home with her boys. When the boys stepped out of the car, the dogs fell apart in the middle of the street. Zeus sat down and trembled. Venus spun in circles at the end of her leash, trying to flee. I calmed them down as best I could while the boys watched. Eventually I coaxed them in the opposite direction. As we walked away, Zeus glanced back several times. *Are they following us?*

"Don't be so paranoid," I said. "Both of you."

But I did mention their reaction to Tod. "We've been leaving Zeus outside when we're gone. I'm worried they're harassing *him* now."

"We need to install video cameras so we can see what's going on around here when we're gone," he said.

I cringed. "That's so creepy. It's like *Spy vs. Spy.* We have to spy on ourselves because Daryl can't stop spying on us."

"There's no other way to know for certain."

"Let me think about it."

"I'll look into the equipment we need," Tod said.

I started paying more attention to Zeus's behavior whenever we returned home. Normally he met us at the porch gate, grinning and wagging his tail. A couple times he didn't. When I found him in the garage he was agitated.

"Maybe a car engine backfired. Or somebody lit a firecracker," Tod said. "You know how he hates loud noises."

"That's possible," I said. "Or maybe he's lonely without Venus. They're back together now, except when we leave."

"It's been almost four months. I think we should start leaving them outside together."

"What if Daryl and his kids torment her again?"

"There's only one way to know for sure ...."

"I know. I know." I rolled my eyes. "Video cameras."

"Home surveillance system," he said like a true salesman. "I have it all figured out. I just need to decide whether I should install the software on a separate server."

I ignored him. "You know the weather is getting warmer. I don't think it's good for Venus to be cooped up in the house."

The first Sunday in March we went downhill skiing. The plan was for Emily to come over and let Venus outside in the afternoon for a few hours with Zeus.

Later she told us, "When I got there around 2:30, I found Zeus in the garage. He wasn't happy to see me like he usually is. He seemed nervous and grumpy. He nearly knocked me over to get in the house. Then he refused to go back out, even after I let Venus out."

That evening Zeus was in a terrible mood, definitely agitated about something. He growled at Venus and snapped at one of the cats. He slept downstairs in my office. The next day at Dogland when Venus tried to play tag with him he knocked her to the ground and growled at her. I responded to his behavior with a "bite," a poke behind his ear with my two fingers. Luckily Venus didn't fight back. She walked away and avoided him.

After our leash walk in the evening, Zeus usually went inside and ate his food. But Monday evening Zeus parked himself on the grass next to the sidewalk and stared at the Harrison house. No amount of prodding made him budge. He stayed out there for 20 minutes. His body language and the look on his face said it all. *I don't trust them.* I finally coaxed him inside with the promise of chicken. "Something happened here while we were gone yesterday," I said to Tod.

He nodded. "If we had a home surveillance system ...."

"Okay." I held up my hands in surrender. "Order the video cameras."

When the equipment arrived, Zeus took quite an interest. He sniffed the cameras as we unpacked them. He watched Tod mount them and string the wires to the server. I don't think he understood how cameras work. I do think he sensed our energy changed.

When the new home surveillance system went live, we started leaving both dogs out again when we weren't home. Some dog experts and dog lovers believe dogs should never be left outside in a fenced yard when their humans are not home. I don't think dogs should be left unattended in a fenced yard or kennel for long hours, day in and day out. They need exercise and human interaction. Leaving our dogs was not a daily occurrence. Every dog and every situation is unique. If the humans take the time to observe and understand their dogs they can usually figure what's best for them.

We learned the hard way what can go wrong. We never dreamed the neighbors we'd known for more than ten years would sink so low as to harass our dogs. We never would have believed police officers would park in our driveway and provoke our dogs to bark. At no time in our lives had we experienced anything remotely like what was happening to us.

Even though keeping the dogs indoors stopped the harassment, it wasn't a real solution. For one thing, Venus and Zeus wanted to be outside. Whenever we prepared to leave they didn't plop down in front of the TV with a bag of cheesy puffs. They both went to the door to be let out.

Naturally we were curious to see what they did while we were gone, so we watched the video replay. They kept an eye on our property and the surrounding neighborhood. Nothing escaped their attention. We fast forwarded through hours and hours of two dogs' heads turning, eyes watching. Every now and then they took turns walking around the yard. They pooped and peed. They slept a lot and rarely ever barked. They were watch dogs. Watching was their job.

Two weeks later, Tod resigned from the town board. The town attorney had filed a complaint with the state Supreme Court against a planning consultant who was representing a local business owner. Tod disagreed with the complaint but the other board members had sided with Wiesel.

"They've succeeded in backing me into a corner. I don't have any choice," Tod explained. "Wiesel didn't bring this complaint before the board for a vote. I wasn't allowed to publicly state my opposition. The way he did it is called tacit approval."

"I don't understand," I said.

"In other words, because I'm a board member and Wiesel represents the board, any action he takes out of public view or without a vote has the board's silent—or tacit—approval."

"So he did it that way on purpose to get rid of you," I said. "He knew you would object."

He nodded. "That's how I see it. But it's for the best. I'm outnumbered and ineffective on the board. The staff dislikes me. And the harassment is so bad we had to put in a surveillance system."

"Your resignation won't stop the harassment," I warned.

"I know. And that's not the point anymore," he said. "Everyone—from the mayor to the trustees to the town attorney to the police chief—everyone knows about the harassment or was a party to it. And we're not alone. Look at what's happening to this consultant. Wiesel doesn't like her so he's filing a false complaint against her. You know as well as I do, others have been harassed. I can't be part of a town government that sanctions bullying."

I sighed. "But it's not just about you. My blog has been a huge issue. And now I'm writing about Venus." For three months I had been blogging about our experiences with Venus and canine compulsive disorder. Sadly, in my research I had learned many dogs were euthanized because of lack of information and understanding about CCD. I thought if I could save one dog's life by sharing Venus's story, it would be worth it. But I worried about repercussions. "When the Harrisons read my blog, if they haven't already, they might make an issue out of her mental illness."

He shrugged. "They bitched about Venus before her breakdown. She's under veterinary care. She's on medication. There's nothing they can do about it."

"Doesn't mean they won't try. I don't want to make things worse. It might be better to stop now and let the whole thing fade away."

"You wouldn't stop writing about Venus if she had cancer," he said.

I stared at him. "What's your point?"

"This has gone way beyond Venus. It doesn't matter what we do. You're right, they won't stop harassing us. So we might as well do some good."

While I mulled over my dilemma I didn't write any new posts about Venus. Then a comment came in from a woman who worked at an animal shelter. She thanked me for my blog posts about Venus. She added: "Most of the dogs that end up in the shelter have anxiety issues. Whether it's CCD or some other issue, people need to know there is medication to treat anxiety and it works! I can't wait to read more about Venus's progress."

I showed it to Tod.

"What more proof do you need?" he asked. "It's important to keep telling her story."

I wrote about Venus playing tag with Trevor and posted it with photos. Another comment came in from "anonymous." It said simply: "You are being watched."

I printed it for Tod. He read it and crumpled the paper. "Oh yeah? Well thanks to the video cameras, now we're watching back."

Chapter 17 - Practice, practice, practice

Throughout the spring we saw drastic improvement in Venus's re-socialization skills. I use the term "re-socialization" because she socialized normally with other dogs before her breakdown.

One of those skills was training her to ignore unbalanced energy in other dogs. A dog who wants to pick a fight is a problem for any dog owner. Quite honestly, the dog doesn't care one way or the other. Take Zeus for instance. At 120 pounds he was often the target of scrappy dogs, especially unneutered males. First he ignored them. If the dog persisted and attacked, he defended himself using his body mass to knock the dog off balance. It worked every time, even with Venus—until her breakdown.

Venus was not so patient. She reacted. Before her breakdown, she skipped the ignore part and pounced. The few times she was attacked, she pinned the dog down. One time Emily's Husky mix, Isis, attacked Venus over a dish of food. Isis had serious food issues. Venus knocked her down and drew blood. Other than that, her scuffles never amounted to much.

Even when she attacked Sasha and the other dog at Dogland, she backed off easily and nothing happened. Afterward Sasha avoided Venus and she returned the favor. As Sasha noticed the change in Venus's personality, she gradually became less fearful. Eventually she was able to greet Venus on the trail instead of beating a path in the opposite direction.

A Pit Bull mix named Moxie had consistently approached Venus with stiff legs, tail straight up, ears back. Sometimes she snarled. Mostly she oozed dominance. Even though the two had never fought, whenever we saw Moxie we put Venus on leash, which made it easier to distract her and keep her moving forward. One day in April, Venus and Trevor were chasing a ball. We ran into Moxie and her human. Venus ignored her and kept playing. The next day and thereafter when those two met on the trail, they ignored each other.

Another day we met up with a Blue Heeler named Zip. He was with his human and on a leash. He lunged at Venus. She stood still. His jaws snapped like an alligator.

"Hey - hey - hey!" Hands on hips I stepped between them and claimed dominance over the situation.

Venus didn't curl her lip or growl. She backed away and walked a wide path around him. Zip snorted and pulled his owner toward the next poor, unsuspecting mutt. It was a big test for Venus but she treated it like a pop quiz. We showered her with praise.

In May, we took the dogs camping in Utah, our first trip with them since her meltdown. In the past, travel and camping had been a challenge for her. She tended to get anxious and squirrely before we even left home. But Venus had changed. She waited calmly during the packing up stage. She and Zeus shared the backseat of the pickup together without any grumbling. We camped on public land north of Moab. We didn't have to tie her at the campsite. She staked out a perimeter and kept us in sight while she checked on things, always the "rain dog." She also hunted for dead things.

Early Saturday morning I sat by the campfire sipping coffee, drinking in the multi-colored desert sunrise. Venus appeared dragging a smelly, stringy rib cage, which she dropped at my feet.

"Good girl. Thank you." I stood up. She crouched to guard her prize. Her lip curled. "Leave it." I pointed toward the camper. "Go. Now."

She sulked off to lick the stinky residue from her paws. I picked up the rib cage with two fingers and stuffed it in a garbage bag, which I hid in the pickup. Fun with dogs.

Our biggest challenge came from Zeus. On Saturday afternoon while we were hiking in a canyon, a storm rolled in complete with lightning, thunder, wind, hail, and torrential rainfall. Storms never bothered Venus. At first Zeus freaked out. He panted. *Let me out of here.* He ran down the trail. I caught up to him and snapped on the leash. We took shelter under a juniper tree next to a rock wall. Venus sat calmly and showed him there was nothing to fear. Tod and I assured him everything was okay. We didn't pet him or touch him because it's not good to give affection when a dog is fearful. We talked to him so he could focus on our voices instead of the thunder. He calmed down. The thunder lasted long after the rain had stopped. Zeus shook off his fear and hiked out of the canyon, unleashed, even as the thunder rumbled.

Back at the campsite, he threw himself down on a smooth rock with a sigh of relief. *No more thunder.* He had barely closed his eyes for a well-deserved nap when some yahoos started shooting guns in the distance. Usually he fled in blind terror when he heard gunshots. His satellite dish ears perked up. He shot a fearful glance in my direction. *Did you hear that?*

"Everything is okay, Zeus," I said calmly.

He snorted with disgust and stood up. *Where can a dog get a little peace and quiet around here?* Tod opened the camper door. Zeus climbed in and Tod turned on the satellite radio to drown out the shooting.

While Zeus chilled out in the camper, three guys on dirt bikes rode into our campsite. As one of them turned his bike around, the engine stalled. Venus charged up to him and barked, then retreated calmly. Her reaction was perfect.

We celebrated Zeus and Venus's big day with barbequed chicken—their favorite. To top it off they shared the table bed that night without any lip curls or grumbling.

After our camping trip Venus and I went to see Dr. Price. It was a milestone for us. Venus had been on clomipramine and undergoing rehabilitation for six months.

"I've done some more research," Dr. Price said. "The general consensus among researchers is that the dog needs to achieve normal, stable behavior on the drug and continue that way for six months. I don't want to seem like I'm moving the carrot but ...."

"No. I get it. It makes sense," I said. "Cesar says play comes last. Once a dog can socialize and play well with other dogs off-leash, then the dog is showing stability. That happened for Venus in March." I described how well she handled meeting other dogs at the park, even the unstable ones. I told her about our camping trip and how Venus had helped Zeus deal with his thunder phobia.

Dr. Price agreed Venus had shown amazing progress. "Let's make sure she can handle all the summer activities, and the changes in her normal routine."

"You're right," I said. "She needs to learn to adapt."

She nodded. "Let's re-evaluate her progress in September."

"There's something else we need to discuss. Her aggression," I said. "We figured out why she turned on Zeus. It was redirected aggression."

"Oh?" She raised her eyebrows. "Tell me more."

"Last fall when you first diagnosed Venus with CCD you asked if she barked a lot. I told you the neighbors complained about her barking but we didn't think it was excessive and they had never proved it was. Well, there's more to it than that." I told her about the harassment. "The neighbors and cops admitted they provoked the dogs several times when we weren't home. You can be sure it happened more times than we know." I explained how Venus had been conditioned to view the neighbors as a threat to her territory. "Eventually she took out her anxiety on Zeus."

She frowned. "I don't disagree. I need to do more research on aggression."

"So do I. But we've learned a lot from paying attention to our dogs' behavior. Just by watching how they react to our neighbors and the cops we can tell there's a problem."

"How do they react?"

"Zeus gets nervous. Venus gets anxious. She barks at the sight of the neighbors or the cops. They even react to their vehicles."

"That's not good." She peered at me. "How are you guys coping with all of this?"

I described our regimen of limiting Venus's time outside and seldom leaving the dogs alone. "It's just easier to take them with us."

She smiled and shook her head. "That's not what I meant. But never mind. Just remember it's important for a dog like Venus to own her territory. It's the Akbash way." She leaned forward and scratched Venus's ears with both hands. Venus licked her wrists. "No dog should be harassed in her territory." She glanced at me. "And neither should you."

I nodded and swallowed the lump in my throat. "We put in a video surveillance system so we can see what goes on when we're not home. We haven't had any complaints or problems with the neighbors lately. But that doesn't mean anything. We've gone for months thinking everything was cool and then they harassed the dogs and called the cops. The mom and kids will be home more during the summer which means there will be a lot of negative energy directed at us and the dogs. The last thing we want is a relapse. Venus is still learning how to cope with her anxiety. She knows how to calm herself down. She knows how to calm Zeus down."

"Good." Dr. Price stroked Venus's head and stood up. "Now she needs to practice, practice, practice."

Chapter 18 - A vicious complaint

A month passed. School let out and summer break commenced. I babysat Kaley (then seven years old) and Henry (six months) so they spent time at our house almost every day. Venus followed Kaley everywhere, guarding her like a little lamb. She was always in the yard so Venus was, too.

On a warm morning in mid-June, the temperature was already 60 degrees at 6:30 a.m. Tod opened the garage door and took out the garbage. Unbeknownst to him, Venus snuck out. Later, when he headed downstairs to go to the office we heard her barking. Tod walked outside and saw Venus in the middle of the street barking at a young man dressed in a long black jacket and black ball cap. Venus had startled him and he stopped, which caused her to bark louder because she sensed his fear. Tod called her and she retreated. He apologized to the young man who grumbled *en español* and walked on.

I witnessed the entire incident from our bedroom window. Venus never stood closer than 15 feet from the guy. She didn't bite him. She didn't touch him. She barked at him.

An hour later I picked up Tod at the office and we took Venus and Zeus to Dogland. Afterward I dropped him off and picked up Kaley and Henry. When I arrived home with the two dogs and two kids there was a police car parked in front of our house.

"She didn't ...." I muttered to myself.

"What did you say?" Kaley asked.

"Oh look. The policeman's here," I said. "Wonder what that's all about." But I knew exactly what it was about. As I unloaded dogs and kids, Officer Fuddle ambled over.

Venus was not happy to see him. She kept her distance and barked. I ushered her through the front gate. Fuddle could see I had my hands full.

"Is there a problem?" I asked.

He pointed at Venus. "Did your Yellow Lab get out this morning by any chance?"

I laughed. "Yes. She snuck out when Tod took out the garbage. She barked at a guy walking by. Tod was on it right away. He apologized. She didn't mean any harm."

He sighed. "Okay. I'm just following up on a complaint about a vicious dog attack."

"Oh? Did the guy complain?" I asked. "He didn't seem upset."

"No. It wasn't him. A woman called in and said she witnessed a vicious dog attack."

I looked over his shoulder at the Harrison house. *Oh yes. She did.* "You mean Margie Harrison."

"Can't say." He glanced around, avoiding eye contact. "So the dog didn't bite anyone or anything like that?"

"Oh no," I said. "She didn't touch him. She just barked. She scared him. That's understandable. Tod apologized. Nothing happened."

Officer Fuddle thanked me and continued on his merry way.

"She didn't," Tod said when I called him.

"I'm sure it was Margie. It happened right in front of their house. The cop said a woman complained."

In some respects it came as no surprise. Margie and the boys were home all day. Their negative energy seeped through the neighborhood like a toxic chemical. They were always lying in wait, ready to pounce if we screwed up. Even so, the vicious dog complaint was a whole new tactic.

I recalled an interesting phone conversation I had with Wiesel a few weeks earlier. Six months had passed since Tod had requested changes to the barking dog ordinance, and nothing had been done. We had assumed Wiesel's foot-dragging was because he didn't want to be accused of a doing a special favor for Tod, even if it meant not doing his job. With Tod off the board, it was no longer an issue.

So I had called Wiesel. "As you are well aware, our neighbors and the police have used the barking dog ordinance to harass us. The ordinance needs to be revised. It should include a warning provision and two witnesses should be required. Plus the issue of someone provoking a dog has to be in there. Tod talked you about this last October yet nothing has been done."

"I'm so glad you called. I've been working on those ordinances. I meant to call you for your input," Wiesel said. *Yeah, right,* I thought. We discussed the changes I recommended. Then he added, "You should know that the vicious dog ordinance was brought to my attention recently. I took a look at it and it needs updating."

I hesitated. Was he trying to tell me something? "Wait a minute. Who talked to you about the vicious dog ordinance?"

"I can't discuss that." He cleared his throat. "Of course I will be looking at all the animal ordinances to see which ones need updating. Not just the barking dog ordinance."

After I hung up I looked up the vicious dog ordinance.

If any dog bites, attacks, snaps at, or tears the clothing in an attempt to bite any person(s), on public or private property, and was not provoked; if any dog kills or injures any domestic animal, and the incident is reported to the police department and is proven in municipal court, that dog shall be deemed and declared by the municipal court to be a vicious animal.

Tod was in Chicago. I called him and recapped my discussion with Wiesel. "It's obvious the Harrisons read my blog posts about Venus. So they talked to Wiesel about the vicious dog ordinance."

"What does it say?" he asked.

I recited the ordinance.

"Right. It says if it's reported to the police, if it's proven in court. None of the incidents involving Venus were ever reported to the police."

"I get that," I said. "You're missing the point. They're going to try and use her mental illness against us."

"Read the ordinance again. If they do, they will have to take us to court. I'd be happy to go to court and present our evidence of harassment to a judge."

I sighed. "Good point."

Back to the morning in June, when Venus escaped. She barked at a guy. She retreated on verbal command. End of story. I realized the vicious dog complaint was the Harrisons' attempt to use the vicious dog ordinance against us. They had made it clear during mediation they wanted to get rid of her. Except no one was attacked.

I told Tod, "Maybe I should call Chief Bickle and ask him why he doesn't send a squad car over to the Harrisons and question Margie about her false complaint."

He winced. "Not a good idea."

I rolled my eyes. "I was being sarcastic."

"The less said about the incident the better," he added.

"Look, if they're going to pursue this vicious dog tactic, I need to re-think the blog series."

He shook his head adamantly. "No way. Now more than ever putting Venus out there on your blog shows we're being open about her condition. We have nothing to hide."

I agreed and let it go. I had something else on my mind. Living with CCD, we had learned to pay attention to changes in behavior. Our summer routine— even though it was late spring—had posed a real dilemma. Kaley spent a lot of time outside. Venus wanted to be with her. All that time outdoors exposed Venus to the Harrisons' hostility while she was in guardian mode. A couple times I coaxed her inside with a treat and urged her to lie next to the air conditioner. As soon as she realized Kaley was still outside she danced frantically at the front door. Even if she sat on the porch and watched Kaley play, she needed to be there. It was her job.

During the incident on the morning in question, Venus had displayed a high level of anxiety. Was she having trouble coping with her anxiety?

Chapter 19 - Wild mood swings

The night before Margie's vicious dog complaint, Tod had put the camper on the pickup because he needed to take it in for minor repairs. But Venus and Zeus didn't know that. Their dog brains interpreted the camper on the pickup one way. *We're going somewhere. Fun will happen.* We had assumed Venus snuck out so she could be closer to the camper, in case we were leaving soon. In her mind it was an extension of our home and thus her territory.

We were indeed planning a trip to Lake Powell, except the dogs had to wait a whole week before the trip actually happened. Venus fixated on the camper because Tod loaded it on the pickup. "Practice, practice, practice" meant she had to learn to cope with changes in routine. By contrast Zeus behaved calmly. I could tell he was excited about the camper being on the pickup, yet he was content to wait.

We left for Lake Powell a week later. Kaley came along so there wasn't room for both dogs in the backseat. Venus rode in the camper. Considering her propensity for anxiety it would have been better for her to be in the pickup with Kaley. But Zeus was older and had the thicker coat. He needed to be near the air conditioner so he sat in the backseat. Venus had ridden in the camper many times but she acted more anxious about it than she needed to be. We used a two-way thermometer to monitor temperature in the camper, which stayed in the low 70s, so she was fine.

For the most part, the trip went well for Venus and Zeus. They had been to Lake Powell with us many times. They enjoyed boating, swimming, and camping. The weather wasn't as hot as usual, high 80s during the day and low 60s at night, which was very comfortable for them. We rented a dock at the marina. To get to our boat, the dogs had to walk out onto the busy docks past boats, kids, adults, carts, and other dogs coming and going. They were so calm I held their leashes with one hand.

We did notice odd behaviors in Venus. She seemed a little off. We took a boat ride out to a favorite spot we called Zeus's Cove. For two solid hours, Venus obsessed about the lizards scurrying over the rocks. She hunted them relentlessly. No matter how many times we distracted her, she always went back to the lizards. She barely swam, and only when we pushed her in. She showed no interest in chasing tennis balls or fetching driftwood. She just chased lizards.

"I realize she likes chasing lizards," Tod said. "But she's way too obsessed about them."

"Maybe it's okay to let her obsess about stuff like lizards and dead things," I said. "As long as nobody gets hurt."

The next day she chased them for about an hour, and then she passed out under the dashboard on the boat.

Our boat is only 19 feet, which makes for close quarters with two adults, one child, and two big dogs. They were always well-behaved on the boat. Venus loved lapping the wind up on the bow. But on the ride back to the marina she stayed on the floor beside Tod. I noticed her staring at Zeus who was stretched out on the bench. I distracted her. She turned around and ignored him.

Back at the campground, a group of teenage boys ran foot races on the road past our campsite. Venus was tethered to the camper. She barked and danced around anxiously. She didn't calm down until they stopped running.

After supper she passed out from exhaustion before sunset. Shortly after dark a man, who was setting up camp across the road from us, walked into our campsite without a flashlight and started asking questions about the campground in a loud voice. Kaley jumped out of her chair. He startled the three of us, so of course he startled the dogs. Venus woke up out of a dead sleep and freaked out. She didn't attack the man or even go near him, but she barked ferociously. I took her inside the camper. She sat beside me on the bench, trembling and growling. I talked to her about lizards and fishes until she calmed down and dozed off.

On the trip back home she was too tired to be agitated about riding in the camper. We talked about her obsessive behavior.

"It's hard to tell whether Venus had fun or if she simply wore herself out," I said.

"Maybe it's because I came along," Kaley said. "She feels like she needs to protect me all the time."

I nodded. "I think you're right. At least that's part of it, anyway."

"She's definitely having some mood swings," Tod said. "We'll see if she calms down when we get home."

The next day at Dogland she seemed like her normal self again. Although I noticed Lucy, the Yellow Lab and Mandy, the Cocker Spaniel, avoided her.

While I cleared the table after dinner someone set off a string of firecrackers. *Pop-pop-pop. Pop-pop-pop.* It sounded like it came from across the street. Both dogs were in the house. Zeus fled downstairs. I walked calmly to the kitchen to fetch the Pet Calm. More firecrackers exploded. Zeus, still agitated, came back upstairs and walked over to his water dish next to the refrigerator. Venus was lying about three feet away from him. In an instant she jumped up.

"Hey! No!" Tod was right there and called her off mid-strike but she didn't listen.

She grabbed Zeus by the neck above his spiked collar, and held on. I filled a pitcher with water and dumped it on her head. She let go.

As Tod separated them, Zeus growled and lashed out at Venus. He bit her on the cheek. By then I held Venus by her collar and Tod held Zeus. We separated them again. The whole thing lasted about two minutes. Zeus had a bite on his neck and Venus had a bite on her cheek. Zeus went downstairs. Venus stayed upstairs. We closed the gate.

After we recovered from the emotional jolt, I collapsed on the sofa in tears. "All those hours of training. All those months of progress. Down the tubes. Return to start. Do not pass go. Do not collect your reward." I felt crushed.

Tod plopped down and wrapped his arms around me. "Venus has had a lot to cope with lately. So have we. This is a setback. But we move on."

"What about Zeus?"

"He fought back this time. He didn't let her knock him down. He bit her."

"Oh great." I tossed up my hands. "What? Are we into dog fighting now? Maybe we should charge people to watch. Hey, we could make videos. Post them on YouTube."

He smiled. "Feel better now?"

"No." I pouted. "I don't want my dogs to fight."

"You said she's on a low dose of the drug, right?"

"Yes and we will—most definitely—be putting her on a higher dose."

"So there. See? We just need to adjust her meds."

But it wasn't quite so simple. Venus and Zeus began living separate lives again. They were only together at Dogland and on leash walks.

The fight happened on Saturday. The following Monday, I took Venus to the vet. Dr. Price was on vacation, so we saw Dr. Landers. He was familiar with her case and I brought him up to speed on her obsessive behavior and mood swings, beginning with the vicious complaint incident and escalating into her attack on Zeus.

"I want to make sure we don't overreact to this one incident," he said as he observed Venus stretched out calmly at my feet, head erect. "Look at her now. She's perfectly normal."

I leaned over and scratched her chin. "We've learned this is all part of her mental illness. Dr. Jekyll and Miss Hyde, if you will. Like schizophrenia."

He nodded. "That's true. But it's also true that sometimes dogs fight."

"But Saturday wasn't the first time Zeus has been freaked out by loud noises since Venus has been on clomipramine. There were fireworks on New Year's and *Cinco de Mayo.* Plus thunderstorms, gunshots, and engines backfiring. Zeus has exhibited fear lots of times and Venus didn't attack him. Sometimes she ignored him on her own. Sometimes we ordered her to ignore him. Sometimes she even helped him calm down. This time she forgot her training. She didn't hesitate. Her brain snapped into attack mode."

"I see what you're getting at," he said. "I'm just hesitant to increase her dosage without discussing it with Dr. Price."

"I understand," I said. "But as you know, 75 milligrams is a low dose for Venus. And since we don't have much to guide us as far as research on CCD, Dr. Price has pretty much left it up to us to decide if and when we think she needs a higher dose. What happened Saturday wasn't an isolated incident. Anxiety at the campground. Obsession with the lizards. It goes back to the vicious dog complaint. She is losing control."

Dr. Landers frowned. "So is that matter settled? I mean, come on, any dog would do what she did."

"As far as I know the cop was satisfied she had not come in contact with the guy," I said. "But we never know what our neighbors are going to do."

"Well if they pursue it, you let us know," he said. "We can vouch for her medical treatment."

I nodded. "Good to know. Thanks."

"Anyway," he said. "I don't think these mood swings—the anxiety, the obsession—even the aggression you're seeing necessarily mean the CCD is progressing."

I sighed and patted Venus's head. "I'm glad you said that. Tod and I think she's having a hard time coping. Dr. Price and I talked about what an important transition this is for her. It's summer. We're busy. Our whole routine changed. I'm babysitting my grandkids more. She's very protective of them. My grandson is only six months old."

He tossed up his hands. "Well that explains a lot. She's part Akbash isn't she?"

We both nodded.

"So here we are," I said. "Summer is just getting started. We want to take the dogs camping. Now fireworks season is here. We're working with Zeus and his fear of fireworks. I have him on two doses of Pet Calm per day. His fear is not really a problem. He's pretty low key. It's how Venus reacts to it."

He exhaled. "Gosh. You've got your hands full with those two big dogs. And you're right, you need to get her anxiety under control so you can get Zeus through fireworks season." He scratched his head. "Okay. Yes. Let's increase the dose to 100 milligrams. But it can still take up to three weeks before you see any change. You will need to supervise them constantly or keep them separated."

I laughed. "You just described my life. Upstairs dog, downstairs dog, inside dog, and outside dog."

He laughed, too.

"If I don't laugh at this I'll end up just as crazy as Venus," I said.

"Hey. Come on. You guys are doing great with her," he said. "I know it isn't easy. Most people would have given up on her by now."

"We can't." I stroked Venus's beautiful white head. "We see this as an opportunity. We're learning a lot. We've never had a dog like her before." She sat up and dropped her head on my lap.

I was on the verge of tears. I sensed Dr. Landers was too.

He stood up abruptly and gulped. "Be sure to call Dr. Price next week and let her know how things are going."

On the drive home I felt sad. No matter how much Dr. Landers had tried to reassure me, it was a setback. Venus had been doing so well on the lower dose. I was disappointed that we had to increase it. But she had to learn to cope with change. In order for her to practice calm, balanced energy, her mind had to be able to focus. Setbacks are common with any illness.

At home I had little time to dwell on my feelings. We were back to Chinese-fire-drill-with-dogs. It was important to keep Venus moving forward. Within two days the increased dose had begun to balance out her highs and lows. We were beginning to see sustained calm energy from her again.

Wednesday night we heard a few firecrackers. Zeus was upstairs, Venus was downstairs. The gate was shut. Zeus perked up his satellite dish ears and looked alarmed. *Did you hear that?* But he didn't get up. I ignored him and he calmed down. Venus didn't react at all.

About an hour later we heard a huge bang. Venus was upstairs, Zeus downstairs, gate shut. Venus jumped to her feet and looked alarmed. *That was bigger than a firecracker.*

Sirens wailed. Zeus howled.

"Everything's okay," I told Venus. "Lie down." She did.

Tod walked outside to the street. When he came back he said, "There was a car accident at the corner of Seventh Street."

Zeus had planted himself on the rug in my office downstairs. But we didn't check on him. If we reacted to loud noises it only encouraged his fearfulness. He didn't come upstairs to the gate so we assumed he heard it, felt fearful, and then calmed down.

In addition to their psychological wounds, both dogs had actual physical wounds from their recent fight. The puncture wound in Zeus's neck worried me. The hole, which was the size of a pencil head, re-opened and oozed blood. I snipped the surrounding fur and plugged it with ointment.

I told Tod, "If it doesn't stop the bleeding by tomorrow I'm taking him to the vet."

He smeared ointment on the three-inch gash on Venus's cheek. "I'm glad Zeus bit her. Maybe she learned a lesson."

"We can always hope," I said. "That hole in his neck bothers me. She came awfully close to hitting an artery. She might have nicked it. He could bleed to death from just a single bite. I don't know if I can ever feel comfortable leaving them home alone together."

"Don't be too discouraged. We knew summer would be a challenge for her." Venus rolled over while he scratched her belly.

"I get all that," I said. "I talked it through with Dr. Landers and I've talked to you about it until I'm blue in the face. The point is, when she snapped it was sudden and without warning. One minute she was fine, the next minute she was on top of Zeus."

"There were signs," he said. "Next time we'll know she's losing control."

"Next time," I repeated. "Right now it's about trust. It's going to take a long time before I can trust her again."

Venus sneezed. *Remember what the doc said. Don't overreact.*

I stuck out my tongue at her.

Chapter 20 - Thunderstorms and fireworks

We assessed the situation. Venus had breezed through more than seven months of training and rehabilitation without incident, on a low dose of clomipramine. When she attacked Zeus there was a trigger—his fearfulness. Perhaps she was also fearful. The incident was less severe than her November meltdown. Dr. Landers didn't think the CCD had progressed. Zeus bit her back, which everyone agreed was a significant development. He had demanded her respect and won. It wasn't a clean win by any means, though he did establish a boundary.

We analyzed all of her behaviors leading up to the fight. In addition to her increasing anxiety, Venus had slid into subtle, dominant behaviors in the house. She had set up camp under the kitchen counter about three feet from Zeus's food dish, the same spot from which she had launched her latest attack. She had chosen the spot so she could sit and stare at him while he ate. She wasn't allowed to sit there anymore, even if Zeus wasn't in the room. She was squirrely on leash walks. She insisted on leading and often lunged at other dogs and kids on bikes. We reined her in.

With a little help from us, Zeus continued to muddle through fireworks season. The Pet Calm helped. He retreated to our bedroom with the air conditioner blasting and the TV on and he was fine—not necessarily calm, but not panic-stricken either. We were wrong to pay attention to Zeus when we heard fireworks. Venus was the one who got aggressive. She was the one who needed to be controlled. When we heard pops and bangs, instead of herding Zeus away from Venus, we switched our attention to her. We distracted her, isolated her, and calmed her down.

Ten days after the fight we started letting them out in the yard together again when we were home. There were no problems. We decided to keep them separated indoors and outdoors when we weren't home through fireworks season because we didn't know when the pops and bangs would occur. The gate at the narrow walkway between the front yard and backyard allowed us to separate them outdoors.

The hole in Zeus's neck stopped leaking, though it healed slowly. As I treated it daily with colloidal silver and calendula ointment, it served as a constant reminder of how easily Venus could do serious damage.

We saw steady improvement in her. The weekend before July 4th, we took them camping at Meadow Lake for two nights. I brought along the pepper spray, just in case. They behaved like normal dogs. They even slept on the table bed together at night. A few thunderstorms rumbled through during the daytime. Zeus waited them out in the backseat of the pickup. Venus left him alone.

Tod took Venus with him while he rode his bike. When they returned he said, "She ran wild. She put a coyote on the run and chased a deer."

Running wild had put a smile on her face. Venus had the most gorgeous wide grin. Even Zeus noticed. He dashed up to her and pawed the dirt with his front feet. Then he ran around in circles. I was on my feet by then. Tod was in the camper but he stepped out as the scene unfolded. We exchanged a quick glance but we couldn't keep our eyes off the dogs.

Zeus stopped and pawed the dirt some more. Venus dropped her tail. I held my breath. He let out a "woof" and wagged his tail. She lowered her head. He turned and lumbered off. Venus chased after him. They ran figure eights through the pine grove. Two powerful, giant dogs at play is an amazing sight under any circumstances. But those two dogs had the most complicated relationship of any two dogs I'd ever known. Venus caught up with Zeus and nipped at him. He body-checked her into a tree. She backed off.

I breathed normally again. "They're working it out."

Later we sat in front of the campfire. Zeus eyeballed me from his position on the mat near the camper door. His ears twitched. *I'm certain I heard something explode on that ridge over there.*

Venus rolled onto her back and braced herself against a six-foot long, two-foot in diameter log while she slept upside down. *A-um-mm....*

"She handles life so much better after she's had a good run," I said. "I almost hate to say this but she needs more exercise."

Tod sighed. "I know what you mean."

We knew there would be plenty of bangs and booms at Meadow Lake on July 4th, so we decided it would be better for both dogs to spend the holiday at home in a calm, controlled environment. In spite of Zeus's fears, Tod and I actually enjoy fireworks. They're fun. But we gave up on our own fireworks years ago when we saw how Zeus reacted to his first fireworks season as an eight-month-old puppy. He was terrified. We couldn't put him through it.

Yet even in his worst nightmare, Zeus could not have imagined the ultimate noise-a-thon that awaited him. Our holiday-at-home rolled out with a thunderstorm. Zeus fled to the bedroom. I shut the gate. Tod played a Moby CD to mask the thunderclaps. Venus paced downstairs.

In the kitchen, I stared at the coffeemaker, willing it to brew faster.

"We're off to a roaring start," Tod grumbled.

I danced in place to Moby and punched the air with my fist. "This is good. Gets us in shape. We're ready for anything."

He scratched his head. "That coffee ready yet?"

The thunderstorms rumbled eastward. By late morning the sun peeked through scattered clouds. The dogs calmed down. Luckily we hadn't opened the gate when Zeus wandered cautiously out of the bedroom. He made a beeline for the deck door in the living room. *Is that sunshine I see?*

Pop-pop-pop. Pop-pop. Pop-pop.

Strings of firecrackers exploded across the street in the Harrisons' yard. Zeus fled to his panic room - our bedroom. Venus barked and whined downstairs. I looked out the kitchen window. Two pickups and a van were parked in the Harrisons' driveway. A car pulled up and parked in front of their fence. Another string of firecrackers exploded, followed by loud, raucous laughter.

"What a surprise," I said. "Margie and Daryl are throwing a party."

Pop-pop-pop. Right on cue.

"Well that's interesting," Tod said. "Remember that one party we had here years ago? Some friends of Emily's set off firecrackers and Margie called the cops."

I nodded. "Funny you should mention it. I was just thinking about it."

More firecrackers popped.

"She is way too paranoid for this," he said.

I shrugged. "Maybe Daryl tied her up in the basement."

We chuckled.

The Harrisons and their guests showed off their abundant supply of firecrackers and cherry bombs by exploding them in rapid succession all the live-long day. The relentless pops and bangs unnerved the dogs, which was obviously their goal. No one else in town was shooting off a constant barrage, not to mention it was illegal.

"Funny thing," Tod commented. "The police station is four blocks away. I saw a cop drive by twice. They were shooting off firecrackers but he didn't stop."

"Of course not. Venus wasn't barking."

We laughed.

"So how does that work?" Tod asked. "I wonder if Daryl called his friends and said, 'Come on over. Let's shoot off fireworks until we drive our neighbors and their dogs crazy'."

I held up a finger. "Don't forget—'and the cops won't do anything'."

Pop-pop. Pop-pop-pop. More loud, raucous laughter.

He rolled his eyes. "Could they be any more obnoxious? I feel like we're under attack here."

I sighed. "Look. They read my blog. They know the dogs get freaked out by fireworks."

"Like most dogs," he added.

"Okay. They're assholes. So let's get the hell out of here."

We took Venus and Zeus to Dogland where they swam and chased sticks. Then we walked them on leashes in town away from the noise. The activity tired them out. Zeus crashed in our bedroom. Venus slept on the couch. A gate in the bedroom doorway separated them. We played loud music to drown out the fireworks across the street.

For dinner we steamed crab legs and sweet corn. Afterward we sat out back on our tree-house deck with a fire in the *chiminea.* Venus sat in the living room. By then Zeus had sequestered himself in the bedroom closet. As night fell the other neighbors set off their fireworks stashes. We could always count on a few outlaw fireworks displays in the sky above Silt and we were not disappointed.

Whenever something exploded Venus slid open the screen door with her paw, and stepped outside. *Incoming!* Then she sniffed us to make sure we were okay and retreated to the living room with a half dozen mosquitoes buzzing over her.

Around midnight I coaxed Zeus outside for a short walk. The Harrisons' fireworks jamboree had ground to a drunken halt hours earlier. Zeus coped with the dwindling pops in the distance. Tod walked Venus. She sniffed in Zeus's direction. *Everything okay now, big guy?* He ignored her.

The next evening there were more pops and bangs which Zeus handled a little better. He still ended up in the bedroom closet. Venus didn't exactly ignore Zeus. She was well aware of his fearful seclusion and she left him alone, mostly because we watched her closely and kept them separated. Managing her aggression not only meant recognizing the triggers, but also avoiding any situations where aggression could occur.

A week later I took Venus to see Dr. Price. We had been playing phone tag and I wanted to update her in person anyway, with Venus.

Dr. Price agreed we did the right thing. "I made sure Dr. Landers understood I had left it up to you when to increase her dosage. He's totally up to speed with that."

"I understood his hesitation," I said. "He just wanted to make sure we weren't overreacting."

"You didn't overreact," she said. "You know, we're all kind of feeling our way through the dark with Venus—so to speak."

I rolled my eyes. "Tell me about it."

"With CCD—or any mental disorder for that matter—each dog is different. That's why it's good to bounce things off each other like this from time to time," she said. "Dr. Landers and I—and everyone else around here—we're all behind you one hundred percent. But you guys have to lead the way because you're the ones living with her—and with Zeus, too. We have to take into consideration his tolerance for stress as well."

With a sigh, Venus rolled over on her side and stretched out at my feet. We discussed how Zeus had handled fireworks season, which led us back to Venus.

"Since the latest incident, we realized there were signs she wasn't coping with her anxiety." I described the trip to Lake Powell and her dominant behaviors.

Dr. Price listened, then said, "It's good to make note of those things but I'm not so sure you should put too much emphasis on signs. If and when the disease progresses—and we can't say for sure at this point whether it will—there won't necessarily be any signs. She could be perfectly normal one day and the next day she could lose her mind. We have no way of predicting her behavior."

On the way home I thought about how lucky we were to have vets like Dr. Price and Dr. Landers. Talking to them helped me work through my own feelings. Periodic evaluation is a key part of living with CCD. We spent as much time analyzing Venus's behavior as we did training her. Their encouragement and support convinced me we were helping Venus.

Dr. Price had said, "It must be frustrating to keep the dogs separated so much."

Sometimes it was, especially in the evenings when we watched TV or sat on the deck listening to music. Very often Zeus stayed downstairs in my office because it was cooler and probably because it was my office. I spent more time down there to keep him company. It wasn't normal for a Malamute to take himself out of the pack circle.

Even though it wasn't the most harmonious way to live, the practice of separating the dogs gave us more authority. It forced us to set boundaries and limitations which helped control their behavior. They knew exactly what was expected of them. We accepted that life with those two big dogs meant they would need to be separated sometimes. Our goal had to be making sure the separation was temporary. But it was up to them. Zeus and Venus had to find a way to make peace with each other.

Chapter 21 - Acceptable risks

Was it fair to make Zeus live under the constant threat of attack from Venus? Was she really a constant threat? I argued with myself daily. I worried Zeus might become aggressive, even though I knew we had the power as pack leaders to prevent that from happening. I worried that living with Venus was too stressful for him, even though I knew if we didn't get stressed out about her mental illness then he wouldn't either. I discovered I was more at ease when Venus was outside or downstairs—away from me. She made me nervous. Maybe I was picking up on her anxiety. Or maybe I was developing my own anxiety. I didn't trust her.

When I had said those words to Dr. Price during our recent visit, she winced. "I don't think you *can* trust her," she said. "And I can certainly appreciate how difficult that can be to live with."

We took Zeus and Venus hiking on the Beaver Creek Trail. They hiked to the top of the ridge together. As we headed back to the trailhead, Venus caught the scent of mule deer, dropped her nose, and wandered into the forest. Thunder rumbled as clouds rolled in so Zeus stayed close to us. Then several gunshots echoed from the opposite ridge. Zeus lowered his head and bolted. *Let me out of here.* Tod caught up to him and leashed him. But where was Venus?

Halfway down the ridge we met another hiker. "I saw a white dog," he said. "Does she belong to you?"

"Yes," Tod said.

"She was chasing a deer." He hiked his thumb over his shoulder. "Down the trail a ways."

We continued on. "At least we know she wasn't shot," I said.

We found her cooling her belly and lapping water in Beaver Creek near the trailhead. The hiker had found out our dirty little secret. Venus chased deer. We weren't proud of the behavior. She didn't actually "chase" them. We had seen her in action with deer and elk. She herded them. It was more of a head-em-up-move-em-out maneuver. She meant no harm. We knew it was wrong and we tried to stop her, but it was hopeless. Herding was in her blood. We also knew we could be fined or she could be shot and we accepted the risks. I couldn't imagine a mountain hike with Venus on a leash. It would have exacerbated her anxiety. We had to let her run wild. She returned home happy, exhausted—and calm.

She and Zeus got along amazingly well away from home. When Venus was distracted she didn't fixate on Zeus. They didn't ignore each other either. They often walked side by side. They romped and played tag. Any stranger would have assumed they were best friends.

At home it was a different story. Venus often fixated on Zeus in the house, but not in the yard. One month after their fight, we allowed them to be together indoors without barrier gates, under strict supervision. We made sure Venus kept her distance from Zeus. We looked to him to read her energy. His reaction was telling. When she walked in a room, he stood up and walked out. He didn't trust her. I accepted his judgment. But a sadness enveloped me. Through all our decades with dogs—eight dogs in all—we had never experienced anything like the relationship between Zeus and Venus.

Did Venus need Zeus? Probably not. At times he was a stabilizing influence in her life. He was the object of her obsession. As far as companionship, he was the Stuart Smalley of dogs. He was big enough, smart enough, calm enough, and stable enough to live with her. Yet she would have been fine without him. She would have obsessed over something else.

Did Zeus need Venus? Definitely not. He was less bored and lazy because of her. Except Zeus kind of liked being bored and lazy. It's what Malamutes do— or rather don't do. In terms of companionship, he could have done a lot better, but he did enjoy her company. His life was certainly less stressful before she entered the picture.

In human terms it seemed like a harsh reality. I knew from a lifetime with dog pairs that they can grow to love each other deeply. They become dependent on each other, even devoted to one another. It wasn't like that with Venus and Zeus. I knew it would never be like that.

In the dog world, her instability was sign of weakness and she would have been rejected by the pack and driven off, or killed. When I looked at their relationship from the perspective of pure canine instinct, Zeus had shown remarkable patience and restraint. Perhaps he considered her anxiety an acceptable risk for her companionship.

Life with Venus was a journey into uncharted territory. Depending on her mood, life was frustrating or exhilarating, challenging or rewarding. At home she was more prone to anxiety. Even though we hadn't given the Harrisons any opportunities to harass Venus, the damage had already been done. On a daily basis their hostility was palpable. Tod and I had to find ways to cope with it ourselves, and we weren't mentally ill like Venus. A daily routine provided her with stability. I had the advantage of working at home. Tod had the ability to take her to the office. Between the two of us, we were able to keep her occupied.

Loving any animal is an acceptable risk. CCD is a chronic illness, like diabetes or alcoholism. A normal life wasn't in the cards for Venus. She was a crazy bitch. A dog on drugs. After their recent fight we realized she would never fully recover. But we had a good chance of stabilizing her and keeping her anxiety under control. We were still committed to helping her live a happy life.

Where did Venus find her happy place? When she hiked with us or ran with Tod's bike in the mountains. When she chased coyotes, or deer, or rabbits along the trail. When she bounded through deep snow, hunting for elk bones. When she hunted lizards in the desert.

Then it hit me. For Venus, happiness meant running wild.

Chapter 22 - Speaking Akbash

Let's take Kaley and the dogs camping at Meadow Lake for the weekend," I suggested. "Venus is doing well on 100 milligrams. She's stable. She deserves some fun."

"We all deserve some fun," Tod said.

We packed up and headed for the mountains. On the drive up Buford Road, Tod talked about his plan to start jogging with Venus to increase her exercise.

I shrugged. "I don't think it'll make any difference."

He glanced sideways. "What do mean?"

"I do think Venus needs more exercise. But not the jogging or treadmill kind. She needs to run wild. In the mountains. Look at how much she has calmed down over these past four weeks. What have we been doing?"

He nodded. "Camping and hiking in the mountains."

When we arrived at Meadow Lake we were confronted with a minor annoyance which mushroomed into a giant hassle. The Boy Scouts were holding a rally on the opposite ridge from the campground, what we call Boy Scout ridge. As we set up camp, rifle shots echoed across the meadow from their encampment. Zeus immediately retreated to the backseat of the pickup. I administered emergency Pet Calm.

Tod-the-Eagle-Scout explained, "There's a rifle safety badge. They probably have a shooting range up there. I'm sure they'll be done by noon."

No such luck. After lunch Tod took Venus along on his bike ride. She had a swell time running wild on Meadow Ridge.

Meanwhile Kaley coaxed Zeus out of the pickup. "Come on, Zeusie. Let's go for a walk down to snack lake."

He stood up and looked toward the ridge, eyes wide with terror. *But—we could all be shot!*

"It's okay Zeus," I said. "I won't let anything happen to you."

He braved the non-stop gunshots and high-tailed it down to the shore. He even showed us a new shortcut. For some odd reason he felt safer near the water, though his satellite dish ears twitched the whole time and he kept one eye on Boy Scout ridge. All things considered, Kaley and I were impressed with his behavior. He was nervous but not panicked. He even played with us and snacked on fish heads. However he beat us back to our campsite and waited beside the pickup. *Let me in.* I knew Venus and Tod would return soon and the dogs would have to be separated anyway so I let him hide in the backseat.

The shooting continued through the afternoon and into the evening.

"This reminds me of the Fourth of July," Kaley grumbled. "Except way more annoying."

"Well I hope you've learned a lesson from this," I said.

She squinted at me. "What lesson?"

"Don't grow up to be a Boy Scout."

She howled with laughter as she collapsed in the camp chair.

We persuaded Zeus to join us on a lake walk after supper. He endured the clatter once again. We ordered Venus to leave him alone and she did. By dusk the shooting had frazzled everyone's nerves.

I was in tears. "We should just pack up and go home."

"No, please," Kaley begged. "The guns don't bother me anymore."

"They don't bother Venus either," Tod said.

I pointed at the truck where Zeus had holed up. "He's miserable."

"Kaley's right. It's not that much different than what we went through on the Fourth," he said. "He'll tough it out."

"What's the point of putting him through it if we don't have to?" I insisted.

"Because you're the one who said Venus needs to run wild," he said. "She's doing that and look how calm she is."

Venus was sprawled in front of the campfire. At the mention of her name she sat up and blinked. *If I get any calmer I'll lapse into a coma.*

I tossed up my hands. "It's settled then. We're staying."

Kaley hugged me. Tod and Venus joined in.

"You need to stop worrying so much about Zeus," he said.

The shooting stopped after dark. Kaley coaxed Zeus out of his panic room. He slept in the tent with her. "He's my protector," she said.

"I pity any man or animal who strays into our campsite." I aimed my flashlight into the pine forest and waved it eerily. "Zeus and Venus will scare them away."

Saturday dawned in blissful silence—until 9:00 a.m., when the shooting started all over again. It continued non-stop, same as the day before. Tod took off with Venus on a bike ride in the morning. Kaley charmed Zeus into another lake walk.

After lunch Tod hopped on his bike. Venus crawled under the camper. *You'll have to chase those deer without me. I'm beat.* He peddled off alone. Kaley and I sought refuge from the biting flies and played cards in the camper. Zeus hid out in the pickup as the gunfire raged on.

A young woman drove by on a four-wheeler. Her Black Lab mix jumped off the back and tore through our campsite. I slipped on my shoes. Venus barked. *What? Who's here?* The woman hopped off her vehicle and chased her dog. Kaley peered through the window.

As I walked out the door I said, "Sure hope it's that dog's lucky day and Venus doesn't tear him to pieces." Venus barked her ferocious intruder bark. I peered under the camper. She was trapped between the cooler and the cooking table, snapping and snarling. *Let me at him. Get me out of here.* The black dog ran toward the road. I let out a sigh of relief.

"I'm sorry! My bad. I'm sorry." The woman apologized repeatedly.

I waved her off. "It's okay. Nobody got hurt." As I freed Venus and ushered her inside the camper she whined and complained. *Not fair. Let me go. He's got it coming.*

That night Zeus slept in the tent again with Kaley. In the middle of the night one cherry bomb exploded—then another. The camper door flew open.

Kaley shuffled in. "Zeus tried to crawl in my sleeping bag."

"Is he still in the tent?" I asked.

"Yeah. He's really scared." She snuggled up with Venus on the table bed. "But it was kinda funny. I mean, it's not like he could even fit. But he hogged the whole air mattress so I had to come in here."

When I went outside to check on him another cherry bomb exploded. Zeus escaped from the tent and headed for the pickup. *Let me in.*

Sunday morning we awoke to silence. The shooting had stopped. After breakfast we hiked along the lake trail and met up with three horseback riders taking a break. Two men sat on a log bench and a woman leaned against a hitching post. We leashed the dogs so they wouldn't scare the horses grazing several feet away in a pine grove. We all nodded and said, "Howdy." They had an older Shepherd mix with them. He rushed up to Venus and me. They sniffed each other and he walked away. Tod and Kaley were ahead of us with Zeus.

The horsewoman pointed at Venus. "She's Akbash."

I stopped in my tracks. "You know Akbash?"

She nodded. "I know Akbash. I have one. At home. He's nine. A real sweetie. But he wasn't always that way."

"I know what you mean. She's the most challenging dog I've ever had," I confessed.

"Akbash dogs are nearly impossible to train. And hard to live with. A friend of mine just had to put her Akbash down. Whatever made you get one?" she asked.

"Her previous owner told us she was part Pyrenees and part

Lab," I said.

"Wow. So you had no clue what you were getting into."

"None. We didn't even know what an Akbash was," I said. "Our friends used to have one and they always said she looks exactly like him. Then last summer we saw some actual Akbash dogs guarding sheep up here and then we knew."

"A-mazing." She shook her head. "So how's it going? She seems pretty mellow."

I sighed. "She's heavily medicated." I told her about Venus's CCD and aggression.

She gave a low whistle. "Whoa, doggies. You've got your hands full with this one."

I rolled my eyes. "Yeah. But I finally figured out something about her. I mean all Akbash dogs. They need to run wild. She needs to run wild. When we bring her up here she's at her best. When we take her cross-country skiing or biking or hiking in the mountains she always takes off on her own. But she always comes back. Then she goes home exhausted and content."

She grinned and nodded while I spoke.

"I'm right, aren't I?"

"Yup. Dead on," she said. "I live in the country on two acres. My Akbash takes off every day. And he always comes back exhausted and happy. He used to be aggressive until I realized I had to let him go." She waved her hand. "Oh, I worried he'd get shot. But hey, if that happens, at least he'll die happy."

I smiled. "I feel the same way. We have a big yard and she gets lots of walks but it's just not enough."

She shrugged. "It's their nature. They're like wild dogs. This dog here." She pointed to the Shepherd mix. "He's half coyote, half German Shepherd and he's the same way."

"It's good to know we're on the right track at least," I said.

"What's her name?"

"Venus."

"Suits her." The horsewoman looked at Venus. Their eyes locked. Then she shook her head and exhaled. "Gawd, she is one beautiful dog." She looked at me. "Powerful too, eh?"

"Ferocious."

"Yes, ma'am. You hang in there. She's lucky to have you."

"Thanks." It felt so good to speak Akbash, I could have hugged her. Instead I walked Venus back to the campground so the horsewoman wouldn't see me cry.

Chapter 23 - The uphill road

We returned home from Meadow Lake on Sunday evening. Tod left for Chicago on Monday. I wasn't looking forward to handling Venus and Zeus on my own for five days.

When he called from the Denver airport my surliness surfaced. "I'm going to complain to the local Boy Scout Council about that shooting rampage."

"Don't," he said. "I'll talk to Danielle at the Forest Service. That's a better way to handle it."

I sniffed. "Easy for you to say. You don't have to live with these dogs 24/7. It's bad enough we have to put up with the worst neighbors in the world. But when we try to catch a break and de-stress we have to put up with a bunch of trigger-happy Boy Scouts."

He sighed. "You worry about the dogs too much. You're letting them dominate your life."

"D'ya think?" I snapped.

Admittedly I felt slighted. His travel schedule gave him a break from our doggie soap opera. I did the math. For 20 months and counting, I had not been apart from Zeus and Venus for more than a few hours.

Were they dominating my life? I analyzed the situation. Apart from her disappointing lack of judgment in June when she picked a fight with Zeus, Venus had not shown any other signs of aggression for more than nine months. She was not aggressive toward humans. She had become more self-confident, less defensive, and generally friendlier toward humans and other dogs. They probably were dominating my life. But we had made progress.

Even though we had our moments of frustration, 99.9% of the time Venus was affectionate, sensitive, calm, sweet, intelligent, strong, and obedient. In other words—a normal dog. After three and a half years, I knew her soul. I loved her. Her genetics, her breed mix, her obsession and anxiety—her disease —none of it was her fault. I was addicted to the challenge. I believed I was the only person who truly understood her. I was the only one capable of handling her. She needed me. I could not quit her.

And I needed her. She was my bodyguard. I chose to have big dogs in my life for a reason. Protection. When Tod traveled, I was a woman living alone. I'd had my share of scary situations. Whether it was a man following me, a bear in my backyard, or a stranger at my door, a big dog had kept me safe. I had never trained my dogs to protect me. It wasn't necessary. Nobody messes with a big dog. With Venus, I was certain no human or animal would dare attack me—or Tod, or Zeus, or any other member of her pack. Her presence alone was a deterrent. I always felt safe with her.

So, as the week began, I decided to look upon the three of us as a team. The three *amigos*—sort of. We all had our jobs to do. Fresh from a weekend of running wild at the lake, Venus's job was to practice calm behavior. After somewhat bravely enduring the Boy Scouts' shooting spree, Zeus's job was to get lots of R&R. As pack leader, my job was to feed, exercise, and discipline them.

Zeus had wanted the stairway gate open for a week. He often sat next to it and cast beseeching looks in my direction. *Can we stop the upstairs-dog-downstairs-dog game now? Please?* I wasn't ready. We had been opening the gate occasionally and my plan was to keep them separated. But the dogs had other ideas.

Tuesday afternoon Venus came inside and slept in the hallway outside my office while I worked. A thunderstorm blew through and Zeus wanted in. I showed him where Venus was lying. *So? What's your point? I'm not going back out in that thunder.* He plopped down about three feet away from her. I wasn't too keen on the arrangement but I trusted his judgment. I let it happen.

From then on, a comfort zone developed between them. I was the pack leader and Zeus was my guide. I learned the signals. He glanced over his shoulder at her, or circled and wouldn't lie down. *Stop looking at me. Stop looking at me.* When I checked out Venus, without fail her beady brown eyes were boring a hole through him. It was both oddly comical and deadly serious. I practiced my own signals on her. When she fixated on him, I stepped in and distracted her. I moved her to a different spot, or sent her downstairs, or upstairs if Zeus was downstairs.

The gate stayed open, except when the occasional firecracker exploded. There again I relied on Zeus. With my deaf ear I didn't always hear it. Whenever he retreated to the bedroom, I listened for firecrackers. Then I gated the doorway to keep Venus out.

We had been keeping them separated in the house during the night since their fight, which I had planned to continue. Instead Venus-the-guardian opted to sleep outside. So I let her. I was concerned she'd bark and I wouldn't hear. But she didn't. She kept watch. I loved that about her.

When she was indoors I reminded her to leave Zeus alone. She was not allowed to sniff him, touch him, or stare at him. I used the commands "leave it" or "leave Zeus alone." The more I enforced the rules, the more Zeus liked being around her. In the process of defining our spaces we created a circle of trust.

Wednesday morning at Dogland a Chow mix named Buffy charged up to Venus. They knew each other but Venus snarled at him to back off, then she sauntered away. She reacted like a normal dog. Audrey, Buffy's human, turned around and walked the other way.

A few minutes later, Jeanne and Trevor caught up with me. "Venus snarled at Buffy. Audrey's upset. You need to put Venus on the leash."

I snapped the leash to her collar. I wasn't in the mood to argue. "If she has a problem with Venus she should tell me to my face."

Jeanne held up her hands. "I don't want to get in the middle of anything."

I laughed. "You already are."

"Come on, Trevor." She tossed her head and they walked away.

The minute they were out of sight, I unhooked the leash. On the other side of the buffaloberry thicket I met up with Keith, who had recently started bringing his Chocolate Lab Duke to the park.

He confronted me. "What's the problem with your white dog?"

"Nothing," I said.

"She snarled at another dog," he said. "That's not nothing."

"What it *was,* was normal dog behavior," I said. "Buffy has an annoying habit of charging other dogs. She put him in his place. Zeus does the same thing when Buffy charges him."

He puffed out his chest and bobbed his chin. "Well I reckon Duke must be the perfect dog. I don't believe he has ever snarled at another dog."

"He's young. Give him time," I said. "And that doesn't mean what my dog did was wrong."

He looked skeptical. "You never know. They could've ended up in a fight."

"But they didn't," I snapped. "Nobody got hurt. Nothing happened."

He held up his hands. "I didn't mean to upset you."

I rolled my eyes. "I'm not upset. I think you're making too much of it, is all."

"Well, some of us think you need to keep her on a leash," he said. "You don't even know where she is right now."

I looked past him. "She's right behind you." He looked startled as Venus stepped out of the bushes. While he recovered from his embarrassment I said, "It seems like my dogs are expected to behave better than everyone else's dogs."

"I think everyone expects all the dogs to get along down here," he said.

"You are talking about a lot of dogs and a lot of people," I said. "Incidents are bound to happen. There's no point in making a big deal about it. That's how everyone gets along." I leashed Venus and walked on. I surprised myself. Usually I apologized for her unpredictable behavior whether it was warranted or not. Her mental illness was no secret. I blogged about it. Most Doglanders knew. When they asked questions, we answered them. Nonetheless, the message was loud and clear. Venus made some people nervous. If they were nervous around her, their dogs would sense it and there could be trouble.

That evening while I pulled weeds in the flower garden, Carol came around the corner on her bike pulling Tommy in the chariot. I waved. She stopped at the end of the driveway. I walked over. Venus barked a greeting from the porch.

"I was hoping to catch you at home," Carol said. "Jeanne told me what happened at the park this morning."

I laughed. "Yes. Venus and I got put on probation for snarling. We have to be leashed from now on." I told her about my conversation with Keith.

Her jaw dropped. "They have no right to make you put Venus on a leash. First off, you're right. Buffy's an asshole. He charges up to Buddha all the time. And not because he wants to play."

"It a dominance thing," I said. "When it happened with Venus, Audrey didn't say anything to me. She just walked away."

"Jeanne told me Audrey said she was scared of Venus and just wanted to get out of there before something bad happened."

I rolled my eyes. "That's ridiculous."

"You're not going to leash her, are you? Please tell me you're not," she begged.

"Of course not. She's been roaming free down there for years. She has checking to do, rituals to perform. She'd go crazy on a leash."

"Wait till I meet up with this Keith dude," she fumed. "He lives a block away from me. So does Audrey. I'll put it to them. They don't get to make the rules down there."

"No. Don't." I shook my head. "Look, they have every right to feel nervous about Venus."

"Excuse me." Carol held up her hand. "Sorry to interrupt, but your neighbor and his kids and that other dude have been sitting over there watching us this whole time."

"I noticed." I glanced over her shoulder.

"What's up with that?" It was a rhetorical question; Carol knew about our history with them.

"This is how we live," I said. "They watch us all the time."

"So who's the other dude?"

"Friend of Daryl's. I don't know his name. So I call him Patsy. It suits him."

Carol laughed. As if on cue, a skateboarder zoomed past. Venus jumped up and barked. *Boy on wheels! Woof-woof-woof!*

"Shut up!" Daryl yelled. "Shut that fucking dog up!"

Carol's head snapped in his direction. "You shut the fuck up!"

I burst out laughing, but I touched her arm. "We don't engage him. It upsets Venus."

"Well, who the fuck does he think he is?" she yelled. "God! How can you stand this? You get non-stop shit from those idiots. Now people at the park are on your case." She paused, looked across the street and yelled, "Why don't you all just mind your own business?"

I giggled. "Aren't we plucky today? But you're going to get me in trouble."

She squinted at me. "How so?"

"I'll have to pay for this," I said. "Somehow. Some day."

"Oh for crap's sake. No wonder Venus is crazy. They'd drive me up a wall."

Tommy woke up and fussed in the chariot.

"Anyway," I changed the subject. "Please don't make an issue about what happened at Dogland today. We can't expect everyone to understand Venus's condition. Hell, we don't even understand it. We can go to Dogland early in the morning when no one's there."

"I guess that would solve the problem," she said. "But it shouldn't even be a problem."

I shrugged. "I don't need the hassle. You know? Like you said, those idiots over there are enough to deal with."

"You got that right." She leaned forward and whispered, "I get a really bad vibe in this neighborhood. Gives me the creeps."

"I know, right?" I patted her shoulder. "You're my witness."

Tommy squawked.

"Gotta get moving." She reached over and hugged me.

"Thanks for your support as always," I said.

As she peddled away she yelled, "Hey! Venus! Woof-woof!"

Venus answered. *Yeah. I get it. Woof-woof.* The she looked at me and grinned. Carol's cackles echoed up the street. *Hell to pay,* I thought.

The next morning Margie and the boys packed their suitcases in their SUV and drove off. Carol was right about the bad vibe. After they left it disappeared, like a sweet rain displaces a bad odor. While they were gone Venus rarely barked and she wanted to be outside all day, until Daryl came home from work. Then she wanted in.

We continued our quest for new places to let Venus run wild. Tod took us to one of his favorite bike trails. A winding uphill road led to a ridge overlooking Harvey Gap, a small reservoir north of town.

Zeus loved hill climbs. He was sure-footed and enjoyed the

slow pace. Venus loped along beside him. Any minute I expected her to drop back and slip away. But she stayed with us. At the crest, the land spread out into rolling hills covered in sagebrush and pinion pines. I could almost smell the mule deer. Venus casually sniffed around. For a moment I wondered if I was wrong about her. As if she read my mind, she meandered through the sagebrush, her nose dropped, then she bolted. She knew. She knew why we'd come. She knew it was okay. I was never so glad to see her go. She returned about 15 minutes later, tongue dripping from her wide grin.

At bedtime that night Venus trotted into the bedroom and lay down next to the bed. For the first time in over a month, Zeus followed her and stretched out on the rug, as cool and smooth as a river rock. *No problem here.*

Chapter 24 - Trappers Lake peace accord

Do dogs love?

Some animal behaviorists believe dogs form bonds with other dogs but the bond has more to do with companionship than love. Others believe dogs do love, whether the feeling is based on need, devotion, or companionship, it is certainly love. Most dog owners would agree.

Did Venus and Zeus love each other? There was no doubt Venus loved Zeus. A crazed, obsessive kind of love, but it was love. From the day they met she was smitten. Yet I had often wondered if Zeus sensed her pistons misfiring way back then.

They worked out their boundaries after the fight and their relationship was okay again. That was all—just okay. Every now and then, Venus sneaked in a little lick on Zeus's nose or ear. It was sweet. But we had learned that a lick could quickly morph into a chomp. One little lick was all she was allowed. She couldn't help herself. She loved the big guy.

Zeus, I wasn't so sure about. He figured out the "leave it" game. He knew it was up to him whether she could be near him. A couple times at Dogland she head butted him to get him to chase her, but he ignored her. Was she too anxious? Did she get snippy? He looked at me. *Just testing her.*

Who could blame him? Life with the mentally ill is often described as "walking on eggshells." Life with Venus often felt like that. If Tod and I walked on eggshells then Zeus was right there with us. But Venus hadn't attacked me and I was not a dog. I didn't know what Zeus was going through. I didn't know what he was thinking. His behavior seemed to say, *I'm just not that into you.*

In August, I said to Tod, "Let's go somewhere we've never been before. I've always wanted to go to Trappers Lake."

Our excuse for avoiding new places was because it was easier to take two big dogs to familiar places, especially after Venus flipped out during our Wisconsin trip. But the time had come to test her ability to handle unfamiliar territory.

We packed up the camper, piled the dogs in the pickup, and headed north. We pulled a fast one on the dogs. We didn't tell them where we were going. Then we waited for their reaction. Big fun. By the time we got to Meeker, they knew we weren't on the road to Meadow Lake. They couldn't sleep. They sat up and slobbered on the windows. After we passed Buford, the road turned to gravel for the long ascent up to 9,900 feet. Venus pressed her nose and forehead against the glass. *I've never seen this place before.*

Zeus paced back and forth. I turned around and gave him the evil eye. He plopped down and hung his giant head over my shoulder panting loudly. *Okay. I give up. I don't know where we are.* He rolled his eyes toward the window and then back at me. His white eyebrows almost formed a question mark. *Are you watching out there? Do you even know where the hell we are?* A long strand of drool landed on my shirt sleeve.

I groaned. "Zeus! That's so rude."

He stood and paced some more, which got Venus's attention. Whenever his mood changed we had to distract her so she didn't fixate and snap at him. She stood up.

"Enough already," I barked. "Just chill. Everything's okay. You'll see." I banished them to their corners. I looked at Tod. "Cesar Millan's golden rule might be 'don't humanize your dogs.' But sometimes they act like bratty kids."

He laughed as he peered through the windshield. "Get a load of this scenery."

The Trappers Lake Wilderness has become a case study in the awesome power of nature. A lightning strike ignited a wildfire near Big Fish Lake on July 19, 2002. Forty-one thousand acres burned between Big Fish and Trappers Lake. In its wake thousands upon thousands of acres of charred dead trees stretched for more than ten miles like monuments to the devastation. Yet the almost cathedral-like, mountainous landscape was no less spectacular.

Only a few campsites were occupied so we had our choice of four campgrounds above the lake. As we drove through and inspected each one, the dogs drooled on the windows as they gobbled up the scenery. The campsites were burrowed in the conifer forest. We chose one with a view of the lake and the Chinese Wall for a backdrop.

While we set up camp, Zeus paced impatiently and Venus darted around anxiously. When we finally headed out for a hike we found a short spur to Scotts Lake, a quiet lagoon. The dogs were ecstatic. They raced down the trail and plunged into the water. Venus bounded into the marsh grass and rolled upside down. Zeus splashed around in the shallow water.

We continued another quarter mile to Trappers Lake, where the dogs practically swooned. We laughed at how we'd fooled them. At the shoreline they seemed to get the joke because they each wiggled over and pressed against our legs. Big dog hugs. We hiked up the Carhart trail for about an hour until we reached the intersection of the Wall Lake trail. Talk about running wild. Zeus pranced from one pond to the next. Venus headed for the forest.

"Dog heaven," I declared.

"I don't think I've ever seen them so happy," Tod said.

Throughout the weekend it felt as though we were watching a peace negotiation in progress a la dog world. Zeus and Venus healed old wounds and forged a new bond before our eyes. The Protestants and Catholics. The Capulets and Montagues, though Zeus and Venus were definitely not Romeo and Juliet. More like *Mr. and Mrs. Smith.*

Venus let her freak flag fly. Out on the trails she slogged through marshes, swam across ponds, snarfed horse apples, and rolled in dead stuff like a typical sloppy Lab. Back at the campsite she was pampered pup. She whined to be let in the camper, crawled up on the comfy bench cushion, and passed out. Part wild dog—part princess.

Early Saturday morning I rousted the lazy mooks and headed down to Scotts Lake. Venus figured out where we were headed and beat us there. When Zeus saw her standing in the water he galloped downhill and plowed into her, totally uncharacteristic behavior for Mr. Smooth. Venus looked startled as she jumped backward. Zeus ran off and she chased him through the tall grass.

The wilderness around Trappers Lake is a maze of trails and intersections. No motorized vehicles or bikes allowed. Hiker's paradise. The dogs weren't used to so many interconnecting trails. Venus got a little carried away with the whole running wild thing. On our Saturday hike, Tod and I had a brief discussion about whether we would take the Carhart trail again or hike along Trappers Lake. He was thinking Carhart trail and I was thinking Trappers Lake. I won. About five minutes later we realized Venus was nowhere around. We stopped. We whistled and called but she didn't appear. Tod figured she took off up the Carhart trail so he headed back the way we came. Sure enough he found her there.

Did she read his mind? Or did he read hers?

Before we packed up on Sunday we hiked the same trail around the north end of the lake because the dogs loved splashing in the water. When we reached a trail intersection Tod said, "This is the trail back to our campsite."

"Let's hike out to the bridge and back," I said.

Within a few minutes we noticed Venus was missing again. We assumed she had trotted on ahead of us through the aspen grove and she would meet us at the bridge. No Venus at the bridge.

On the way back to the trail intersection, I asked Zeus, "Where's Venus?"

He glanced around. *She's not here.* A half hour passed and still no sign of Venus.

"We haven't even heard her barking or howling," I said.

"I bet she got her signals crossed like yesterday and took off on the trail toward our campsite," Tod said.

As we headed back I considered the alternatives if she wasn't there. Tod could start packing up and I could hike the trail in reverse and look for her. Our phone number was printed on her collar. The Trappers Lake Lodge served food in case we had to stay another day to look for her.

At our campsite I glanced around nervously but didn't see her. I opened my mouth to describe my plan to Tod.

"There she is," he said.

She crawled out from underneath the picnic table and grinned sheepishly. Her tail thumped in the dirt. *Boy am I ever glad to see you guys. I was afraid you were lost.* I scratched her ears and praised her for being such a smart dog. She trembled, indicating fearfulness and/or anxiety. She stayed put while we packed up, though I kept an eye on her because of her intense anxiety.

"I don't understand why she didn't track us on the trail," I said.

"It's pretty windy up here," Tod said. "And the wind changes direction a lot. That and the maze of trails probably confused her."

"Tracking dogs use the wind to pick up scent," I said. "I wonder if clomipramine affects her sense of smell."

I Googled it when I got home. The results of a University of France study showed a significant decrease in olfactory sensitivity in mice that were given clomipramine. We could tell from Venus's overall demeanor she still had her sense of smell. Perhaps it was impaired by the drug, not wiped out completely.

When I told Tod he shrugged. "As side effects go, it's not so bad. At least now we know we need to pay more attention on hikes. Maybe she will, too."

After the Trappers Lake weekend things changed at home. Zeus was happier. He had a spring in his step as though a weight had been lifted off his back. He stopped peering over his shoulder. Venus smiled more. She was less intense, less fixated on his every move. If he blocked the stairway she woofed. *Move, please.* He either moved voluntarily or I stepped in and made him move. She didn't stare at him while he ate. Sometimes Zeus plopped down next to her. *No problem here.* Sometimes they rubbed shoulders when they walked. In their own inimitable way, they had achieved a peaceful settlement.

Chapter 25 - Magic words

Self-esteem is as important to dogs as it is to humans. In fact, it's so important I would bet most of the dogs in shelters have self-esteem issues.

Venus did. Zeus didn't. From the time he was seven weeks old, he heard the word "good" a lot. "Good puppy. Good boy. Good dog. Good Zeus." He knew he was good. I was pretty sure when Venus was a puppy she heard the words "bad dog" far too often. By the time she came to live with us she was convinced of her "badness." Her lack of self-esteem contributed to her anxiety.

In mid-August, school resumed and my babysitting schedule changed. Venus adjusted easily with little more than a hiccup, which was a good sign. Our house is a block and a half from the elementary school. A parade of kids walked, biked, and scootered to and from school. Venus barked at them, a sure sign of anxiety. I decided to try something new. I focused on Venus instead of her barking, I went out on the porch and praised her.

"Good girl," I said repeatedly. She stopped barking. After a week of consistent praise, her barking diminished. I don't know why it took me so long to figure out she responded best to praise. Perhaps I was too focused on training. Or maybe I'm just a stupid human. Whatever the case, I started saying "good girl" when I wanted her to do anything. "Good girl. Sit. Good girl. Come. Good girl. Leave it. Good girl. Hold." I used the "hold" command when she was on-leash and wanted to chase another dog, or cat, or kids on bikes.

Even though we knew Venus had calmed down over the summer, we looked for more ways to challenge her. Labor Day weekend we took Kaley and the dogs back to Lake Powell. The difference in Venus's behavior was evident from the start. She had to ride in the camper again but showed no anxiety because we kept saying, "Good girl." She pranced in and out of the camper like a princess with her royal carriage.

The first evening we took the dogs down to Hobie Cat Beach for a swim. They rode in the backseat with Kaley. As we turned a corner a coyote crossed the road in front of us. Tod stopped. The coyote halted about 20 feet away and stared at Zeus and Venus. I held my breath. The window was open. They sat head-to-head and stared back at him. They didn't bark. They didn't try to jump out. Mouths agape, their noses bobbed slightly as they inhaled his scent. Eventually he trotted off and they watched spellbound until he disappeared over the red sand berm.

He made quite an impression on Venus. At the beach instead of bounding into the water like she usually did, Venus put her nose to the ground and took off. I wondered if she would try to track the coyote so I kept an eye on her. She dashed back and forth on the berm, stopping to pee every few feet. She was setting up a safety perimeter. She barked at three women and herded them onto their beached boat, much to their chagrin.

I jogged over and apologized. “Sorry. She means no harm. We saw a coyote along the road and she’s just trying to protect you.” Once I explained, they didn’t mind her behavior.

All three nights the coyotes were active on the ridge above our campsite, howling and barking. Venus and Zeus remained alert and listened quietly. Even though they were supposed to be leashed, when the park ranger wasn’t around we allowed them to roam freely and establish a perimeter of pee around our campsite because that’s what dogs do. It helped Venus control her anxiety about the coyotes. She had a job to do.

During the day she chased lizards for a few minutes, then swam, fetched the ball, explored, and played with Kaley and Zeus. In other words, she behaved like a normal dog, a stark contrast from our previous trip in June.

In the campground she was so friendly she happily greeted the park ranger as he scolded me for not having her leashed. She ignored the other campers. A large group arrived in the middle of the night and noisily set up camp. Engines roared. Car alarms blared. Headlights shone in our camper. Loud voices talked and laughed. During all the commotion Venus barked once.

When it came time to head home, it was too hot for her to ride in the camper so she rode in the backseat with Zeus and Kaley. The pickup’s backseat folded down into a flat space for the dogs, leaving a single passenger seat for Kaley. Neither of the dogs could stretch out like they usually did. We made several stops to give them a break. They persevered without any snarling or snapping. Whenever Venus grew restless I repeated the mantra, “Good girl.” She responded with a goofy grin and settled down. Our Lake Powell encore was like an obedience trial. Venus won a blue ribbon. Two simple words worked like magic.

Chapter 26 - An unexpected surprise

At Dogland one morning, the dogs and I ran into Kathy with her Lab mix, Buddy, and Beagle mutt, Sheba. She was the shelter volunteer who had recommended I carry pepper spray. Venus stole Buddy's tennis ball and ran. He chased after her. Game on.

"I haven't seen you guys in a while," Kathy nodded at Venus. "She's doing great."

"Yup. We put her on 100 milligrams of clomipramine. She's reached a whole new level of calm."

Venus danced around Buddy, teasing him with the green ball. She stopped and tossed it in the air. It landed in the river. Both dogs splashed in after it.

"Look at her. She's like her old self again," Kathy said.

"We figured out she's much happier when we take her up in the mountains and let her run wild," I said.

"Yeah, well who isn't?"

I smiled. "Exactly. It's good for all of us."

"Have you ever run across any sheep herds while you're up there?" she asked.

"Yes, but only from a distance. The Akbash were with them."

"The reason I ask is cuz I met this guy who has an Akbash. It's a purebred. But anyway, the dog has some anxiety issues. Long story short, the guy found a sheep rancher. I guess it was a friend-of-a-friend kind of thing. The rancher let him bring his Akbash up to spend some time with the sheep. He said it worked like a drug. Calmed the dog right down."

"Interesting," I said. "Maybe I should get a sheep."

Kathy laughed. "No, seriously. I think you should find a rancher who will let Venus hang out with his sheep. Let her live out her fantasy. Express her inner Akbash."

It was my turn to laugh. Venus snatched the ball again and ran circles around Buddy and Zeus. Sheba waddled into the melee and barked. "What rancher in his right mind would let a crazy bitch on drugs, up from the city, anywhere near his sheep?"

"Well, when you put it that way ...."

"I'm not saying it wouldn't be good for her," I said. "I wish I knew a rancher well enough to ask him to take the risk."

"Why risk?"

"Venus has to maintain stability on the drug for six months. We're not even there yet."

She shrugged. “Well. It’s something to consider whenever you think she’s ready.”

Later I told Tod about Kathy’s suggestion. “They hold sheepdog trials every year in Meeker,” he said. “Maybe there’s a sheepherding school for dogs.”

I Googled “sheepherding training.” The closest school was 200 miles away. I did some research to learn more about the rigors of formal sheepherding training. It’s highly competitive. The real risk is setting up the dog to fail, which would have done nothing to ease Venus’s anxiety—or mine. Yet the more I read, the more the act of herding sheep seemed like an effective way to address her obsessive nature. If only we knew a sheep rancher.

In late August, Tod bought a 1979 Jeep CJ5. The dogs loved it because it was open like a convertible and took us deeper into the back country than hiking. I had mixed feelings. The jungle-black, guerilla-taxi look gave it character. But the giant Mud Runner tires made climbing in an athletic event. Before Tod turned the key I always said a little prayer to the Jeep god. If it started, I breathed a sigh of relief. If it didn’t, we relied on the kindness of strangers.

For me, a CJ adventure meant inevitable risk followed by an unpredictable outcome. For the dogs it meant the wind in their faces, effortless and guaranteed.

We needed to do some trail maintenance up on West Elk before the snowfall. The first Saturday in October was our last opportunity before rifle hunting season. Under a classic, cloudless blue sky, I stood in the driveway and sucked coffee from a thermal mug in the frost-kissed morning air. I watched Zeus, then Venus stumble onto the dog ramp and into the CJ. I shrugged, handed Tod my coffee mug, and followed them. It sure beat ropes and ladders.

The Jeep god smiled on us. The CJ’s engine growled to life.

Up at the West Elk trailhead we spotted two hunting camps, so I tied a blaze orange scarf around Venus’s neck. Zeus wore a nylon blaze orange vest. Even though rifle season hadn’t opened, hunters often came up early to set up camp and do some target practice. We didn’t take any chances with the dogs’ safety. Tod brought the chainsaw to clear fallen trees. He drove the CJ around the trail while the dogs and I hiked in the opposite direction. I cleared limbs and brush.

As we climbed out of the gully, Venus’s nose hit the ground. She took off uphill like a bullet. Zeus lumbered after her. I heard bells—tinkling bells.

“Oh shit,” I muttered. “Sheep.”

I couldn’t see them—or the dogs. I called but they were not in listening mode. I heard Venus bark once. I also heard a smattering of “baahs.” I kept walking and figured I’d assess the situation once I reached the hilltop. I hoped they didn't cross paths with an Akbash on duty, but I didn't hear barking.

Zeus reappeared on the crest of the hill about a hundred yards ahead of me. He shot me a frantic look, then he galloped in circles as his tail whirled like a lasso. *Warning! Sheep! Lots of sheep!* The corners of his blaze orange vest flapped in the breeze.

I laughed. "Come on back, Zeus." He ignored me. Venus had never attacked or harmed another species so it was pointless to panic.

On the hilltop I saw the herd huddled together in an aspen grove on the edge of the trail. I guesstimated there were about 75 sheep. But I couldn't see Venus. I called her. Zeus trotted toward the sheep with an air of authority. *My mom's here. You sheep need to move along now.* Problem was, he knew nothing about sheep and didn't possess an ounce of herding instinct. Bleating and squealing erupted as they scattered across the trail. The scene was reminiscent of the movie Babe when the anthropomorphic sheep cried *Wolf! Wolf!* as Fly charged them. These sheep probably mistook Zeus for a wolf and panicked.

"Come back Zeus," I called.

He retreated with a plaintive look. *Your turn. See if you can get those sheep to move.*

Like a flash of white lightning Venus appeared from the back of the herd. She dashed to the front, then she cut back and forth, back and forth. My mouth fell open. Silently, she made all the right moves. In less than a minute she herded the sheep in a tight circle and held them there.

"Good girl. Leave it," I yelled. Venus crouched like a sphinx in front of the woolly masses. Imitating Farmer Hoggett, I called out, "That'll do, that'll do." I even tried "Bah-ram-ewe," but Venus had entered an altered state of consciousness. Her head moved side-to-side as she eyed the herd for stragglers. The sheep stayed calm and surprisingly quiet. I figured they were used to Akbash.

Zeus, on the other hand, scared the hell out of them. They cowered and backed away if his tail so much as twitched. I thought it best to keep him moving. They were safe with Venus. I heard the chainsaw so I knew Tod was nearby.

I steered Zeus up the trail, then I stopped and turned around. Our movements had caused a commotion on the other side of the herd. As Venus trotted over, the stray sheep moved back toward the masses. She walked all the way around. Then she turned and trotted back the way she came.

As I stood frozen in place, I realized I wasn't watching Venus live out her fantasy. The Venus I knew watched TV upside down on the couch while eating pizza. She didn't know the first thing about herding sheep. Yet there she was in all her glory, herding sheep. Only this Venus could not hear me or see me. It was as though she had been hypnotized.

I wanted to be happy for her. She was having the thrill of a lifetime. Tears streamed down my face as I walked up the trail. But I didn't know why. Zeus had already found Tod. I wiped my eyes before I reached them. "Venus found a herd of sheep. She's exploring her inner Akbash."

He rolled his eyes. "So that's why Zeus is all bent out of shape." He hopped in the CJ. "I'll drive down there. She'll chase the Jeep."

Which was exactly how her big adventure ended.

Afterward Venus was totally exhausted and completely calm, though she walked a little stiff-legged. She vomited a couple times when we got home. I remembered Zeus's bout with gastritis. No doubt a huge adrenaline rush on top of an empty stomach was the problem. I fed her half a can of chicken and rice dog food, which settled her stomach.

That evening while she slept upside down on the couch, utterly spent, Tod scratched her belly. "I think it's pretty neat Venus got to herd sheep. We're lucky nobody got hurt."

"You should've seen her in action," I said. "Pure instinct. She's a natural."

The experience haunted me. I couldn't deny what I saw with my own eyes. Underneath that gorgeous fur coat lived two completely different dogs. In humans it's called dissociative identity disorder (DID). Split personality. She could not be both. Which one would win?

Chapter 27 - Clicker training

Who says you can't teach an old dog new tricks? Meaning me, of course.

"Our sheep herding adventure got me thinking," I said to Tod. "I need more than voice commands to get Venus's attention in sticky situations. I've been reading about clicker training."

"Do you really think she would have responded to a clicker in the middle of all those sheep?" he asked.

"I consider that more than a sticky situation," I said. "I mean like when she takes off running wild and we want her to come back. A clicker might have worked when she lost us at Trappers Lake."

"Or maybe a dog whistle," he suggested.

"Supposedly dogs respond better to the clicker than the whistle," I said.

He looked skeptical. "Somehow I can't picture Venus responding to a clicking sound."

"I think she might like it," I said. "It's Zeus I'm not so sure about. With his noise phobia, the sound might annoy him. Or he might even be insulted."

"Yeah. One more thing he has to put up with," he added. "I'll pick up a dog whistle at the pet store."

I had ordered a copy of *Aggression in Dogs: Practical Management, Prevention & Behavior Modification* by Brenda Aloff. It arrived in my mailbox the next day, like a sign. It is the bible on canine aggression, and just as big as the actual one. Aloff covers all types of dog aggression; how to recognize it and how to deal with it. She has lived with dog aggression and handled aggression in training situations, so it was written from her own life experience.

The book is structured like a reference manual, or textbook. I concentrated on the chapters that applied to our situation. Of course I started with Chapter 53: "Aggression Directed Toward a Canine Housemate." According to Aloff, it is the most difficult to deal with—and didn't we know it. In the case of housemates, the aggressive dog has plenty of opportunities to make life miserable for the other dog in ways we humans have no way of deciphering because we don't live in the dog world. We don't know how they communicate unless we constantly observe their behavior, which is impossible. That's why housemate aggression is such a challenge. That's why life with Venus was like a roller coaster ride.

Since we were already one year into our housemate

aggression, the chapter provided validation more than anything. It was the same reason we became *Dog Whisperer* fanatics. Besides Drs. Price and Landers, Tod and I were on our own with Venus. We relied heavily on our own instincts. Any validation from expert sources gave us confidence to keep doing what we were doing. For example, Aloff emphasized how important it is to separate the dogs after an altercation, then bring them back together gradually under strict supervision. Even though we had done that with Zeus and Venus and Dr. Price had approved, it was reassuring to know our instincts were right on.

Much less comforting was Aloff's ominous warning that housemate aggression rarely goes away: "You need to be ever watchful. Resist complacency when the dogs have 'been good' for a month or a year. This problem is not one that you can put to bed. You can manage, minimize, modify. But you can never rest on your laurels!"

I'm a happy-clappy person. I tend to cling to the best possible outcome. I wanted to believe Venus's aggression would go away. Aloff's warning set me back a notch. I had finally found expert advice and it wasn't what I wanted to hear.

Another chapter grabbed my attention, Chapter 35: "Establishing a Communication System—The RM/NRM and Release Cue." I was all about learning how to better communicate with my dogs. According to Aloff this method is useful because a RM/NRM (Reward Mark/No Reward Mark) gives the dog information: "The dog understands when he is on 'your time' and working vs. 'on his own time.'" The purpose of an RM is to serve as a memory aid to help the dog remember "to do a certain behavior at a certain time or on a particular cue."

Like, pay attention, I thought.

Aloff recommended: "Clickers make an excellent Reward Mark. Because the Clicker is a unique sound in the dog's environment, it is very salient for the dog." Her explanation made sense to me and supported everything else I had read about clicker training. I found a clicker for less than two dollars at the pet store, so I bought two—one for each dog.

Aloff also advised not to ask for any particular behavior when "installing," or introducing, the dog to the clicker. Treats were optional. We tried out the clicker the next day at Dogland. I forgot about not asking for a behavior and I didn't use treats. I jumped right into it. When Venus disappeared, I took the clicker out of my pocket.

"Well, this will either work or it won't," I told Tod.

Zeus was walking with us. I figured if he didn't like the sound he'd let me know. I clicked it several times. His ears twitched. *Did you hear that?* I showed it to him. He sniffed it. I clickered. He looked at me. He grinned. *Do it again.* I did.

Then—surprise—Venus showed up. She nosed in on the clicker

and licked my hand. *Do it again.* I clickered.

"They're definitely curious," Tod said.

I nodded. "But will they actually respond to it like a voice command?"

When rifle hunting season opened we took them hiking at Sunlight Mountain ski resort to avoid any possibility of meeting up with hunters. I used the clicker when they chased a mule deer that crossed our path. Zeus stopped immediately, Venus stopped about a half minute later. The more I clickered, the more they liked it, and the quicker they responded. We only used it when they were off-leash because we were training them that the clicker meant "come back."

The little, blue plastic box was far more effective than advertised. Hunting season was also the busiest time of year at Dogland. People who usually took their dogs up to the high country to run wild were forced to settle for our little island of misfits for the duration. On the weekends there could be up to 20 or 30 dogs at the park. Dogs that Venus and Zeus had never seen before. Many of them unaccustomed to dog parks, or just plain unsociable.

One crisp October Saturday, an Aussie Cattle Dog charged through the thicket tugging on his leash. Instantly the leash triggered a warning flag for me. It meant his human, a 20-something dude, didn't trust him off-leash with other dogs. Tod and I stopped to let them pass. Venus and Zeus stopped, too. As the Aussie approached Venus he gave her the skank eye. Then he attacked. His human dropped the leash. We had us a dog fight.

I clickered as I moved in with authority. By then Venus had the Aussie on his back and held him with her feet, no teeth involved. He snapped at her. I clickered again and called her off. She let him go. Tod snapped the leash on Venus. The Aussie's human grabbed his leash and muttered apologies.

"Go! Just keep moving," I said. He fled as fast as he could tugging the Aussie.

"Wow." I held the clicker aloft. "Who knew a two-dollar piece of plastic with a bendy metal thingy inside could stop a dog fight?"

Tod exhaled. "I'm impressed."

Venus calmed down and we were able to finish our walk without further incident, though we did keep her on the leash. Once a dog's aggression has flared, any spark could re-ignite it. Tod jogged with her on the trail to help her let off steam.

I had often wondered if I expected too much from my dogs. Clicker training showed me I didn't expect enough from them.

Chapter 28 - Team players

The first weekend in November, we took the dogs camping in Utah for Zeus's ninth birthday, and the one year anniversary of Venus's big meltdown. During a late afternoon hike we took a break. Venus plopped down in the shade. *So many critters. So little time.* Zeus walked over and sat behind her. *I'm hot. Somebody turn down the sun.* Tongues lolled from their grinning faces.

Or, maybe they were just hot and tired, that was the coolest spot, and Zeus wasn't going to let her hog all the shade.

Along the trail, Venus found a blanket of snow under a thicket of

junipers. She collapsed and rolled in it. *Ah. Snow bath.*

Zeus stretched out in front of her. *Move over lard butt.* It was uncharacteristic of him to choose to share his space with Venus. But they licked the crusty snow together and looked content.

Or, maybe Zeus didn't want to let Venus have all the fun with snow.

From that weekend forward, their relationship continued to improve because Venus's mental health improved. Her obsession was replaced with affection. They were able to lounge next to each other for longer periods of time in quiet contemplation, almost as if she soaked up his calm energy.

One morning at Dogland, the dogs and I ran into a couple with a pair of beautiful German Shepherds. We had never seen them before. As the dogs and I approached the Shepherds, the male lowered his head and growled. Zeus stopped. The Shepherd charged and knocked Zeus to the ground. It happened so quickly I didn't have time to grab Venus. She bolted toward them, head down. *Don't you dare mess with Zeus!*

I clickered and yelled, "Halt!" To my amazement she obeyed. I leashed her. "Good girl."

The male Shepherd's human leashed him. Then the female, who had not reacted, suddenly rushed up to Zeus and barked in his face. He rolled his eyes and flattened his ears. *No need to shout.*

By then Venus was barking, too, and doing her anxiety dance. The only barrier keeping all 90 pounds of her from knocking the snot out of those two bossy German Shepherds was her woven nylon collar and leash. If she had really wanted to mess them up I could not have stopped her. She barked and snarled and gnashed her teeth. She read them the riot act. *Rude dogs! Get out of my park! And don't come back!* Connected to her through my hold on her leash, I sensed her energy. She was angry all right. But she didn't want to kill them.

"Your big Husky shouldn't have run up to my dogs like that," the man said.

People often accused Zeus of being a Husky so I let it go. But it annoyed me. "This is a dog park," I said. "That's what dogs do. He didn't mean any harm." I could have pointed out that Zeus hadn't done anything to provoke the female and she got all up in his face anyway. But the man had blamed Zeus for his dogs' bad behavior which put me on the defensive. I wasn't in the mood for a debate. My arm ached from holding Venus back.

With our dogs leashed, we humans urged them forward—in opposite directions. The couple struggled with their Shepherds all the way back to the parking lot. I, on the other hand, was ecstatic. Those unstable dogs had presented Venus with an incredible challenge and she behaved like a normal dog. Once their negative energy left the park, she calmed down and forgot about it. While we completed our rounds, I beamed and repeated, "Good girl," over and over.

Tod was in Chicago. When he called, I related the incident. "Venus showed some amazing self-control today. She really is getting better."

In December a new guy, Jason, and his exquisite English Setter, Blizzard, joined the regular morning crew at Dogland. With his sleek white coat and opaque gray spots, Blizzard looked like a long-haired Dalmatian. Venus nosed up to him. *You're cute.*

Zeus trotted over. *Who's the new dog?*

Blizzard snarled. *Back off.*

Jason scolded him. Venus tensed. *Do not mess with Zeus.*

I clickered. "Sorry if that annoys you," I said to Jason. "It distracts her."

"No. I'm the one who's sorry," he said. "Blizzard was attacked by a big Samoyed down here a couple weeks ago. He wasn't hurt badly, just freaked out. I was bringing him down here in the evenings. But that dog and his owner kept showing up and he couldn't handle it. I decided to change to mornings."

"It is a lot more mellow here in the morning," I said. "Eventually Blizzard will learn Zeus is a big teddy bear. He won't hurt him. He loves everybody."

As we got to know Blizzard and Jason over the next several weeks we witnessed more remarkable dog behavior. Venus delighted in Blizzard's shy charm. Zeus liked him, too. But Blizzard didn't like him back, which bothered Zeus. Venus took on the role of peacemaker. As part of her strategy, she teased Blizzard into a game of tag. When she got him going, Zeus joined in. Blizzard forgot himself and romped with them. His fear gradually faded. Venus led and Blizzard followed while Zeus figured out his comfort zone.

It was amazing to witness as Blizzard emerged from his shell. But after everything we had been through, seeing Zeus and Venus act like a team again was nothing short of a miracle.

Chapter 29 - Déjà vu all over again

Two feet of snow fell during one day in December. Big snow meant big fun. As the volunteer managers of the West Elk cross-country ski trails for the Forest Service, our weekends were busy with skiing and trail grooming. The dogs lived to run those trails. All things considered, life was swell.

As had become our habit by then, we rarely left the dogs outside when we weren't home. Most of the time they were with us. No cops had been to our house since Margie's vicious complaint the previous June.

"That doesn't mean they haven't complained," I reminded Tod. "It just means the cops haven't told us about it."

"I've been off the town board for almost a year," he said. "Maybe Bickle got what he wanted when I resigned."

I shrugged. "Anything's possible."

Super Bowl Sunday fell on the first weekend in February. We took Kaley downhill skiing. We had a great time. Then we came home. To Silt. And a calling card from Officer Tuttle and two very agitated dogs. We could hardly believe it. *Déjà vu* all over again. What mischief had occurred while we were gone all day? If Venus, guard dog extraordinaire, was barking then we knew something must have happened.

The video cameras on our home surveillance system had been recording. With the Super Bowl playing in the background, we fast forwarded through hour upon hour of Zeus and Venus asleep on the front porch, or walking around the yard sniffing and peeing. Zeus pooped around 10:30 a.m.

"Good doggie," I muttered.

Nothing happened all day until 2:00 p.m. The backyard camera showed three middle school-age boys messing around in the alley outside our backyard fence. They stayed there for about 20 minutes, during which Venus barked on and off, but not steadily. When the boys left, she stopped barking.

About 15 minutes after the boys disappeared, the front yard camera showed two cop cars in front of our house. Venus and Zeus barked at them. Officer Tuttle left his card in the front door. The dogs barked again. The cops stayed for about four minutes.

"I wonder what Officer Tuttle will have to say about this," Tod said. He put in a call and left a message.

Tuttle arrived 20 minutes later as I was taking the pizza out of the oven. The Saints were behind 10-zip. I lost my appetite. Tod returned from his lengthy discussion on the porch with Tuttle waving a pink barking dog citation.

I was dumbfounded. “You’re kidding, right?”

“Nope,” he said. “When I told Tuttle we had surveillance video of the boys outside the fence, he actually said ‘tell it to the judge’.”

I sighed. “Unbelievable.”

“I argued with him. I told him the kids were trespassing and the dogs were protecting our property. But he said it didn’t matter because Daryl filed a complaint against us.”

“Say what? You mean what Daryl says carries more weight than what actually happened?”

He shrugged. “Looks that way.”

“You know as well as I do Daryl saw the kids in the alley. He knew they weren’t supposed to be there. If he’s such a neighborhood watch dog, why didn’t he call the cops on them? Why didn’t he file a complaint against them?”

“Because those kids did him a favor,’ he said. “He’s been waiting months for this.”

“I swear if Daryl saw some guy breaking down our front door and the dogs attacked, he’d file a vicious dog complaint.”

He nodded. “Exactly. This is more of the same old harassment by cop.”

“By any chance did you ask Tuttle why it took two cops to respond to a barking dog complaint?” I asked.

“Oh.” He laughed. “You’ll love this. Tuttle said he and another cop sat outside our house for ten minutes and the dogs barked the whole time.”

“Wow. He lied.”

“Yeah. I told him that according to the video they were here for less than five minutes. He said it didn’t matter how long they were here, the dogs barked the whole time. Then I told him the video showed the dogs barked for less than a minute, and again when he came to the door. I invited him to come inside and watch the video. He said he didn’t have time. So I asked him, ‘aren’t you supposed to investigate a complaint before you issue a citation?’ He said he witnessed the dogs barking and that’s all he needs to issue a citation.”

“And you can tell it to the judge,” I added.

“That’s right.”

The second half of the Super Bowl had commenced. The Saints were behind by four points. We discussed our options.

“The fine is forty dollars,” Tod said. “Big deal. Pay it and forget about it.”

“Then what’s the point of having the surveillance system?” I asked.

"Okay. So I go to court, plead not guilty, and the judge sets a trial date." He sighed. "What a hassle."

"But this isn't about Venus barking. Or Zeus barking. This is about harassment. Daryl lied. The cop lied. We have proof."

We picked at our barbeque chicken pizza, which was actually pretty good cold, and watched the football game. Venus and Zeus drooled at our feet.

As the Saints took possession of the ball, Tod said, "If I file a harassment complaint against Daryl, the cops will have to investigate. They will have to look at the video."

Touchdown. Saints took the lead 24-17, and went on to win the Super Bowl. Venus and Zeus gobbled up the leftover pizza.

Chapter 30 - Even good dogs need a "little brother"

Monday morning Tod filed a harassment complaint against Daryl. He called me on his way to the airport. "I talked to both cops who were at our house. I described what we saw on the video. The kids were trespassing. They were messing around behind our boat, which provoked the dogs. But Tuttle said that was a separate issue. He said he'd turn my complaint over to Bickle but it probably wouldn't go any further."

"Okay. Then we go to court and show the video of police harassment to the judge," I said. "This is not about forty dollars."

"Let's wait and see what happens," he said. "As far as I'm concerned I dropped this right back on the cops."

Officer Tuttle called me the next day. "If you can find out the names of the boys that were in your alley, we'll go after them," he said.

"I'm not interested in getting them in trouble with the cops," I said. "Besides, I think that's your job, not mine. Aren't you supposed to investigate a complaint?"

"Your husband was the one who complained about them," he said.

"No he didn't. He complained about Daryl Harrison filing a false complaint."

"Ma'am, do you want me to do anything about the boys or not?"

"No. We weren't even home when they were in the alley. They didn't bother us. They bothered the dogs. That's why they barked."

"Okay ma'am. I don't think there's anything more I can do for you," he said.

"Fine. Whatever. You called me," I reminded him and hung up.

I confessed later on the phone with Tod. "I found out the boys' names yesterday. Betty Paxton told me. But I'm not going to give their names to the police or contact their parents. I just wanted to be sure it wasn't the Harrison boys. Betty said they were just horsing around. She said they were making more noise than our dogs and her dog was barking, too."

"If all the commotion bothered Daryl so much he should have complained about that, instead of complaining about our dogs," Tod said.

"Betty said the same thing."

Later in the week Carol called with interesting news. "I happened to see a replay of the town board meeting on TV. Tommy woke up in the middle of the night. After he fell back asleep, I couldn't get back to sleep. So I figured watching the meeting would put me to sleep."

I laughed. "Did it work?"

"Oh yeah," she said. "Anyway, before I fell asleep the town attorney said he was making changes to the barking dog ordinance and wants feedback from the community. You should find out what's going on."

After we hung up, I went straight over to the town hall and asked for a copy of the proposed changes to the barking dog ordinance. The secretary on duty phoned the town attorney and told him what I was asking for. Wiesel came out of his office and introduced himself, which struck me as odd.

"You know who I am," I said. "I understand you're finally making changes to the barking dog ordinance. We asked for changes over a year ago."

"Yes, but once I started looking into the animal ordinances I realized several of them needed to be updated," he said. "That all takes time."

"Yeah. Well in the meantime under the current ordinance, anyone can use the barking dog ordinance to harass someone," I said.

"And you are speaking from experience. I know," he said.

"This has been going on for nearly four years," I said.

"And there has been another incident," he said. "I have Tod's complaint on my desk. I understand you have a video."

"Yes, we have video surveillance that shows kids playing in the alley, which was why the dogs were barking," I said. "The kids were making noise. Other dogs were barking. But we got the citation."

"I just need to see a copy of that video and I would be inclined to dismiss the citation," he said.

"Look, if Daryl Harrison is so concerned about our neighborhood, he should have complained about the boys playing in the alley," I said. "I swear to you if someone was breaking down our front door and our dogs barked, he would complain and we would get a citation."

"Well, what you described is a somewhat similar circumstance," he said. "So it would seem the right thing to do is just dismiss the citation."

But I wasn't going to let him off so easy once I had his attention, though I had sense enough to refrain from uttering "and furthermore." I pressed on. "In mediation with the Harrisons two years ago, we established ground rules with them and with the police department. But we are the only ones abiding by those rules. The police are not supposed to sit outside our house and provoke the dogs to bark. And that's exactly what they did. Two of them. You'll see it on the video. It was totally ridiculous."

"Yes, well, you should know that Chief Bickle did talk to me about the situation and he's aware of the procedural problems there—with how it all went down," he said. "He was not happy about that."

"And how do you think we feel?" I was on a roll. Our conversation was not private. We were standing in the hallway in the center of the town hall. Anyone who wanted to could hear every word we said. "Two cops on a barking dog complaint. Neither of them investigated the incident. They didn't ask the other neighbors what was going on. Tuttle wouldn't even look at the video."

He nodded. "I understand. There were some issues with police procedure. Unfortunately our police officers don't have much experience with home surveillance videos."

"They don't seem too eager to learn," I said.

"Chief Bickle assured me it won't happen again," he said.

I rolled my eyes. "We've heard that before." I hesitated. "And one more thing. You should know that Venus—the dog in question—is on medication. She's not even capable of sustained barking."

"Okay. That only adds to the substance of your dispute with the citation," he said. "Which is why I would be inclined to dismiss it. We don't want this thing to escalate."

"We aren't escalating anything. *He* filed a false complaint against us," I said. "And the cops went along with it."

Wiesel changed the subject and asked for my input on changes to the dog barking ordinance. We discussed the need for more than one complaint and an allowable defense for provocation.

When Tod called that evening I told him about the meeting. "It felt really good to unload on him in front of God and everybody at the town hall."

He laughed. "If Bickle was in his office and he heard all that, I'm sure you're on his shit list."

"Because I wasn't before this? Oh please."

"I've been thinking. After the way the cops handled this thing, I'm not comfortable with Wiesel looking at a copy of the video. I don't want to be accused of editing it."

"You're right," I said. "He should come over here and look at it on the computer."

The following week, Wiesel sent me an email me with a copy of the revised animals ordinances attached. The "Dogs disturbing the peace and quiet" ordinance—aka barking dog ordinance—included all the provisions we had requested: a dog can't be provoked, no citation without a warning first, and only after two or more complaints from two unrelated people.

On Friday afternoon, the same week, Wiesel stopped by and viewed the video evidence on our computer. "Because the existing ordinance is still in effect and does not contain an allowable defense for provocation, I can't consider that," he said. "However I can see from the video that even with the commotion in the alley, neither of the dogs barked excessively or could be considered a nuisance." He said he would file a motion to dismiss the citation. "And I would ask that you drop your harassment complaint."

It seemed like a reasonable request so we agreed.

"I would also recommend posting a sign on your property that it's protected by video surveillance," he added. "For one thing, it may keep kids out of the alley and away from your fence so they don't bother your dogs. And it might make your neighbors stop and think before calling the police to complain."

We were satisfied with the outcome. There was only one problem. Wiesel's motives were purely political. A town election was coming up in April. Mayor Minnifield and three trustee candidates were running on a shared platform of slashing the budget by firing the overpaid town manager, town planner, and town attorney. The mayor had hand-picked those people for their positions. Evidently they had not proven to be unscrupulous enough to satisfy him. He disliked them as much as everybody else did. I had openly supported the trustee candidates' platform on my blog, but Tod and I had steadfastly refused to support the mayor's re-election campaign.

I told Tod, "Dismissing the citation was the right thing to do. But the only reason Wiesel did it was to gain political favor with us. Notice how he threw in the barking dog ordinance with all the changes we asked for, just to sweeten the deal."

He nodded. "That's how things work in this town. That's why I left the board. There's no reason to think it will change after the election. No matter who wins."

We posted three signs on our fence in three different places: *Property Protected by Video Surveillance.* It had taken a year for me to embrace the whole concept of counter surveillance, which has been coined "little brother" in this postmodern world. Protecting our property and privacy by spying on others seemed obsessive. But we're not spying on anybody. All four cameras are trained on our property. Aside from my misgivings, I felt confident the system would prove itself one day and it did.

I still believe a good dog is the best protection. But sometimes even good dogs need a "little brother."

Chapter 31 - Chucky

The revised barking dog ordinance went into effect on a Sunday in April. By 10:10 a.m. there was a warning ticket on our doorknob. Video surveillance—aka "little brother"—showed Tod and me leaving in the pickup at 9:15 a.m. At 9:22 a.m. a police car drove up a dead end street a half block from our house. Twenty-five minutes later the same cop pulled up in front of our house. He rang the doorbell, waited about two minutes, then left his card in the door.

After he left, the Harrison boys ran back and forth in the street in front of our house. Then another character from the neighborhood walked over with his dog and stood in the street in front of our fence. Neither of the dogs barked during those performances. At 10:09 a.m. the cop returned and left a red warning ticket on our doorknob. We returned home around 2:00 p.m.

The character from the neighborhood was a familiar face. We didn't know his name, only that he lived on the same dead end street where we saw the cop car headed in the video. I named him Chucky because he looked like the horror film character with a bad case of Progeria. He was 60-ish and used a cane when he walked his dog. We had never actually seen him anywhere other than in his car until the previous autumn when he got the dog. A Red Heeler. I called him Red.

In mid-October, I saw him walking Red and said to Tod, "Isn't that the hermit crab from up the street? He got a dog."

"No way." Tod stared out the kitchen window.

I shook my head. "Poor dog."

When Chucky first got Red, he walked past our house every day. Venus barked at them in the beginning. Then she lost interest and only barked sometimes. Eventually she stopped barking at them. So Chucky made a habit of stopping at the end of our sidewalk, or in the grass between our fence and the street, which made Venus bark. Sometimes Venus barked first. Sometimes Red barked first. Venus usually lost interest and walked away. When I was home I brought her inside. One day I came home from the grocery store and saw Chucky and Red loitering in our yard at the end of the fence.

"Henry was with me or I would have said something to him," I told Tod later.

"Like what?" he asked.

"Like, you're provoking our dog. Move along."

"Don't you think he already knows that? Seems to me that's the whole purpose."

"I think we should call him on it."

He laughed. "Oh yeah. Like that's worked so well for us in this neighborhood."

I frowned. "Then he'll just keep doing it."

"But it's not working," Tod said. "Venus is learning to ignore them. It's good practice for her."

He was right. Allowing her to go through the exercise with Chucky and Red helped assure us that when we were not home, she would behave the same way. Chucky grew bored with his game and went back to walking his dog.

Reporting on the town election campaigns had taken up most of my time and blog space. I had deliberately avoided posting anything about Wiesel dismissing the citation because I knew the Harrisons read my blog. I figured if they found out Wiesel intended to dismiss the citation, Daryl would conjure up a reason to file another false complaint.

I finally broke the news on my blog on the last Friday in March. The next day while I was washing dishes, I looked out our second story kitchen window. Margie and Daryl stood in the middle of the street talking to Chucky, which wasn't all that unusual. His mobile home was behind their house. I assumed they knew each other, which was probably why he never spoke to us. But 30 minutes later when I looked outside again, they were still there.

"Uh-oh. Looks like the Margie and Daryl are recruiting a co-conspirator," I said.

Tod peered over my shoulder. "I see what you mean. They need to find one more complainer when the revised ordinance takes effect."

From then on, like an obnoxious wind-up toy, Chucky resumed the stop-and-stand game. If I saw him coming, I brought Venus inside. One evening he loitered with his dog in front of our house for almost ten minutes. Tod wasn't home. Both dogs were inside. It appeared to me he was looking for the video cameras which totally creeped me out. I checked the video feed, but he had stood out of camera range.

Fast forward to the Sunday the revised barking dog ordinance went into effect and we got a warning ticket. Later in the afternoon I was in the front yard cleaning the porch. Chucky drove up in his old green pickup and idled in front of our house. He watched me for two minutes. From there he drove into the alley beside our camper and stared at me for a few more minutes, then he slowly backed across the street into the opposite alley. I found Tod in the backyard and told him what happened. "He's a creep."

The next morning I went out to get the paper at 5:41 a.m. I was startled to see Chucky and Red standing in the grass in front of our fence. Zeus was outside. Venus was inside. I didn't say anything to him and went inside. Red started barking. Venus barked and ran to the door.

I let her out in the yard. Chucky had moved to the end of the sidewalk. Red was still barking.

I stepped out on the porch and said, "You are provoking my dog. You need to leave."

"I can't hear you," he said.

Wearing a T-shirt, pajama pants, and flip-flops, I stomped out to the end of the sidewalk and shouted, "You can't hear me because your dog is barking. You are provoking my dog. You need to leave."

"Call the police," he said.

I squinted at him in the pre-dawn darkness. "You called the police yesterday and complained about my dogs, didn't you?"

"I have complained about your dogs many times and I will do it again." He jerked Red's leash which kept him agitated and barking.

"Well now *your* dog's barking is bothering me. You need to leave."

"Call the police," he said again.

"Okay." I tossed up my hands. "This is like talking to a three-year-old."

I went back inside and called dispatch. Chucky and Red dug in their heels. I reported the man and his barking dog in front of my house.

The dispatcher said, "I need you to hang up. Chief Bickle is monitoring this call and will call you back."

I hung up. Call me? I had just reported a man standing outside my house and the police chief was going to call me. The phone rang.

"Hey, this is Chief Bickle. What's going on there?"

I explained everything as it had unfolded.

"Is Tod home?" he asked.

"Yes. He's in the shower."

"Do you know the man?"

"He lives up the dead end street. Walks his dog with a cane. I don't know his name."

"Wait a minute." He hesitated. "He's your neighbor and you don't know his name?"

I pulled the phone back and stared at it for a second, then put it back to my ear. "What does that have to do with anything? He's a man who lives in my neighborhood. I've never met him. I don't know his name."

"Is he still there?"

"Yes." I held the phone out toward the kitchen window and pulled it back. "Can't you hear his dog barking?"

"I hear two dogs barking."

"Yes. Venus is barking, too."

"Where is she?"

"In the yard."

"Why did you let her outside?"

"Because there's a man standing outside my house with his dog!" I said with the same tone I used with eight-year-old Kaley when she tried to con me with a circular argument in order to avoid the point I was trying to make. Meanwhile, Red stopped barking and Chucky shuffled off toward his dead end street. I exhaled. "He's leaving now." While I had Bickle's ear, I brought up the previous day's monkey business.

"It's just a warning ticket," he said. "I don't know what you're upset about."

"Who said I was upset?" I said. "The point is they were walking back and forth in front of our house to provoke the dogs. And that's not all that happened." I described Chucky staring at me from his pickup and pulling into the alley. "Add to that his stunt this morning and it sure looks like irrational behavior to me. I call it creepy."

"I'll go talk to him and get back to you," Bickle said.

I hung up and looked at Tod. "Wow." Six a.m. was too early for the fury I might have otherwise felt. The sun was coming up. I sighed. Who could be angry at the dawn? "That was surreal."

"What did he say?"

"He said I should know the guy's name and I shouldn't have let Venus out."

"Good ol' Chief Bickle. Blame the victim."

I laughed. "Can you buh-lieve it? Yesterday Chucky's barking dog complaint got a squad car immediately. Two months ago, Daryl got two squad cars. A man stands outside with his barking dog at o-dark-thirty and I get a phone call. What's wrong with this picture?"

Tod shook his head. "Plenty."

At 7:45 a.m., Chief Bickle arrived at my door, which was another thing that stuck in my bridgework. The cops showed up our place so much the casual observer might have thought we ran a crack house. After every appearance by the Silt PD, one-by-one, Irma, Betty, and Randy Flinch asked, "What's going on?" I knew they were merely concerned, and said as much, with Tod gone so often. Their questions didn't irritate me. The police did.

My irritated self let Venus bark her fool head off before answering the door. She hated cops. Besides, there was a gate between her and him. Eventually I opened the door and stepped out on the porch. I attempted to calm Venus but she focused on Bickle and kept barking. I stepped down to the sidewalk. Bickle followed me. The minute he stepped off the porch, her barking stopped. He looked at her and then raised his eyebrows at me.

I shrugged. "She's a guard dog."

He cleared his throat. "I just spent a half hour with Don Fowler." I assumed that was Chucky's real name. "He said he's fed up with your dogs barking."

"Oh really. That's news to me. Funny how he's never mentioned it before now," I said.

"He has called and complained before but he didn't give his name."

"Then how did you know it was him?"

"He told me. Just now. When I talked to him."

"And you believe him?"

"We did have one complaint from someone who didn't give his name."

I felt another circular argument coming on so I changed the subject. "Why did we get a warning when there was only one complaint? The way I read the ordinance, there have to be two separate complaints."

"You're reading the ordinance wrong. Subsection D says an officer may issue a warning after receiving a complaint of a disturbance."

"Yeah. *May.* Not *shall.* In other words, he could have chosen not to issue a warning."

"I told the officer to issue the warning. In light of all the problems we've had with you and your dogs I felt it was warranted."

So this was payback for busting his officers on procedure and getting the citation dismissed, I thought. But I said, "What about the problems we've had with the Harrisons and now this guy Fowler? We proved the harassment from Daryl and the police two months ago."

"I certainly don't see it that way." It was his turn to change the subject. He handed me a printed form. "Here's this voluntary statement I need you to fill out. And I'll need copies of the surveillance video from yesterday and also this morning. Now if you could show me where Mr. Fowler was walking and where he stood this morning."

While I re-enacted Chucky's pre-dawn antics, Bickle tossed out fresh Chucky-isms, still steaming from their conversation. Thus ensued the most bizarre discussion I have ever had with anyone, much less a police chief.

"Mr. Fowler said Venus started barking as soon as you and Tod left yesterday. He said he complained right away because he didn't want to listen to her bark all day."

I stopped in front of the prickly, yellow rose bush. "Let me get this straight. You authorized a warning ticket because one guy was afraid our dog *might* become a nuisance."

He shook his finger at me. "I didn't say that."

"I just did." I continued my demonstration skit. As we approached the mailbox stand, I explained, "When I picked up the newspaper from the end of the sidewalk I saw him standing right here with his dog." I stood in the grass about four feet from the corner of our fence.

"He said he was getting his mail," Bickle said.

"His mailbox is over there." I pointed to the mailbox stand, more than ten feet away. "His dog pooped right here." I pointed at the pile a foot away.

Bickle stuck his nose in the air. "That could've been from any dog."

"I saw him do it."

"You never mentioned that."

"I just did."

"Maybe he picked up his mail before you came outside."

"He didn't have any mail in his hands when he stood in front of my house."

"Maybe he didn't get any."

"Are you making excuses for him?"

With a look of utter chagrin he declared, "He's not well, you know. He's on medication. He said he tires easily and needs to stop and rest when he walks his dog."

I sniffed. "He gets around pretty good for someone so frail. He's caused a lot of trouble in the last 24 hours."

"So you can see why I might be inclined to question whether he's even capable of all the activity you described."

"I have it all on video." I marched across the grass in front of the fence. Venus shadowed me on the opposite side, snorting in disgust. *I don't like this guy. What is he doing here? He doesn't like you. Are you okay?* Zeus observed everything from his front porch throne. "He walked along here with his dog and …."

"That's public right-of-way," Bickle interrupted. "He can walk there. Anyone can."

"Try telling that to my dogs. As far as they're concerned it's their yard."

"If you don't want people walking between the mailboxes and the end of the fence you need to post a 'no trespassing' sign."

"Okay. We will."

"He said the reason he has to get his mail at that time of day is because your dog barks at him whenever he gets his mail."

I rolled my eyes. "She does not."

"He said she barks at everyone at the mailboxes."

"That's not true. If someone—like him—brings his dog and stands around, then yeah, she barks."

Bickle glanced around. "That mailbox stand needs to be moved."

"What?" I shook my head in confusion. "Are you talking about?"

"If the mailboxes aren't there, that solves the problem."

"That's ridiculous. The mailboxes aren't the problem. When Emily gets her mail at the other end of town, the dogs across the street bark at her. So what? If he doesn't want Venus to bark at him when he gets his mail, or when he walks in front of our fence and taunts her, tell him to leave his dog at home. Or better yet, quit harassing her." I trudged through the dewy grass. Venus scratched at the fence board and whined. *Let me out. I'll get rid of him.* I whispered, "Shh. It's okay." I walked toward the street and stopped where the sidewalk ends. Shel Silverstein crossed my mind. He would have been amused by the absurdity of it all. I aimed for the same bemusement. I sensed Bickle wanted me to come unglued. Venus appeared on the front porch with Zeus, watching every move he made. "This is where he stopped and stood for more than ten minutes. His dog barked first."

"Before or after you confronted him."

"*Before.* And I wouldn't call it a confrontation. I told him to shut the dog up and leave. This is my house."

"He said he told you to call the police because he wanted the officer to witness you assaulting him."

I laughed. "That doesn't even make sense. How could I simultaneously assault him and call the police?"

"The point is, maybe you overreacted. He just happened to stop and rest here."

"For more than ten minutes. So he gets to take a nap on my sidewalk now?"

"I'm just telling you what he told me."

"And none of that sounds irrational to you?" I asked.

"I think there's some of that on both sides."

I marched up the sidewalk. He followed me. Zeus poked his nose between the porch rails. *Are you going to smack him? Or should I?* He glanced at Venus. *You could let her out.*

She couldn't take her eyes off Bickle. From deep in her throat a low, barely audible growl emerged. Let me put him on the run.

I was finished with Bickle. But he obviously knew he'd tweaked a nerve so he dug up a few more Chucky-isms. "By the way, Mr. Fowler also said your dogs bark pretty much constantly for two hours when the kids are walking home from school."

"Maybe they should move the school," I muttered.

"Excuse me?" Bickle said.

But he heard me. I headed for the porch. Venus gave him the skank eye and growled. *Do not come any closer to my mom. Do not step on my porch.*

"According to him everyone in the neighborhood hates you because of your dogs." He hesitated a beat, then he said, "Those were his words. Not mine."

"And they sound rather childish," I said. "Besides being provably false."

"It's not like I'm going to survey the neighbors or anything but ...."

"Well, we *have* surveyed the neighbors." I put my hands on my hips. "Look, this is getting pretty silly. The man is obviously lying. I don't know why and I don't really care. But he doesn't have the right to harass us or our dogs."

"I'm just investigating your complaint. Isn't that what you wanted?"

"Okay. Then let's investigate. If all the neighbors hate us," I waved my arms, "because we let our dogs bark all the time, you'd think someone else would have complained by now."

"The Harrisons complained."

"And only them. No one else."

"And they said you let your dogs bark to get back at them."

I squinted at him. "You know very well what we've done to appease them. In return they have harassed and provoked Venus. Her anxiety got so bad we had to put her on medication."

"What do you mean?"

"She's heavily medicated. She's not even capable of barking for two minutes. Two hours is a joke."

On the other side of the gate, Venus crouched low in front of Zeus, her chin perched on her front paws. At a glance one might have thought she was supine. I knew better.

Perhaps Bickle did, too, because he stared at her and said, "I wouldn't keep a dog like that around very long."

I turned away until the stench from his words faded. Then I said, "Dogs bark. Mr. Fowler has a dog. His dog barks. Venus doesn't even bark as much as his dog. Or Flinch's dog. Or Paxton's dog."

"He said the only time his dog barks is when your dog provokes him."

I rolled my eyes. "Boy, you have a comeback for everything."

He held up his hands. "I'm just repeating what he told me."

"Fine. I've heard enough of his lies. I'll have Tod make copies of the video and get them to you." *You're dismissed,* I wanted to say.

"Is he in town all week?" he asked.

"Yes."

"Good. I need to talk to him, too." He turned to leave, then he paused. "You know there's one way you could end all the trouble."

I bowed my head. I felt the blood rush to my cheeks. I gritted my teeth and refused to look at him.

"Get rid of the dog," he said.

My head snapped back. He had pulled out all the stops to

provoke me. "So is that where this is headed? You're going to force us to get rid of her."

"I didn't say that."

"Oh yes, you did." I glared at him. "But I can assure you it would not end the harassment. This is not about Venus. This is about harassment. From the Harrisons and the cops and now this guy."

He shook his head. "You're exaggerating the situation."

Still clutching the form, I waved it at him. "I'll get back to you." I went inside and shut the door. Trembling, I collapsed onto the bottom step in tears. I didn't have a feather of respect for the man. I should not have let him get to me. But his cold, cruel words echoed in my brain. *Get rid of the dog.* I glanced at the clock—8:15 a.m. Sometimes life in Silt was just plain exhausting.

Chapter 32 - Chucky's revenge

Tod was already annoyed with Bickle by the time they met up. Afterward he said, "Take your meeting with him and re-run it."

"That bad, huh," I said.

"Worse. Now he's latched onto the fact that Venus is on medication."

"What do you mean? What did he say?"

"He said we shouldn't keep a dog like that—excuse me—*he* wouldn't. Same as he told you."

"But she's stable," I said. "We can get a letter from Dr. Price."

"I told him all that. He said with all the complaints they've had about her lately it doesn't look that way to him."

"Oh my god. What have I done?" Tears welled on my eyelids.

He squeezed my shoulder. "It's not your fault."

I grabbed a tissue. "I shouldn't have said anything about her medication."

"It doesn't matter. Between your blog and the vet, everything is documented. The cops can't touch her."

"Doesn't mean Daryl and Chucky won't try and make something of it."

"They would have to take us to court and I don't see that happening," Tod said. "By the way, Bickle said we should keep her inside when we're not home."

"Oh great. More rules," I grumbled.

He shrugged. "I tend to agree. He wants us to keep her inside because he thinks she's unstable. But the reality is, they're all crazy. And I'm afraid the cops will shoot her."

"They wouldn't dare."

He was dead serious. "Think about it. We're gone. One of the neighbors sneaks over and flips the latch on one of the gates. Venus gets out. They call the cops. Bickle tells the cop to shoot her. Won't matter if we have video. She'll be dead."

"Stop it!" I shook my head to get the disturbing image out of my brain.

"Believe me. I pushed back. I told him the constant harassment from the Harrisons and the cops contributed to her mental illness. The fact that she's on medication proves it and we can get our vet to back us up."

"I'm sure he had some cocky comeback."

"No. For once he didn't. That shut him up."

"I'll call Dr. Price and get a letter," I said.

He shook his head. "No. Don't. We don't have to prove anything."

From then on, we either took Venus with us or left her inside when we were gone.

Chucky's little chat with Chief Bickle emboldened him. No doubt he thought Bickle was on his side. We certainly did. The next morning when I came home from Dogland, Chucky was waiting for me at the corner of his dead end street. He sat in his car and watched while I unloaded the dogs from the Jeep. He didn't leave until after I closed the garage door and went inside.

Wednesday evening—same week—Tod and I walked the dogs on leashes in town. Three blocks from home we stopped for traffic. Chucky's station wagon pulled up on the cross street and signaled a left turn. While we waited, Zeus pooped in the dirt on the right-of-way. The station wagon careened around the corner and screeched to a stop. Chucky hopped out and strutted toward the rear gate with amazing speed and agility for such a frail man. I didn't see his cane anywhere.

"Are you going to pick that up?" he demanded.

"I forgot to bring a bag," Tod said.

"Did you pick up your dog's poop in our yard?" I asked him.

He didn't look at me. "I can't hear you!" He sang the words like a mouthy middle-schooler. He opened the rear gate and pulled out a plastic grocery sack. He thrust it at Tod. "You should always carry a bag with you."

"Do you carry a bag?" I asked. "Do you pick up after your dog?"

"I can't hear you!" The second time he sounded like a braying jackass. He returned to the driver's seat with the same ease and swiftness as he exited.

Tod picked up the poop. "Man that guy is nuts. This is the fourth time this week he's harassed us. Bickle's gonna hear about this."

"He'll probably give you a citation for dog poop," I said.

We continued walking.

"Then I'll make him give Chucky one for his dog pooping in our yard on Monday."

I burst out laughing. "So now we're fighting over dog poop. This is hilarious."

He smiled. "It is pretty juvenile."

I held Venus's leash. She fell in step next to my right leg and nudged me as she peered over her shoulder. *Look behind you.* I glanced back. Chucky had turned his car around and was slowly following us while we walked. "Maybe we should stand out in the street and throw dog shit at each other." We both laughed. Venus snorted and nudged me insistently. *Are you paying attention here? He's following us.* I halted.

Chucky's station wagon idled.

Tod didn't stop. "Keep walking."

I did and Chucky's station wagon rolled along behind us. "This is creepy. I wish you had your cell phone."

"Why?"

"So you could take a picture or call the cops."

"Now that's funny. Bickle would probably say the guy has to stop and idle his car because he's on medication."

We dawdled. The dogs took full advantage. They sniffed and peed on every weed and shrub. At the same time they both kept one eye on the station wagon. Whenever we stopped, Chucky stopped. At the mailbox stand, Zeus staged a sit-in. *I won't budge until he goes home.* He glanced over his shoulder. Chucky pulled up and parked a block away.

"This is too much tension for her," Tod grabbed Venus's leash out of my hand. "I'll take her inside."

Zeus refused to move. Chucky waited. And waited. Finally he blinked first and drove home. I took Zeus in the house.

I checked my watch. "It took ten minutes to walk two and a half blocks."

"Now that's what I call stalking," Tod said.

We started a log of Chucky incidents. Thursday morning at 9:30 a.m., Chucky drove by slowly in his pickup and stopped long enough to make sure I noticed. He turned into the alley across the street which dead ended behind his mobile home. Five minutes later he showed up in his station wagon and did the same thing. At 10:00 a.m., I opened the garage door and shuddered. His station wagon was parked in the alley across the street facing our house. He sat and watched while I loaded the dogs in the Jeep. My hands trembled as I closed the rear gate. I didn't want the dogs to pick up on my anxiety so I went in the house. He waited another minute, then drove off.

Later the same day Tod met with Bickle for the second time that week. He turned in our log of encounters with Chucky and told him he was in the process of making copies of the video for most of them. Bickle said he would talk to Chucky again.

We never knew whether he did but the incidents ceased. Chucky quit walking Red. We noticed them in Harrisons' yard several times because they were impossible to ignore. Red ran around in frantic circles barking like a trapped hyena. And they thought Venus was unstable. She had never behaved like Red.

In early April, Mayor Minnifield and three trustee candidates had swept the town election with their budget-slashing platform. The axes fell during the next town board meeting. Wiesel, plus the town manager and town planner, were fired during a five-hour spectacle that put reality TV to shame. Much to our dismay, Chief Bickle was spared the axe at midnight.

A couple weeks after the firings, Wiesel called me out of the blue. "I visited your blog recently. I see you've been writing about the problems with your dogs."

"So what?"

"Well, I'm not sure that's such a good idea," he said. "Certain people might use it against you."

"You mean like you used my blog against Tod?"

"That was what? Two years ago?" he scoffed. "That's all behind us now."

"Is it?"

"Look, this a friendly call. I have to ask you to take down the recent posts that mention my name. Let me see, there is one, two, three ...."

I heard papers rustling. He must have printed them. "What?"

"I'm looking for a job and in these particular posts, I felt you portrayed me rather harshly."

"Why? Because it took you two years to update the animal ordinances? Because you stood by and did nothing even though you knew our neighbors and the cops were harassing us and our dogs?"

"You didn't allow me the opportunity to present my side of the story."

I laughed. "It's a blog. Not *FOX News.* Or a courtroom. I don't have to present your side."

He sighed with exasperation. "I know you and Tod are having a lot of problems with your neighbors. Now that I can speak more freely, you should know that I am inclined to agree with you about your harassment claim. Especially concerning the latest incidents with Mr. Fowler. I did see the log you turned in to Chief Bickle."

"Well there's nothing you can do about it now," I said. "Bickle should've been fired along with the rest of you."

"Look, you've got a real problem there. The police are more involved in the situation than you know."

"We're not stupid," I said.

"Well ...." He hesitated. "It goes even further than the department. I have information that would definitely be helpful to you. I'd be inclined to share it with you—if you remove the posts from your blog. I can email you with the list."

Stunned, I sucked in my breath.

"Hello? Still there?" he asked.

"I'm just wondering. How do you sleep at night?"

"Very well, thank you. Again, I know your situation has escalated. I know Tod is gone a lot. You and your dogs could be in danger."

I sniffed. "So far you haven't told me anything we don't already know. Unless you can stop the harassment, there's nothing you can do for me. I wish you luck. Have a nice life." I hung up.

The next day around noon I stood in the front yard watering the flower garden with the hose. Zeus and Venus were asleep on the front porch. I noticed a streak of fur in the alley. Venus jumped up first, then Zeus. They ran around to the backyard. I opened the gate and followed them. Red dashed back and forth in the alley on the other side of the fence. Venus and Zeus copied him on the inside. Red ran toward the street. Venus and Zeus raced back to the front porch with me on their tails. Red stopped next to our camper in the front yard, about six feet from the porch and barked. The camper was like their doghouse. They went nuts and a bark fest ensued.

Chucky appeared in the alley across the street walking briskly. He held a leash, but no cane. I stood between Venus and Zeus on the porch. Chucky crossed the street and stopped at the end of our sidewalk. Red bolted toward the street. Chucky glared at me and the dogs, then he headed for the mailbox stand. Instead of snapping the leash on Red he let him run back and forth in the grass in front of our fence. Venus and Zeus bounced around and barked until they left. A police SUV rolled by slowly 15 minutes later.

I showed Tod the video replay of the incident.

"He's deliberately provoking the dogs," Tod said. "He knows Venus is on medication. He's trying to agitate her."

"Hey. Not just Venus," I said. "He's driving me crazy."

Tod rocked back in the chair and look at me. "But you can rationalize. You can even laugh about it. Venus just sees that as a threat." He pointed at the screen.

"I know." I sighed. "I told Wiesel I wouldn't take down the blog posts about him and I meant it. But I'm not going to post anything about Venus anymore. I'm sick of this."

He shook his head. "Your blog isn't the problem."

"They're using the information about her mental illness to drive her insane."

"They would have found out anyway," he said. "I still think it's better to have it all out in the open. They can't do anything about it."

"Except harass us," I said. "I'm serious. No more posts about Venus."

Chapter 33 - Band of bullies

As we reviewed and copied the videos of Chucky incidents, another character and his Shepherd mix emerged on the screen.

Tod paused the replay. "I've seen this guy before." He pulled up the playback from Super Bowl Sunday and put all four cameras on screen. "Watch the front yard camera. This was about 15 minutes before the boys showed up in the alley."

The man walked slowly past our house, stopping often to let his Shepherd mix sniff and poop and pee in our yard. Venus and Zeus were asleep on the front porch so they didn't react.

I peered at the screen. "That's the guy I call Patsy. Friend of Daryl's. He started walking his dog by our house a couple months ago, around the same time Chucky got weird. He always walks with traffic in front of our fence then crosses to the other side. It's so obvious he's trying to provoke the dogs."

"I see what's going on. Daryl is pissed off because we got the citation dismissed and the ordinance revised. So he's recruiting his friends and neighbors to harass us. First it was Chucky. Now this guy." He pointed at the screen. "Patsy."

I stared at the stocky figure and his dog. "Daryl and his band of bullies. At least they're motivated to walk their dogs. Even if it's just to harass us."

Tod rolled his eyes. "I don't get it. We've never done anything to this guy. We don't even know his name."

I shrugged. "We've never done anything to the Harrisons either. Or Chucky."

"The problem is the cops are in on it. Those guys know they can get away with it."

I nodded. "This is like a game to them."

Tod stood up. "And we don't have to play. Most of the harassment goes on when we're not home. We're already keeping the dogs inside. We need to get them out of here as much as possible."

I exhaled with relief. "I could definitely use a break from this town."

We headed for Utah. We had planned to camp on public land as we had for many years. Instead we were greeted with a new sign: *No Primitive Camping Allowed—Camp in Approved Campgrounds Only.*

As Tod drove away Zeus paced and snorted in disgust. *This is my favorite place. Why are we leaving?*

Venus ignored him and slobbered on the window as she lapped

up the scenery. *Maybe we'll stumble on a herd of sheep. A girl can dream.*

Zeus wanted to do what we always did. We shared his disappointment.

The lure of public land had always been the maze of Jeep trails for hiking and the fact that we didn't have to tie the dogs. Not to mention trees and shade, a must with two big dogs in the desert. We knew the area well. The "approved" campgrounds near Moab were hot, flat, and crowded.

Our search for a campground with trees and hiking trails led us to the Visitor Information Center in town. Gateway to Canyonlands and Arches National Parks, Moab is an energetic tourist town. That morning walkers, joggers, and dogs swarmed the sidewalks. A non-stop parade of bicycles, dirt bikes, motorcycles, cars, and trucks zoomed past.

I opened the rear passenger door to leash the dogs and walk them. Venus jumped out as I snapped the leash to her collar. A motorcycle engine revved up across the parking lot. Zeus retreated. Tod grabbed Venus's leash and I coaxed Zeus.

I walked the dogs while Tod went inside to get camping information. But the cacophony of noise put Zeus on edge. For once he was the anxious one and Venus took it all in stride with her nose to the ground. If she was aware of his vexation she didn't let on until I sat on a bench under a stunted cottonwood. Zeus plopped down in the shade, stretched out and groaned. *It's hot. It's crowded. It's noisy. I hope we're not camping here.*

Venus went over, lowered her head, and pawed the ground next to where his head lay. *Remember Trappers Lake? They're going to surprise us. You wait and see.*

Concerned he might snap at her and start something, I said, "Just leave it Venus. He's decided to be grumpy. Let him wallow in it."

She looked at me for a second and crouched on the ground behind him. She rested her chin on her front paws and blinked at me. *This is a game we play. Right? There's a surprise coming. Right?*

Eventually we headed south to the Canyon Rims Recreation Area. We chose Hatch Point Campground for its remoteness and hiking trails. We were not disappointed. Only one of the ten campsites was occupied when we arrived. The sites were small and close together so we paid for two—one for us and one for the dogs. The site for us had the best view. The site for the dogs had shade trees.

Upon inspection, the accommodations met with their approval. Venus nudged Zeus. *See? I told you so.*

He sneezed. *What do you know? You're a dog.*

Venus's good mood carried on through the weekend. On our Saturday hike as we crossed an open field, a lone pronghorn antelope grazed a couple hundred yards away. Tod snapped the leash on Venus. She danced and whined when she spotted the antelope. He stared at us for a few minutes. She fell silent. Then he bounded off like a giant jackrabbit.

As we sat by the campfire after supper, two contented dogs slept nose-to-nose within inches of one another.

"Did you notice Venus never took off today?" I asked.

At the mention of her name, she stood up and shook all over. Zeus groaned. *Let sleeping dogs lie, would you please?*

"She would have chased that antelope if we let her," Tod said.

"She didn't even see it until we practically pointed it out."

"She was having too much fun with her buddy Zeus." Venus sat down next to his camp chair and rested her chin on Tod's knee. *Pet me.* He did.

"She turns five at the end of the month. Maybe she's slowing down."

"Are you slowing down?" he asked her. She licked his hand.

"She seems less anxious." I paused, as though I dare not say it. Then I blurted, "Happier."

He nodded. "She and Zeus are getting along better than ever."

As calm and peaceful as our weekend was, we still had to return home to the band of bullies. I checked the video replay often. Whenever we left our house, Chucky and/or Patsy walked by with their dogs, looking for Venus and hoping to provoke her. But our dogs were in the house. Normal people would have given up and found another hobby. But they were not normal people.

They changed their strategy. At the end of May, there was another weird incident involving Chucky. At 7:30 a.m., he showed up with Red and stood in the pouring rain on the other side of the street, across from our front porch, where Zeus and Venus slept. They didn't react. He jerked Red's leash until he started barking. Venus woke up and barked. When I walked out to the porch he said something to me but I couldn't hear him. I brought the dogs indoors. He stayed another five minutes and jerked on Red's leash, which made him bark.

From then on, Chucky and Patsy showed up with their dogs, at different times of course, while we were home and Venus was outside. Except walking their dogs on the street wasn't enough to get her barking. So they loitered in front of fence, letting their dogs pee and poop in grass.

I described their behavior for Tod when he returned from New York. "They hang out on the other side of our fence like it's a city park."

"And they double dare you to do anything about it." He shook his head. "Hard to believe these are grown men."

"Daryl and Patsy are quite the role models. Their boys will have black belts in bullying by the time they reach high school."

He sighed. "Just bring the dogs inside so they can't provoke them."

"I think we're the ones they're trying to provoke," I said. "And right now it's working. I'm about ready to call bullshit on their stupid game."

"That's exactly what they want you to do."

"So what?"

"So don't do it," he insisted. "They're trying to provoke us into a confrontation."

Instead I adjusted to their change in strategy. Whenever I saw Chucky and Red, or Patsy and Shep coming, I brought the dogs inside. The temperature outside heated up into the 90s. They were happy to hang out near the air conditioner and watch Kaley and Henry play while I babysat. Patsy and Chucky quit walking their dogs in the heat. We walked Venus and Zeus at dusk, or after dark, when it cooled down.

In mid-June they switched tactics. Whenever we took the dogs out for their evening walk, we ran into Patsy and Shep, or Chucky and Red.

"Daryl must call them and tell them when we leave the house," I said.

"What's the point of this?" Tod asked, irritated.

"You assume there is one," I replied.

We adapted and changed our route, or ducked down alleys and side streets to avoid them. Chucky wasn't much of a walker to begin with, more of a stopper and stander. Besides, all that effort contradicted his frail image. He dropped out of the game first.

Patsy soldiered on with a renewed gusto. He figured out we were purposefully avoiding him, though it took him a few days. Not the brightest bulb in town. One evening he switched directions. As we walked in the direction of our house, he turned the corner and walked toward us with Shep, on our side of the street. We were walking against traffic. As he approached, he refused to move over to let us pass. Then he lifted his foot and kicked his dog in the ribs. Shep let out a yelp.

"Stop," I said to Tod. I couldn't believe it. Patsy was trying to provoke Venus to attack his dog.

He grinned stupidly like the Jeff Daniels character in *Dumb and Dumber.* He walked within two feet of us with Shep agitated and straining at the end of his leash. Zeus stood there while Venus did her anxiety dance.

I looked at Tod. "Did you see him kick his dog?"

"Yeah. What a jerk."

Patsy didn't say a word. He just kept walking. We headed home.

"I am so sick of this," I muttered.

"I know." Tod put his arm around me. "We need to get you and the dogs out of this fish bowl again."

He took some vacation days and we headed to Lake Powell with Kaley and the dogs. Both dogs rode in the backseat with her with no grumbling. We enjoyed a long, lazy weekend camping and boating. No one bothered us and nothing happened.

On the drive home I said, "Venus was so calm this trip."

"She loves the lake," Tod said.

"She didn't take off and run wild this time."

"She stayed close to Kaley," he said. "Gave her a job to do."

"Yeah." But I wondered about the change in her. Was the call of the wild fading as she grew older?

The weekend before July 4th, we towed the CJ up to Meadow Lake. Kaley came along again. The reason we had always camped in the campground was because it was near the lake, a short hike with the dogs and Kaley. With the CJ, we could drive them to the lake. We climbed up Boy Scout ridge and found a primitive campsite in a grove of towering white pines—but no Boy Scouts. Kaley and the dogs were free to roam the surrounding meadows.

After dark we sat around the campfire roasting marshmallows.

"We should give the CJ a name," Kaley suggested.

"We could call it CJ," Tod said.

Kaley groaned. "Bor-ring." Flames licked the marshmallow on the end of her stick. It slid off into the fire. "Oops." Venus drooled when she reached in the bag for another. *I prefer mine raw, thank you.*

"I agree," I said. "It has way too much character for just CJ. It has this whole guerilla taxi thing going on."

Kaley looked puzzled as she fed a marshmallow to Venus. "As in gorilla? Like an ape?"

"No. As in guerilla." I spelled it. "Like a South American soldier of the jungle. They ride around in black Jeeps like that."

"Oh." Kaley thought about that. "How do you know?"

"I saw it in a movie," I said.

She laughed. "Does Zeus like marshmallows?"

I shook my head.

"All it needs is up armor and we're battle ready." Tod offered Kaley a golden brown marshmallow.

"Yum." She slid it off the stick and tossed it in her hands to cool. Venus jumped up and stood guard in case she accidentally dropped it. "What's up armor?"

"A machine gun," Tod said. "I was just kidding."

"Oh." She squished the gooey marshmallow between her fingers and ate it. "We have dog armor." Venus licked her sticky fingers as she giggled.

Like a spark from the campfire, the name popped in my head. "Let's call it Hugo."

"I like it," Tod said.

Kaley wrinkled her nose. "I'll have to think about it."

The next day we meandered along the Jeep trails. The dogs loved riding in Hugo. But whenever it tipped too far to one side they had no way to hang on. So I got out with them and walked through the gnarly uphill sections. Venus seemed content to shadow Kaley so I wasn't concerned that she didn't take off and run wild.

I noticed something else about Venus that weekend. I had also noticed it in Utah and Lake Powell. But I had kept it to myself. When it came time to pack up and go home, her mood changed from happy to sad—maybe even a little depressed. I wondered if she had picked up on my energy. Between camping trips, Tod was traveling—a lot. Life in the fishbowl had become tedious. I, too, felt sad about going home, especially that particular Saturday. July 4th was the next day and I dreaded it. I felt certain Daryl and his band of bullies had some mischief planned to annoy us and the dogs.

Instead we returned home to a pleasant surprise. The Harrisons were gone and stayed gone for two incredibly peaceful weeks. Apart from the usual intermittent fireworks eruptions, July 4th was calm and uneventful.

While I was at the grocery store, Sally the clerk asked, "Are you going to see the fireworks show tonight?"

I shook my head. "We have to babysit our big dogs. They hate fireworks."

"My Border Collie does, too," she said. "He hides in the bathtub. It seems to help."

That evening as the firecrackers, cherry bombs, and bottle rockets exploded Zeus retreated to the bedroom. I showed him the bathtub in the master bath. It's an oversize tub with a Jacuzzi.

He shot me a miserable glance. *That racket out there isn't torture enough? Now you're making me take a bath?* A string of firecrackers popped off in the distance. He climbed right in.

After dark, Tod and I sat on our tree-house deck and drank tequila. We toasted to one year plus 14 days of emotional stability with Venus. At the mention of her name Venus, who was keeping watch from the living room, whipped open the sliding screen door with her paw and stepped outside. *Everybody okay out here?* She didn't like the pops and bangs either but her need to check on us overwhelmed her fear. She buried her nose in Tod's armpit and snorted. *Pet me.*

He scratched her ears. "Hard to believe it's the Fourth of July. Zeus is asleep in the bedroom. Venus is ignoring him. We don't even have the gate up. The dogs are so calm."

"The Harrisons are gone. No one's harassing them," I said.

A volley of pops and bangs burst in the air. Venus stretched out and rubbed her ear on the deck floor. *Make it stop.*

"I think the noise hurts their ears," Tod said.

She lifted her head and looked expectantly at him as she panted. *Yes. It hurts. Make it stop.*

"Look at her," I said. "She wants you to make it stop."

A single firework burst in the sky above the trees. Venus sighed and lay down again.

"In a lot of ways she seems like the Venus before her breakdown," Tod said. "Like a normal dog."

I nodded. "I think we have to accept the fact that she will be on clomipramine for the rest of her life."

He looked at me. "That's okay with me. What about you? I know you always hoped we could stabilize her off the drug."

I shrugged. "Venus is crazy. Mentally ill. Doesn't matter whether it's her breed, her upbringing, or genetics. She is unable to function as a normal dog unless she's medicated."

"You won't get any argument from me," he said.

I stretched my open palm toward Venus. "Look at her. She's calm. She's happy. She and Zeus have worked out their differences. I say, don't mess with success."

Her tail thumped on the deck. *I'm a good girl.*

Chapter 34 - Lunatics are running the asylum

With their commander away the first two weeks of July, Chucky and Patsy took a vacation from walking their dogs to our house.

Daryl returned some time mid-day on Friday, July 16. I noticed his car in the driveway when I looked out the window while making supper. I thought little of it because we were in the midst of a heat wave. The dogs were inside close to the air conditioner. At 6:00 p.m. it was 95 degrees.

Tod had been in New York all week. He arrived home around 8:00 p.m. We split a couple beers and discussed the previous week. In the cloudless sky, twilight lingered longer than usual. By 8:30 it had cooled down to 80 degrees. The dogs were restless so we took them out for a walk. Zeus and I walked in the grass in front of our fence. He liked to sniff out who'd been traipsing through his yard. Tod and Venus were in the street. She was on the flexi-leash and headed for the public right-of-way in front of the Harrisons' fence.

The instant she stepped off the pavement onto a patch of dirt, Daryl jumped over his four-foot fence, nearly falling on his face. Venus squatted and peed in the weeds. Daryl waved his arms and shouted a string of obscenities. "Get your goddamn dog off my yard! Get the fuck out of here!"

Zeus and I stopped in our tracks. He lunged toward the action but I held him back. A deep growl rose up from his throat. *I don't trust that guy.*

Tod stood his ground in the middle of the street and pulled Venus toward him. Still shouting, Daryl charged at them waving his arms. Venus planted her feet in front of Tod and barked, which kept Daryl from stepping any closer.

He shook his fist and yelled, "Call off your dog, asshole. Call off your dog!"

But he was the attacker, not Venus.

"If you calm down and stop shouting she'll stop barking," Tod said.

"Get off my street!" Daryl shouted. Obviously he'd been drinking.

Venus's bark turned to growling.

Zeus was beside himself, whimpering and panting. *Let me at him. Just this once.* It took all my strength to hold onto his collar with both hands. I didn't dare move or he'd bolt. I had never felt such anger in him. His intention was clear. *I'm going to charge over there and knock him on his ass.* As much as I wanted to, I couldn't let that happen.

"I have every right to walk in the street with my dog," Tod was saying.

"You can't let your dog piss in my yard," Daryl spat. "That's illegal."

"She was in the public right-of-way. I don't think that's illegal." Tod shrugged. "But you can call the cops if you want. I'll wait right here."

"Fuck you. Smartass son-of-a-bitch!" Daryl shouted. "Keep your dogs away from my yard. I don't want you walking on my side of the street."

Right then a jacked-up white pickup with green flames careened around the corner and headed straight for Tod and Venus. The truck swerved and braked.

The woman driver yelled out the window, "Fuck you and your dogs!" Then she flipped me off as she drove past. Venus jumped up and down and barked again.

Patsy's green mini-van raced toward us from the opposite direction. He zoomed past me and Zeus. He braked as he drove around Tod and Venus. Then he stopped in front of Daryl's driveway.

Patsy jumped out and yelled, "Get the hell out of the street! Who the hell do you think you are?"

Tod didn't respond. Venus growled and snapped her jaws at him. *Stay back.* Patsy didn't take another step forward.

My head was spinning. Tod and Venus were trapped. Did Daryl have a gun?

"Answer him!" Daryl pointed at Patsy. "Who the hell do you think you are?"

Tod tossed his head, steered Venus in my direction, and walked away.

Daryl pursued him. "What the hell's the matter with you? Come back here and fight like a man."

"Okay. That's it," I said. "Let's go Zeus." He lunged toward Daryl. *I've got this.*

Tod stepped in front of us and shook his head. We pulled our dogs to opposite sides. But they weren't interested in each other. They wanted Daryl.

He staggered. "Go on! Hide behind your fucking vicious dogs. Chicken shit."

Zeus and Venus bounced up and down anxiously and complained. *He's too close. Push him back.* I didn't look at Daryl. I had my hands full with Zeus. Tod kept his back to him.

Daryl retreated finally muttering, "You goddamn assholes."

I felt like I was watching a movie. The whole thing seemed somehow staged. I shuddered. "Wow. The lunatics are running the asylum."

"You can say that again." Tod rolled his eyes. "They're all crazy."

"Are you okay?" I asked.

Venus danced around at the end of her leash and whined.

"Yeah. But Venus needs to get away from here and let off some steam." He exhaled. "So do I." He turned toward our sidewalk. "Let's go."

I grabbed his arm. "I don't want to walk past them."

He shook off my grasp. "Fuck them. It's our damn house. We can do whatever we want."

He took off with Venus. Zeus and I caught up to them. Daryl and Patsy leaned against the side of his van drinking beer and watching us.

As we walked past Patsy yelled, "Go on! Take your dogs and get the hell out of here."

"You disgust me. Fucking assholes," Daryl added.

I looked at Tod. "I think we just died and went to junior high."

He burst out laughing. I joined in.

"What's so funny?" Daryl called after us.

We ignored them. Venus calmed down within a few blocks. But not Tod. His face was ashen and his breathing shallow.

"Are you sure you're okay?"

"Yeah." He stopped, sucked in a deep breath and let it all out. "He scared the shit out of me. I didn't know if he had a gun. Or if Patsy was going to hit us with his van."

"And the bitch in the flaming green pickup. What was up with that?"

He shook his head.

"Bullies. Why do they pick on old people like us?" I teased.

He smiled.

I rubbed his shoulder as we walked on. "I know we laughed at them but it's not funny. We should file a complaint."

"You mean call the cops?" He shook his head. "Now that's funny."

"He attacked you. I'm a witness."

"And the cop will ask me what I did to piss him off."

I sighed. He was right. "You know, the whole thing felt staged. I think Daryl planned it, right down to that wacko in the pickup."

"I had the same feeling."

"Okay then. If you won't call the cops, I will," I insisted.

"That's exactly what he wants us to do. It's like he's fighting a war against us. The problem is we don't fight back. So he's frustrated as hell."

"So tell me. How is calling the cops fighting back? He attacked you."

"Then he'll do something to get back at us. And it never ends."

"But doing nothing hasn't ended it either." I tossed up my hands which jerked Zeus's leash. He stopped and snorted. "Sorry Zeus. Look, what just happened was pure insanity. It was like—I don't know." I waved my arms. Zeus gave me a dirty look. "Like a temper tantrum—with a Greek chorus."

"That's funny." Tod smiled again. "I don't know what else to say. I just got home from a long week. The last thing I want to do is spend the rest of the night talking to the Silt cops."

I kicked a stone. Zeus ducked. But it didn't go anywhere near him. "I'm so sick of this."

Tod put his arm around me. We stopped walking. "So am I." Venus and Zeus leaned against us in big dog hugs.

"Calling the cops will only make things worse," he said.

"I guess you're right."

"I know I'm right."

I sniffed. "I think you'd feel differently if it was me he attacked."

"Of course I would. That's not the point."

I walked away with Zeus. He looked forlornly at Tod and Venus. *Are we mad at them?*

They caught up to us. "Listen to me," Tod said. "He didn't attack you. He attacked me. I stood right there in the middle of the street. I looked him in the eye. I saw the rage. I felt the hatred. I felt like he wanted to kill me. I told you he scared the hell out of me. The guy is dangerous."

"Duh. I was there," I snapped. "I totally get that. He's dangerous. That's why we need to call the cops."

"You're not hearing me. He's looking for an excuse to retaliate. He wanted to fight with me. Over dog pee."

"I know. He's nuts."

"Right. And you're home alone a lot. I'm not going to give that maniac any ammunition to come after you and these dogs."

They sensed his anger. Venus whined. *Should I be upset?* Zeus shuffled impatiently. *You can walk and talk at the same time. Let's go.* We resumed our walk.

I exhaled with exasperation. "Okay. So we don't call the cops. What do we do?"

"Nothing. If we don't react, he can't do anything to retaliate."

I fumed. "I'm too angry to do nothing."

"By nothing I don't mean nothing," he said. "We keep doing what we've been doing. We keep a log. We lock our doors. We keep the dogs inside as much as possible."

We checked the video replay when we got home. Unfortunately most of the action occurred out of camera range, only the vehicle activity was visible.

The confrontation must have been cathartic for Daryl. Everything was finally out in the open. After that night the hatred flowed like liquid lava. He was more demonstrative, stomping around and glaring angrily at us when he was outside. Patsy often stopped by in the evenings. They sat outside, drank beer and watched our house. If Tod or I was outside, they jeered and laughed at us.

Our lack of response seemed to egg them on more. The intensity had been ratcheted up. Their war against us raged on with a vengeance. Chucky made his rounds daily with Red. He didn't always appear at the same time so I never knew when to bring Venus inside. It didn't matter if she was out or in, he stopped in the street in front of our house and jerked Red's leash until he barked. Sometimes I let Venus stay outside and bark at them. She was doing her job. She seemed to enjoy it, like a game.

Patsy also pitched in with frequent walks with Shep. He always showed up when Venus was outside. One evening I glanced out the window as Patsy and Shep arrived in the street out front.

"Amazing," I said to Tod. "I let Venus outside about ten minutes ago and Patsy and Shep just showed up. It's like someone called to tell them she's outside."

Tod groaned. "Yeah. Daryl. God. That's sick."

Venus barked a few times. Patsy and Shep walked on the grass in the public right-of-way in front of our fence. I heard Venus run across the porch into the yard. She barked again.

"I'll bring her in," Tod said.

The images of Daryl's attack were seared into my brain. Add to that the constant drip of harassment every time I stepped outside my front door, and coping became a struggle. I had my own anxiety issues. I wasn't good at doing nothing. I Googled "sociopath" and "sociopathic behavior," which I immediately discovered was a bad idea. I would have been better off not knowing what Daryl and friends were capable of. Insomnia gradually set in.

"Forget about Venus," I told Emily. "This is driving *me* insane."

"I know," she said. "You just have to pretend it's all a game."

"Okay." I held up my hands. "I quit."

She rolled her eyes.

"See?" I taunted her. "Not so easy is it?"

I Googled "adult bully" and "adult bullying." Everything I read validated Tod's "do not engage" strategy. Avoid escalation at all costs. As perverted as our situation had become, it still helped. The more stories I read about adult bullies the more it stood out that when the police acknowledged the bully's behavior and dealt with it, everything turned out okay. But in cases where the police ignored victims' pleas for help or worse, behaved like bullies themselves, then things always ended badly.

While I was busy feeling anxious, Venus and Zeus were busy being dogs. Suddenly the tables were turned. I needed their calm, stable energy. If Zeus wasn't by my side, Venus smothered me with affection. She had given up trying to dominate him or compete for my attention. She waited her turn. My reservations about Zeus dealing with the stress of living with her mental illness had faded away.

Much less soothing was the constant routine of watching for Chucky and Patsy, bringing the dogs inside, and letting them out again. It aggravated me. For Zeus and Venus it really was a game. They didn't care if Shep peed all over my rose bushes. They didn't care if Red pooped in the shrubs outside our fence. For their sake and my own peace of mind, I needed to let it go, too.

I explained it to Emily. "It's not the fact that they bring their dogs over here to poop and pee in our yard. It's the irrational motives behind it that keeps me awake at night. I mean, really? These men have nothing better to do?"

"Nope." She shook her head. "But you need to stop thinking like that. You'll scare yourself. And me."

I waved my hand. "Don't worry. I'm not scared. It's more like, I've been living in a cave. Or I just fell down the rabbit hole. I didn't know grown men were capable of this kind of lowdown behavior. I thought mankind had evolved."

"I know, right? Really sucks." She sighed. "What a letdown."

"Exactly. I feel like I'm going back and forth between two totally different universes. One is where the calm, rational people live and the other one—"

"Is a bunch of morons tripping over each other." She finished my sentence.

"The Three Stooges."

We laughed.

The first week of August, as Tod was packing to leave, he said, "If it makes you feel any better, you have nothing to worry about with Venus here. I've never been more sure of that." At the mention of her name, she rolled over and showed her belly for a scratch. Tod obliged. He looked at me. "Daryl's afraid of Venus. I saw it that night. As long as she's with you, he won't come near you."

I nodded. "I know." I crumpled onto the rug and rubbed her belly and played with her feet while he finished packing. "I've always felt safe with her. Now more than ever. She's changed."

Two weeks later she showed us how much she had changed. The weekend before school started we took Kaley and the dogs to Trappers Lake. Other people had the same idea and the campgrounds filled up with kids and dogs. What could have been an anxiety-riddled weekend with Venus turned out completely the opposite. She ignored or greeted other dogs. We rarely had to tie her. She stayed in our campsite or followed Kaley. On a hike along the lakeshore Venus waded in up to her belly. Then she walked in circles lapping water, as though immersing herself in the wilderness and drinking it all in.

As we roasted marshmallows around the campfire Saturday night, Venus and Zeus snoozed at our feet, exhausted from our romp to the lakeshore at sunset. Tod remarked how well Venus was doing. We talked about the changes in her over the summer.

Even Kaley chimed in. "It's more fun to walk Venus on the leash now. She's not all nervous. She doesn't pull me all over the place."

Venus sat up and stretched, her nose pointing up at the stars. Her white fur looked golden in the firelight, as though she was basking in the glow of our praise.

"What a pretty girl," I cooed.

Kaley reached over and hugged her. "I love you, Venus."

"What amazes me is how well she's handling the harassment from the neighbors," Tod said.

"I think that has more to do with me," I said. "If I don't let it bother me, it doesn't bother them. I'm working on it."

He nodded. "You're less paranoid."

I reached over and punched his arm. "Sometimes I wonder who's the real crazy bitch? Me or Venus."

"Nana," Kaley piped up. "You shouldn't call Venus a crazy bitch." She giggled and fed a marshmallow to Venus.

"Very funny," I said.

When it came time to pack up and leave on Sunday, Venus's mood changed. She seemed a little depressed. She curled up in a corner behind Zeus and slept all the way home. I figured she was tired.

We hadn't been home more than a half hour when Patsy appeared from around the corner with Shep while we unloaded the camper. The dogs were sacked out on the porch. Patsy dawdled in front of our house. Venus and Zeus jumped up and barked at them.

"Look, it's the welcome home committee," I said to Tod loud enough for Patsy to hear. "Daryl must have called to tell him we're back so he rushed right over."

Patsy walked Shep in the grass in front of our fence. But Venus and Zeus were too tired to chase them and went back to sleep. He lingered as though daring us to say something to him. We didn't.

Coming home was a huge let down. I understood how Venus felt.

Chapter 35 - Meadow Lake

I had made a habit of watching the video replay whenever we returned home. As we suspected Chucky never walked Red by our house when we gone. Nor did Patsy walk Shep.

"Never, as in not ever," I told Tod. "They didn't even accidently walk by."

"Be sure to make a note about that in the logs."

The first day of school arrived and Kaley entered fourth grade. She always stayed with me until Emily picked her and Henry up after work. While the school kids walked home in the afternoon, Chucky and Red showed up as Kaley walked up the sidewalk. Venus was on the front porch and wiggled with excitement at the sight of her. Zeus was asleep in the yard. I stood indoors, behind the screen door. Chucky jerked on Red's leash until he yelped. Venus looked at them and barked.

"It's okay Venus," I said. "I'm here. Good girl."

She calmed down and whined at Kaley for attention.

Kaley turned and looked at Chucky as Red strained at the leash and barked. "Why does that scary man keep standing there?" She looked at me. "He's staring at me."

"I see that," I said. "He's trying to make Venus bark."

"He's scaring me," she said.

Venus danced around on the porch, torn between happiness at seeing Kaley and her need to protect her. I brought her inside away from Chucky's bad energy.

When Emily came to pick up the kids I told her about the incident. "I checked the video. He hung around for more than five minutes. He didn't leave until after I brought Kaley and the dogs inside and shut the door."

"That's creepy." She shuddered. "What's even creepier is I saw him this morning when Henry and I walked Kaley to school. He was hanging around at the corner by the stop sign watching the kids while they walked to school."

"If you see him again, take his picture," I said.

The next morning she snapped a picture of him with her cell phone as he loitered on the street corner with his dog watching the kids walk to school.

"He saw me take his picture," she told me later.

"Good," I said. "Maybe he'll stop acting like a creepy stalker."

Two days later at 7:30 a.m., during a sudden downpour, Chucky and Red appeared in the alley across from our house. Zeus and Venus were asleep on the front porch. Chucky jerked on Red's leash but he didn't respond. Instead he shook his drenched fur and sat down. Chucky tugged on the leash to make him stand up. Red barked, more at Chucky than Venus. She was curled up on the wicker loveseat ignoring them. I opened the front door and stood inside behind the screen door. He walked toward our house and stopped in the street across from the end of our sidewalk. Red kept barking because Chucky kept jerking his leash. Venus stood up and barked, then lay down. He hung around long enough for me to find the camera, come back, and take a photo.

When he saw the camera, he crossed the street and walked Red in the grass in front of our fence trying to provoke a reaction from Venus and Zeus. But they didn't care. They were warm and dry on the porch. Chucky and Red were sopping wet in the rain. For several more minutes he walked around the area between the end of our fence and the mailboxes. Then he headed home.

An hour later the meter reader's pickup pulled into our driveway. Venus barked at him. Two minutes later I saw Chucky trotting down the street with Red toward our sidewalk. He jerked on Red's leash until he barked. Venus continued barking. I walked out the front door, opened the gate and stood on the porch with Venus. She stopped barking. I had left the gate open. I considered letting her go after them. But I knew it would get us both in trouble.

Chucky's lips were moving. He was talking to me but Red was barking so loud I couldn't hear him. I assumed he was trying to provoke me into walking out there so he could claim I assaulted him. Eventually he gave up and walked up the alley with Red. Ten minutes later, a cop drove by slowly. Venus and I were inside by then.

Tod was home that week. Thursday evening we discussed the recent Chucky incidents while we watched Patsy stroll by leisurely with Shep.

"I don't like this," I said. "Why is Chucky paying attention to Emily and the kids?"

"He wants to provoke us."

"Okay. I'm provoked," I said. "It's creepy. He's a stalker. We need to do something."

"Let's take the dogs camping at Meadow Lake this weekend," Tod said. "I'll take tomorrow off. We can tow Hugo up there and go Jeeping."

"That's not what I meant."

"I don't know what else to do," he said. "The cops won't do anything."

"We're talking about the kids here," I insisted.

"Collect the evidence. Take photos, check the video, log the incidents. If he keeps it up next week, I'll talk to Bickle."

Friday morning Venus was tied out in the driveway while Tod loaded the camper onto the pickup. Marybeth Christianson's Black Lab mix Eddie ran down the alley, crossed the street, and ran into our driveway. Venus jumped up and leaped to the end of her tether, yelping and barking. Eddie dashed around the pickup into the front yard. Venus was beside herself. Even Zeus darted back and forth on the porch, barking. Eddie ran toward home. Zeus calmed down.

Tod brought Venus inside. "She needs to calm down." She growled and snorted and hugged the door. *Letmeout-letmeout-letmeout.* He shook his head. "She went nuts. She hates that dog."

"What was he doing down here anyway? I've never seen him running loose before."

He rolled his eyes. "How should I know?"

"You know what I mean." I peered at him. "Did Marybeth let him loose on purpose?"

He tossed up his hands. "Let's just get the hell out of here. I'll finish loading the camper."

Venus sat next to me panting. "Shh.... It's okay. Good girl."

The incident made our drive to Meadow Lake feel even more like an escape from the insane asylum. I sensed Venus's anxiety evaporate as we rumbled up the Buford Road. But I couldn't stop thinking about Marybeth's dog showing up at our house all of a sudden. Living with harassment I had learned that no detail is insignificant, and there's no such thing as coincidence. I had developed a healthy paranoia.

My suspicions about Marybeth Christianson nagged at me. She had run against Mayor Minnifield in the April election and lost. She was a close ally of the town manager who was fired. She had made no secret of her opposition to the "coup," which was how she referred to the mayor and the three newly-elected trustees. She liked Tod and me even less than before because we supported the coup and the mass firings. The rumor was she blamed my blog for her defeat. During the campaign I had put out the word that Tod and I didn't support either candidate for mayor. A lot of voters read my blog. Not everyone was a fan. Marybeth had always hated my blog. There was no doubt she knew about Daryl and his band of bullies. Everyone did.

When we arrived at Meadow Lake, luck was on our side. Our favorite campsite on Boy Scout ridge was all ours. The minute her feet touched the dirt, Venus bolted. I had brought the clicker so I let her go. She checked in periodically but most of the afternoon she pursued the call of the wild. She showed up when we started cooking supper. She ate and wandered into the forest again.

While Tod did supper dishes in the camper, Zeus stood at the screen door and stared into the grove. I walked over and opened the door. "Come out, Zeus." He looked over my shoulder and backed away. The skin on the back of my neck tingled. I turned sharply. Venus stepped out of the shadows. I exhaled. "It's just Venus. Come on, Zeus." He sat down and looked away. *I like it here just fine.*

Venus slept near the campfire all evening.

"She was quite the explorer today," I said. "She hasn't taken off like that in a long time."

"She definitely needed to run wild," Tod said.

"Don't we all."

He exhaled. "Look. I didn't mean to dismiss the situation with Chucky. It bothers me, too."

"And don't forget Marybeth Christianson's dog showing up in our yard this morning. That was no accident."

He winced. "I wouldn't jump to any conclusions about that."

I fetched a couple beers out of the cooler and opened them. I handed him one and collapsed in my camp chair. I took a long, slow swig. Then I said, "I've been doing some research on bullies and harassment. I read this quote, 'sometimes paranoia's just having all the facts.' When you're under siege like we are, when you're being harassed, paranoia can be a good thing. It's important to pay attention to details. You learn to see patterns in people's behavior. And you learn to make connections. Sort of a healthy paranoia."

"Okay. So how is Marybeth Christianson connected to all this?"

"Bullies almost always recruit other weaker people to do their dirty work."

He almost spit out a mouthful of beer. "Daryl."

"Marybeth didn't like us during the recall. She's still bitter about the election and the firings. And she's made it perfectly clear to anyone who will listen she hates my blog. She wanted to make an ordinance against it. Remember? It's no big leap to assume Daryl recruited her for his little war. But she's not about to waddle past our house with Eddie. That's beneath her."

He nodded. "When I was on the board with her, she preferred to do things behind people's backs."

"So it's more her style to open the door and let Eddie escape. Then she's not directly involved in the harassment."

Tod leaned forward and tossed another log on the fire. He sat back and finished his beer. "Think I'll have another. Want one?"

I still had a half a bottle. "No. I'm good."

When he sat down again, I said, "It's not easy living like this. You're the one who said I shouldn't do anything to retaliate. So I put that energy into research. Into learning how to live with this harassment. With bullies."

He picked at the wet label on his beer bottle. "You're right. It's not easy. What you said about Marybeth getting involved—as sickening as it is—I know it's possible."

"Reality bites." I finished my beer.

"Even if Marybeth isn't involved, the situation with Chucky is pretty bad. He shouldn't be paying attention to Kaley's comings and goings. This week let's organize our logs and photos and put together whatever video evidence we have. I'll take it to the police. But this time I'll ask the new town attorney to be there."

"Now there's an idea," I said. "Maybe he will listen to you."

When it was time for bed, Venus refused to come inside the camper.

"I wonder if she saw a coyote or two in her travels today. Zeus was acting weird earlier," I said.

Tod shrugged. "Let her sleep outside. She'll be okay here. I'll check on her."

Saturday we all climbed in Hugo and spent the day Jeeping and hiking. We wore them out. While we washed supper dishes in the camper, gunshots rang out from a group of campers up the road. Zeus wanted in but Venus was already sitting on the bench.

"Let him in," Tod said. "They'll be fine."

I opened the door, Zeus climbed in and Tod helped him onto the bench. The two dogs sat calmly side by side and stared out the window.

Venus slept outside again. We awoke to her barking once. Tod went out and checked on her.

"Whatever it was, she scared it away," he said.

I rolled over and went back to sleep. I knew she wouldn't let any critter near our campsite.

Sunday morning, Venus disappeared again after breakfast. I grabbed the camera and went looking for her. Zeus followed me across the meadow until we could see the lake. I walked in a circle. But even with a 360-degree view I saw no sign of her. I paused to shoot a couple photos. When I lowered the camera and turned around, she was standing ten feet away, panting, tail wagging.

"Good girl. Where did you come from?" I asked. "For a moment I thought we'd lost you." She wiggled over to me. I smoothed her ears. "Glad you came back."

As we headed back to the campsite, Venus and Zeus romped around sniffing and bumping into each other. She even teased him into a quick game of tag.

Tod called out to us, "Let's take a ride down to the lake before we pack up."

Venus stopped in her tracks and sniffed the air. Then she stared across the meadow as though something beckoned her. I snapped a photo and then I peered in the direction of her gaze. Whatever mesmerized her was not accessible to my human senses.

"Come on you two. Let's go," Tod called again.

The dogs ran up the ramp, stumbled into the back, and off we went. We hiked out to the dam. The dogs splashed around in the shallow water. Venus pawed at the fish. On the hike back we met up with a woman and her Blue Heeler. For a second he seemed startled by our big dogs. Then he snarled and attacked Venus. I clickered. She knocked him down and pinned him to the ground. He yelped. I clickered again. She let him go and walked away.

"Sorry," the woman said. "I don't know what got into him."

"It's fine. Nobody got hurt," I said.

"Wow. Close call for that dog," Tod said.

"I wonder why he attacked Venus. She's so mellow today," I drawled.

He shrugged. "Not very bright I guess."

While we broke camp Venus curled up under a fir tree and slept. At home as we pulled in our driveway we saw Patsy and Daryl drinking beer in his backyard. When Venus hopped out of the pickup, she stopped and stared across the street. Her left eye twitched rapidly. Was she reading their energy? For an instant I thought she might charge over there. Then she dropped her head and followed me inside. She collapsed in front of the air conditioner and passed out. Zeus stayed outside. We endured a few cackles and jeers as we unloaded the camper.

Later Venus picked at her food and went back to sleep.

"Guess she had too much fun," Tod said.

"Yeah." I sighed. "It's such a downer coming home to this neighborhood. Even I find it hard to adjust to the negative energy."

"She's just tired." He looked at me. "So are you. Things will look better in the morning."

Chapter 36 - Casualties of war

The next morning Venus acted listless. Usually she waited by the door to go out in the yard. Instead she hugged the cool tile in the foyer and ignored me. She balked at taking her pills.

I stood at the bathroom door and reported to Tod. "It took two tablespoons of peanut butter and three tries to get her pills down. And she won't go outside."

He stopped shaving. "I wonder if she ate something nasty when she was out wandering."

"Do the sheepherders poison the coyotes?"

"I don't think so," he said. "Why would they? They'd risk the Akbash getting into it. Maybe she chewed on a deer carcass and it made her sick."

"But she didn't puke."

"She didn't eat."

I tossed up my hands. "I'll keep an eye on her this morning. If she's not better by noon, I'll call the vet."

Venus slept until 9:00 a.m. She woke up, drank a bowl of water, and stood at the door in my office to go out. Zeus was asleep on the front porch.

An hour later I was upstairs in the bedroom putting on my shoes and socks before taking them to Dogland. I heard a commotion on the front porch. Venus barked in rapid succession—her thunderous intruder bark. I looked out the window in time to see Eddie wandering through the flower garden. He darted between Hugo and the camper. Then he ran off toward the elementary school.

I headed downstairs. I wanted to make sure Eddie was long gone before I opened the garage door. I heard growling and snarling from outside.

"Dammit!" I pushed open the screen door. Eddie must have returned.

I didn't see any dogs but I still heard a dog fight. The adrenalin surge almost knocked me over. I swung the gate open. I couldn't feel my feet when my shoes hit the porch floor.

The dogs were in the yard. I felt confused. Venus was on top of another dog. For a split second it looked like Eddie. But how did he get in the yard? It couldn't possibly be Zeus. The dog was down on his back.

"Venus! No!" I screamed.

The dog wailed. It was Zeus.

There was no time for the hose. I jumped off the porch onto

Venus and straddled her back. I clutched her collar with both hands. She held the skin from Zeus's groin between her teeth. She shook him hard. He wailed in agony. *Halp! Me!*

"No-no-no-no. Venus. No. You don't want to do this. Listen to me. It's Zeus. Zeus. Please," I begged. "Don't do this!"

If she took one more chomp she would tear his gut open. I let go of her collar and shoved my hands in her mouth. When she bit down her tooth sunk into my left middle finger. The ring finger on my right hand cracked. I felt my heart break. She hesitated and lost her grip on Zeus. He kicked at us with his right leg as I grasped her collar with my index fingers and thumbs. I pulled her off him.

"Run, Zeus, run," I cried. He rolled over and tried to stand. She snarled and lunged forward. The blood made my hands slippery and I lost my grip. She jumped on his back and bit into his shoulder. Zeus threw back his head and yelped. I wrapped my forearm around her neck, grabbed her collar with my left hand and lifted her off him. "Run, Zeus! Run!" I screamed.

She snapped and snarled and struggled as I held on. I said her name over and over. "Venus. Venus. Venus." Her jaws clacked and her body trembled. She glared in front of her as though facing down an invisible intruder. She whined and yelped. As we stood there together in the grass, smeared with blood, connected by my grip on her, I sensed her mental anguish. She didn't know who she was or where she was. She had snapped. Lost her mind. I could almost feel her brain thudding against her skull. I felt the enormity of her suffering.

I slowly eased her through the door into my office. She walked stiff-legged as though each step was painful. She collapsed on the rug, panting, waiting for the intruder to return.

I called Tod at his office. "Come home. Right now. Venus attacked Zeus. It's bad."

He gasped and hung up on me. I wrapped my right hand in a dish towel and headed outside to find Zeus. My head pounded as I checked the front yard, backyard, the garage. I saw drops of blood. But no Zeus. A feeling of dread washed over me as I stared at the service door. Was he in the house? With Venus? I couldn't remember. I searched the entire house including the bathtub. No sign of Zeus.

Tod met me at the front door. "What the hell?"

"I can't find Zeus."

"The front gate is open."

"Shit. My fault."

"Where's Venus?"

"My office. She's out of it. She lost her mind."

I pushed him out of the way. "I gotta find Zeus. He's hurt." I held up my towel-wrapped hand. "Worse than me."

"How bad is that?"

"Finger."

"Still attached?"

"Think so."

He grabbed my other arm. "Stay here. I'll find Zeus."

"No way. Get on your bike. I'll go on foot."

He sighed with exasperation.

"Go! Now!" I ran out the door.

As I turned the corner Irma Nossie called out to me from her front gate. "Are you all right? Where are you going?"

I stopped. "Zeus ran off. Have you seen him?"

"What's going on? We heard dogs fighting. And screaming. What's the matter with your hand? Did they attack you?"

I shuddered. "No. No. They had a fight." I broke down. "I have to go." I jogged toward the park. As I crossed the bridge over the irrigation canal I saw him standing in the middle of the playground looking like a lost circus pony.

"Zeus!" He didn't respond. "Zeus!" I ran.

He turned and plodded toward the shade under the crabapple tree. When I reached him he collapsed at my feet. I knelt down.

Tod appeared out of somewhere and jumped off his bike. "He's in shock." He grabbed the water bottle from his bike and squirted Zeus's mouth and head.

Joe Nossie showed up behind him.

"Hi." I looked at Tod.

"He was helping me look for Zeus," Tod said.

Joe looked down at Zeus's hind quarters. "He's hurt bad."

Zeus had relaxed enough to reveal the carnage. His skin was splayed open from his left lower rib to his groin and oozing blood.

"Stay with him. I'll get the Jeep," Tod ordered.

"You need to get them both to the doctor," Joe said. "Do you need my help?"

"No. I got this. Thanks." Tod took off.

Joe looked at me. "You need to be careful. Sometimes an injured dog will snap at you and bite because he's in pain."

I shook my head. "Zeus won't hurt me."

"What happened to your hand?" he asked.

I knew it was the first of many questions I would have to answer. "I stuck my hands in Venus's mouth to make her let go of him."

"Did she attack you?"

"No. I attacked her."

He considered that. "Do you want me to stay until Tod gets back?"

"No. We'll be okay." I glanced up at him. "Thank you. I

appreciate your help. Really. I do. What's happening right now is just ...." I exhaled. "Really h-hard." My voice croaked and tears dripped down my face.

He left. Too much doggie drama for him.

While we waited I stroked Zeus's head and ears and talked to him. "I hope Tod gets here before the cops. This is a no-dogs-allowed park. We're gonna be in big trouble. They'll probably haul the whole lot of us off to jail." He didn't think it was funny.

When Tod returned he brought the dog ramp. "I think we can roll him onto it—like a stretcher—and carry him over to the Jeep."

Zeus lifted his head and raised his eyebrows at Tod. *I don't think so.* Slowly he struggled to his feet and stumbled off toward the Jeep.

"Guess he nixed that idea." I smiled weakly. But it was a good sign he could walk.

On the two-block drive home Tod explained, "I called Emily. She's dropping Henry off at Carol's so she can take you to the hospital. I'll take Zeus to the vet."

Emily met us in the driveway. "Let me see your hand." She grabbed my arm. She used to be an EMT. I peeled off the towel. My right ring finger appeared oddly out of place. Emily tapped it lightly. "Yup. It's broken."

I looked at her. "She bit it in two. When it cracked she let go of Zeus." I looked at Tod. "I saved his life."

Emily turned pale. "We gotta go. Now."

We climbed in the pickup and headed to the hospital in Glenwood Springs, about 20 miles away. Emily drove.

"Mom," she said. "You need to understand something. You might lose that finger."

Tears ran like sweat. I turned my hand and studied my finger. "Then I will always have something to remember Venus."

Emily sobbed.

At the ER, as soon as the receptionist saw I had a possible severed digit, she sent us straight up to the orthopedics floor. When the elevator door opened a nurse met us. She ushered me into x-ray. Of course the technician wanted to know what happened.

Afterward I waited in Dr. Kirchoff's office with Emily. A parade of nurses flowed in and out. More questions. Different questions. The same questions. Emily filled out forms. It was a kind and gentle interrogation. I understood why they needed to know what happened. There were big dogs involved.

Dr. Kirchoff arrived and examined my hands and fingers. More questions. He seemed satisfied with my answers.

"The broken finger. The puncture wound on the other finger. Both are consistent with sticking your hands in a dog's mouth," he said to his nurse. She nodded. He looked at me. "Sometimes we see a little kid who stuck his fingers in the dog's mouth. Not adults."

I bit my lip. "I saved my other dog's life."

He glanced at Emily. "Is that what happened?"

She shrugged. "I don't know. I wasn't there."

"I see." He looked at me. "So you were alone with these dogs?"

"Yes."

"Well, you either did a very brave thing or a very stupid thing," he said.

"Can you save my finger?"

He smiled. "Of course I can. But we need to pin the finger so that means surgery." He looked at his nurse. "Schedule it for six o'clock." As he stood up to leave he hesitated. "What are you going to do about your dog? The one with the mental illness."

I breathed in sharply. "There's nothing we can do." Tears dripped down my face again. "We have to let her go."

The nurse burst into tears and fled the room. Dr. Kirchoff shook his head and walked out.

I brought Emily up to speed on the drive home. "I swear to you she didn't know it was Zeus. She thought he was Eddie. I thought he was Eddie. The whole thing was a total mind fuck. I need to look at the video. I need to see when she snapped."

"I don't think that's such a good idea," Emily said. "I'll take your word for it. She snapped. What difference does it make?"

"I need to know."

"Mom, I know you have to put her down." She gripped the steering wheel and swallowed. "I'm just not sure Dad does."

I nodded.

"He makes excuses for her. He's having a hard time with this. You know?"

"I'll talk to him." I called him on Emily's cell phone. "Dr. Kirchoff says he can save my finger."

"That's a relief," he said.

"I'm scheduled for surgery at six. I have to be back by four. But it's one o'clock now so we decided to come back home. Can you meet us there?"

"Sure."

"How's Zeus?"

"He's scheduled for surgery at six, too."

"Oh. That's funny."

He didn't laugh. "I had to leave him there. He's still in shock. He was a handful. Thrashing around. They gave him something for the pain."

"Oh no. Poor baby." I sniffed. "Will he be okay?"

"We'll know more after the surgery."

Back at home Tod waited for us on the front porch. Venus lay at his feet. "Did the doctor's office notify the Silt police?" he asked.

"What? No. Why? Did Bickle call you?" His question confused me. I opened the gate.

"No," he said. "I was worried they would come and take her away from us."

Venus sat upright and sniffed the air. Her body trembled and her teeth chattered as I approached her. Her eyes rolled back. She stood and backed away.

"Tod," I said. "She's confused. She can't handle this."

"Let's go inside," he said.

As we headed upstairs to the kitchen Emily explained, "Dr. Kirchoff doesn't have to report this. It's not technically a dog bite. Mom stuck her hands in Venus's mouth."

He looked me. "That's what you said earlier. What happened?"

I perched on the chair at the kitchen counter and began with, "Eddie showed up here again this morning and she lost her mind." I explained what happened as far as I knew.

"Goddammit," he fumed. "Eddie was down here on Friday. Now again this morning? Damn right it was no accident. We're getting a lawyer and we're going after these assholes."

"No. We're not," I said. "We have to let her go, Tod. She's sick. She's suffering. You saw what happened when she saw me." Tears slipped out.

He shook his head. "We can try another medication. Dr. Price said so."

"No. This is different. She didn't bite Zeus in the neck this time. She tried to kill him. She would have if I wasn't here. She didn't know who he was. She didn't know me. Her mental illness has progressed."

He turned away in tears. "So they won. They tormented her until they drove her insane."

I broke down. When I could speak again, I said, "Nobody won. This is a tragedy. She can't cope with the harassment anymore." I sniffed. "Hell, I don't know if I can."

"That's exactly my point. We'll get a lawyer. We'll get the harassment to stop."

"Tod, forget about the neighbors for a minute. Think about Venus. She's not happy here anymore. Don't tell me you haven't noticed. Whenever we take her camping she's a different dog."

"Right. We have to find a way to deal with the harassment."

"You're forgetting something. Venus has a serious mental illness. She's a dog. Zeus has endured the same negative energy. The same harassment. But he didn't flip out. She did."

"So we can try new medication. Give it couple months."

"Dad," Emily spoke up. "We can't trust her with Kaley and Henry anymore. She can't go near Zeus. She can't even handle being around Mom."

"We just need to isolate her for a little while," he said.

"Is that really what you want for her? You want to drug her into a stupor and keep her away from everyone she loves?" I wrapped my arms around him. "Please. Think about Venus. Think about her at Meadow Lake. She's happy there. We can't release her into the wild. But we *can* set her soul free. No more drugs. No more torment." We held onto each other and wept.

My surgery went well. Dr. Kirchoff pinned my finger back together and cleaned out the puncture wound on the other finger. Emily and I arrived back home around 8:30 p.m. with a box of dressings and special bandage goop. The bandages on my hands looked like white catcher's mitts.

Venus jumped up and down behind the porch gate, whining and yelping. Her anxiety level was off the charts. My heart ached. I wanted to go to her and soothe her pain. But the minute she sniffed my bandages she trembled. Her feet dropped to the porch deck and she cowered.

I looked at Emily. "I'm the only one who understands what she's going through. But there's nothing I can do to help her."

We retreated inside. I found Zeus in my office, laid out on the rug. He lifted his head when I walked in. *There you are. Finally. Pet me.* I crumpled to the floor and buried my face in his neck, too tired to cry. "I'm so sorry." He sniffed my bandages, groaned, and dropped his head on the floor. "We'll be okay Zeus. Get some rest."

I joined Tod and Emily upstairs in the kitchen. "Will Zeus be okay?" I asked.

"I think so," Tod said. "Dr. Landers is an amazing surgeon. Zeus had 18 stitches. There were no internal injuries. He got lucky. You really did save his life."

I sighed. "Thank God. At least we don't lose two dogs in all this."

Emily said, "It's getting late. I'm exhausted. I need to pick up the kids."

"Tell Carol thank you. We love her," I said. "Kiss the kids for me."

"She will babysit as much as we need her," she said. "You better get some rest. When that local anesthetic wears off you're gonna be in a world of hurt."

"Okay." We hugged. "Love you."

Tod poured two shots of tequila and set one on the counter in front of me. I sipped mine. He polished his off. "I talked to Dr. Landers when I picked up Zeus."

"About Venus."

He nodded. "You're right. The disease has progressed. We don't have any way of knowing how much she's suffering. Dr. Landers said once the disease progresses the dog can be fine one minute and confused the next. We could sedate her with more drugs but it's like you said, it's a quality of life issue. Mental anguish is just that—anguish."

I emptied my shot glass.

"I just want you to know I thought it through," he said. "We have to set her free."

I leaned my elbows on the counter and rested my head against the palms of my catcher's mitts. "I'm on emotional overload. My fingers are broken. My dogs are broken. My heart is broken. I need to go lie down."

"One more thing," Tod said. "The neighbors."

"Oh please. I beg you. I don't even want to think about them."

"Neither do I. But we have to. The harassment won't stop even after Venus is gone."

"Probably not."

"Remember earlier when I asked you if the Silt police were notified?"

I pushed my shot glass toward him.

He poured two more shots. "Irma asked me if we called the police."

"Oh no," I groaned. "She and Joe both asked if the dogs attacked me. What did you say?"

"I told her we didn't. She got pretty indignant and insisted it's the law. I changed the subject. Then when I brought Zeus home about an hour ago, I saw her talking to Margie and Daryl."

"Ohmygod. You think they're gonna come after Zeus next." I shook my head. "I'll get a letter from Dr. Landers to vouch for Zeus's sanity."

"Maybe I should go ahead and report it to the police."

"No way. She didn't attack me. She didn't bite me. I shoved my hands in her mouth. It's none of their goddamn business."

"They might make it their business."

"Fuck 'em all. Let 'em come after me."

"They will."

Zeus and I slept all morning on Tuesday. Tod took Venus to the office. By mid-afternoon my curiosity beckoned me to the video surveillance server. I instinctively knew something about the incident was different. In my heart there was no doubt we had to set her free from her mental anguish. I was there. I felt it. I knew her brain had snapped. Because of everything we had learned about CCD, everything we had been through with her, I needed to see what triggered it. I pulled up the replay of Monday morning. The resolution on the front porch camera was the best of all of them, and the closest range.

Zeus was asleep on the front porch when Venus went out at 9:00 a.m. She did her business in the yard and climbed onto the wicker glider. After about ten minutes, Zeus walked around back, through the dog door and disappeared into the garage. Did he sense something in her energy? We'll never know. Maybe he was just eager to go to Dogland, which he knew would happen soon.

Eddie appeared in the front yard about ten o'clock. He sniffed around the flower garden and peed on the roses. Venus was on her feet and barking. Then he did a stupid thing. He dashed up to the porch, put his front feet on the bottom rail, and snarled at her. Her chest slammed against the railing with the ferocity of a mama grizzly. It looked like it knocked the wind out of her for a split second. Eddie bolted toward the driveway and ducked between the camper and Hugo. From the camera angle, which was about the same as her perspective, he simply vanished. She jumped around, barking. Her head darted back and forth, searching for him.

Right then Zeus appeared around the corner from the side porch, no doubt to see what all the fuss was about. His timing was deadly. Venus turned sharply. The instant he caught her eye, she snapped. The moment was visible on camera. Her head rolled back, she reared up like a horse, and lunged. Poor Zeus panicked. Instead of backing up, he tried to turn around and got wedged between the glider and the railing. She landed on his back and knocked him down. He used all his strength to crawl toward the side porch with the full weight of her on his back. His spiked collar bought him precious time as she tried to sink her teeth into his neck. For a couple seconds they disappeared out of camera range.

The video from the side yard camera showed them rolling off the side porch onto the grass. Zeus landed on his back. She pinned him down. That's when I appeared. All of that occurred in less than three minutes.

It was clear what had happened. When Eddie jumped up on the railing and snarled he became an aggressive intruder—a threat—which put her into the red zone. When he bolted, she lost sight of him. Because Zeus was in the garage, she had probably forgotten he was even outside. She had been conditioned from Chucky letting his dog run loose in our yard to expect the intruder to return. Zeus was in the wrong place at the wrong time. As I suspected, she thought he was Eddie.

I focused on the moment her brain snapped, when her head rolled back and she reared up. I re-played it over and over. She had never done that before. It confirmed everything I had sensed when I was in the middle of it.

After work Tod took Venus to Dogland, then they went to the vet. I wanted to be there but she couldn't handle being near me. I couldn't even say goodbye.

Carol called while Tod was gone. "I know Tod is at the vet with Venus. I figured you might need a friend."

"With every fiber of my being I know this is the right thing to do," I said. "But it still hurts like hell."

We cried and talked and laughed a little.

When Tod returned I could tell he needed to talk.

I hugged him. "I'm so sorry you had to go through this alone."

"Dr. Landers talked me through it. He understands what we're going through."

"I know he does," I said. "Carol called." I told him about our phone call. "She got me through it."

"Oh God." He wiped away tears. "Everything happened so fast. She was doing so well."

"She was drugged," I said. "And the drug worked. Until it didn't anymore. Then she snapped. I think her mental illness was worse than any of us realized."

"I just wish …." He hesitated, then said, "Oh, never mind."

"What? What do you wish?"

"I don't know." He sighed. "I wish there was more we could've done."

"We ended her suffering."

He nodded. "Dr. Landers said we did everything we could. He said he doesn't know too many people who would've had the patience to do what we did. At least we gave Venus a good life."

I smiled. "We gave her the best damn life a dog could ask for."

Chapter 37 - Zeus

For the first two days Zeus stayed downstairs, mostly in my office. By the door. His escape route. Whenever he got up and moved into the hallway or foyer he stopped and peeked around the corner—just in case.

"I'm pretty sure he thinks Venus is upstairs," I told Tod.

"He'll figure it out. He's still really groggy."

Of course we were right. Zeus was the next target. We didn't even have time to grieve. They used poor, old Irma Nossie to deliver the message to us. When I went out to get the mail on Thursday afternoon, she stood at her back fence waiting for me.

"Peggy! Come over here," she hollered.

I crossed the alley. "What's up?"

"You poor thing. How are your hands?"

"It's my fingers. They'll be fine."

"How are your dogs doing?"

"Well, Venus is dead. And Zeus is recovering from surgery."

She put her hand over her heart. "Oh my goodness. What happened?"

"We put her down. She had a mental disorder."

She raised her eyebrows. "You know the neighbors have been talking to me."

"I just bet they have," I snapped. "Let me guess. Margie and Daryl and Mr. Fowler." Or Chucky as we knew him.

"They said your Venus was a vicious dog."

"No. She had a mental disorder. She was on medication."

"But she attacked you." She nodded at my bandage mitts.

"No. She didn't. She attacked Zeus. I stuck my hands in her mouth."

"They said she was dangerous. You shouldn't keep a dog like that."

"We didn't. She's dead."

"But you did keep her all this time. What if she attacked your grandkids?"

"She didn't."

"But she could have."

"Irma, she never looked cross-eyed at those kids. She never attacked a human."

"Well you're just lucky."

"Oh." I clenched my teeth.. "Is that what I am?"

"Mr. Fowler said those dogs have fought before. He heard them."

"He doesn't know what he's talking about."

"He said you wrote about it on the Internet."

I rolled my eyes. "And he's exaggerating what I wrote. Look, I don't think we owe you or anyone else in this neighborhood an explanation or apology. Venus was mentally ill and now she's dead. Period. End of story."

She tossed her head. "I have to say I'm shocked that Tod would let you do such a thing."

I let go a bitter laugh. "What? Take care of sick dog?"

"You put a lot of people in danger," she scolded.

"Did anyone get hurt?"

"You did."

"And that's my problem."

"Well, what about Zeus?"

"The vet said he'll recover."

"But—he lived with that dog."

"Her name was Venus. You liked her. You said she was a good dog."

She was taken aback. "Well I didn't know she was a vicious dog. I guess I'm lucky she didn't attack me."

I pointed my bandage mitt at her. "You need to get something straight, Irma. Venus was not a vicious dog. And I don't appreciate you spreading false rumors."

"I'm only telling you what they told me."

"Then show us some respect and don't repeat it." I turned away. "I need to go lie down. I have a headache."

"Wait! I'm not finished," she called out.

"Well I am," I muttered. I took two steps toward the driveway.

"They said Zeus is a vicious dog, too, and he should be put down."

I gritted my teeth and spun around so stiffly I thought my knees would buckle. Then I growled, "You tell them they will have to kill me first."

"Oh my goodness." She put her hand over her heart again. "I think we all need to sit down and talk about this." She took a deep breath. "What do you say Joe and I have a little get together and you can all work out your differences."

"I'd sooner burn in hell." I walked away.

"Wait!" she cried.

I waved my arms and kept going. I called Tod at the office and warned him.

"At least they didn't send the cops," he said.

"I can't believe they dragged Irma Nossie into this."

"Sounds like she was an eager participant."

"Look, I know they can't do anything about Zeus. But they are going to try. I'm just warning you."

"And we expected this. So we'll deal with it like we do everything else with these morons."

"I'll get a letter from Dr. Landers."

Zeus's fog lifted significantly in the afternoon. Tod grilled turkey burgers on the tree-house deck. The aroma lured Zeus out of hiding. He climbed the stairs and joined us.

"Hey Zeuser. Welcome back to the land of the living." I leaned over and hugged and kissed him. "I hate to be the one to tell you this, but the lunatics are still running the asylum. Nothing's changed." I stood upright. "Oh by the way, watch out for old Irma. She thinks you're a vicious dog."

Zeus lifted his nose and drooled. *Do I smell turkey burgers?* Tod laughed.

Venus died between 6:00 and 6:30 p.m. That evening, two days after her death, at a few minutes after six, Zeus picked up his stuffed bunny and loped into our bedroom. He sat on the rug and whined. I abandoned my turkey burger. As I walked through the bedroom doorway a low hum rose from deep inside his chest. He rested like a sphinx. As he slowly raised his head he opened his mouth and howled long and loud.

I collapsed on the rug next to him. Tod showed up. Zeus howled again. And again. Tears saturated the fur under his eyes. "He's grieving." I whispered.

He chewed on his stuffed bunny and whined. *I miss her.*

Tod sniffed. "Just when I thought I couldn't cry anymore."

"Don't you see? He loved her," I said. "I never knew for sure. Now we do. He loved Venus."

To drive home his message, every evening between 6:00 and 6:30 p.m. for almost two months, Zeus sat on the rug in our bedroom and howled. *We miss you!*

Epi-dogue

"Sometimes paranoia's just having all the facts." — William S. Burroughs

This quote from my research on bullies and harassment became the foundation for my healthy paranoia. The mistake we had made with the neighbors and the cops was thinking they would somehow all come to their senses and behave like rational human beings. Yet nothing in my research or our experience backed up such a naïve assumption.

After Venus's final breakdown and death, the neighbors made sure we got the message. They thought Zeus was a vicious dog and we should get rid of him. Therefore, we presumed Daryl, Chucky, or Patsy (or all three) would file a vicious dog complaint against Zeus with the police department. Based on past experience, we supposed Chief Bickle would respond to their complaint. Even though he had no legal grounds, that hadn't stopped him in the past.

In a pre-emptive move, I submitted a voluntary written statement to Chief Bickle explaining the incident between Venus and Zeus, along with a letter from Dr. Landers stating Zeus had never been diagnosed with aggression and he wasn't on medication for behavioral problems. Bickle called Tod and said the information had cleared up any questions about the incident. I was spared the agony of interrogation.

The harassment reached a fevered pitch. Daryl, Chucky, and Patsy were out to get us any way they could. They rang the doorbell and prowled around the property after dark, so we installed motion sensor lights everywhere. They followed me when I walked Zeus, especially after dark. I felt like I was under attack. On the surface their actions seemed random—harassment for the sake of harassment. But I knew better. I felt certain a vicious dog compliant had been filed against Zeus, but my statement and Dr. Landers' letter had quashed any basis for Chief Bickle to pursue it. In frustration they had taken matters into their own hands. They intended to harass us into a confrontation and provoke Zeus until he snapped.

My healthy paranoia was validated ten days after Venus's breakdown. Chucky arrived at our house while Zeus and I were in the front yard. He told me Zeus was a vicious dog and they were going to make sure he was destroyed. He said he would not stop following me or coming over to our house until they got rid of him. I ordered him to leave but he refused. He finally left after Zeus and I fled indoors. I filed a complaint but Bickle didn't do anything. On the advice of a friend I filed another complaint in district court and asked for a protection order against Chucky. Our logs and videos proved quite damning. A temporary protection order was granted four weeks after Venus's death.

One month later Chucky faced me in court. Under the judge's skillful line of questioning, he revealed his deep-seeded contempt and hatred for me—and he didn't like my blog either. In legal terms, he hung himself. The judge made the protection order permanent.

The protection order sent shock waves through the neighborhood. Our popularity sunk to a new low and has never recovered. What Bickle had said about all the neighbors hating us eventually came true. I wish I could say the harassment stopped. But it didn't. Bickle is still Chief of Police. Minnifield is still the mayor. We hired a lawyer. Gradually the incidents have subsided but there's no sign this is a lasting peace.

As I write this in January 2013, Zeus is still with us. He is 12 years old, which is ancient for a Malamute. We feel very fortunate. The combination of nerve damage from the injury to his groin, arthritis, and old age has slowed him down considerably but his kind and gentle spirit remains steadfast as ever. For his own protection we never leave him outside when we're not home.

As I expected, his life without Venus has been less stressful. But he does miss her. He shows a definite preference and fondness for female Yellow Labs. Evidently it was the Lab in her he loved. More than anything, we sensed he missed their canine companionship. When I looked back on Zeus with Venus and our other dog pairs in the past, I appreciated the importance of canine companionship. Dogs are, after all, pack animals. Love grows between humans through companionship. Companionship and love with other humans gives us a feeling of security. It's the same with dogs.

Finding a suitable companion for a senior dog is a challenge under the best circumstances and Zeus was a special case. He was turning ten years old and recovering from serious trauma and injury. We didn't know how many more months or years we had left with him. Even though we wanted to make his life as easy as possible, we had a slight dilemma. Zeus was lonely and we weren't ready for another dog. Zeus loves puppies but we knew he couldn't handle a puppy crawling all over him and pestering him to play on a daily basis. Adopting an adult dog didn't seem like a good idea either. None of us—especially Zeus—could handle the emotional hurdles that come with a shelter dog. Plus we had an awful lot of baggage for a shelter dog to overcome: kids, cats, a senior dog, and an environment of harassment with neighbors and cops who could not be trusted. It hardly seemed fair, or humane, to put an insecure shelter dog into the middle of what was still a very tense situation.

While we wallowed in angst, a little Chihuahua Dachshund named Pepé noticed the hole Venus had left in our lives and jumped through it. Pepé had shown up at Emily's house one day the previous year. We had tried to find his owner but no one claimed him, so he stayed with her and the kids. Around the time of Venus's death, Pepé entered his bratty phase. He was getting way too much affection and not enough exercise and discipline. Between work, two kids, and two senior Huskies, Emily didn't have time to walk him. Tod and I started taking him with us to Dogland. Then we let him stay at our house for more training. Zeus got a kick out of training him. It gave him a job to do. When Pepé went back to Emily and the kids, Zeus missed him. Emily confessed that Pepé was calmer and happier at our house. By Thanksgiving he moved in.

Pepé adores Zeus. He treats him like a god. They share a friendship, a mutual respect, which has been remarkably healing for Zeus. In return Pepé, who used to be anxious and fearful, has learned from Zeus how to be calm.

Last summer we added another dog to our pack, a one-year-old Reindeer Chihuahua named Lupe Lu. Pepé had way too much energy for Zeus and needed a playmate to wrestle with and play tag. Together Pepé and Lupe Lu are cute as bug's teeth and full of mischief. Because they have each other they never pester Zeus. He loves to watch them play and sometimes joins in the fun. He feeds off their energy which keeps him from fixating on his aches and pains and the limitations of growing older.

For hard core, big dog lovers like us, Chihuahuas are a whole new learning experience. They are amazing athletes and incredibly brave. Life with these clown dogs, as I call them, is like a circus at times. They keep us laughing.

My right ring finger has healed. It's slightly misshapen and the knuckle at the fingertip doesn't bend so I will never forget her, as if I would have if there wasn't any permanent damage. Venus was, and is, unforgettable. Her legend lives on.

Last summer when I was talking to a Dogland friend about this book, she said, "Everyone has a Venus story. You should include some of those."

"This is Venus's story," I said.

Venus definitely made an impact on everyone she met. Reactions to her final breakdown and death ranged from sympathy and support to criticism and blame, and of course more harassment. As we sifted through the process we discovered, in spite of our candidness about her mental illness, Venus was very much misunderstood.

Canine compulsive disorder is a mental disease. Minus any other complications, such as physical illness or aggression, it is treatable with prescription drugs. Along with treatment, human commitment to rehabilitation is the key to a longer, fuller life for the dog. A diagnosis of CCD is not a death sentence.

In January 2010, the Cummings School of Veterinary Medicine, in conjunction with the University of Massachusetts Medical School and the Massachusetts Institute of Technology, identified the canine gene "chromosome 7 locus" as an indicator of susceptibility to compulsive disorder, in breeds carrying that gene. Breeds at risk for CCD include German Shepherds, Dobermans, Border Collies, Jack Russell Terriers, Great Danes, Retrievers and English Bull-Terriers. The discovery of chromosome 7 will eventually lead to the development of genetic tests that will enable early intervention, treatment, or prevention of compulsive disorders in high-risk canines. Perhaps one day breeders will be able to isolate the chromosome and avoid adding it to their bloodlines.

In Venus's case the aggression was an overwhelming obstacle to her long term stability. On the basis of our experience, I believe when CCD is accompanied by aggression there is a greater chance the disease will progress. Aggression is caused by triggers and it's impossible to remove all triggers from the dog's life, especially if the dog has CCD. The provoking and harassment from the neighbors created the anxiety that triggered Venus's aggression. Removing her from their negative energy worked only because it was temporary. Aggression was a relatively minor aspect of her disease. Once the triggers were gone it disappeared like magic. However her major issue on a daily basis was coping with obsession and anxiety caused by CCD. Even if we had moved away from the neighborhood, thus removing the harassment that triggered her aggression, Venus would have found new obsessions and anxieties which could have led to triggers and then further aggression. We will never know for certain because none of that happened. However, I did keep copious diaries and logs during her illness, plus hundreds of photos and hours of video. In studying her behavior an unmistakable pattern emerged: obsession followed by extreme anxiety, if unchecked, peaked with aggression. It was a pattern we couldn't control and its progression toward a total breakdown was inevitable. But patterns are only visible in hindsight and not in the experience of living through them.

We packed a lot of life experience into our four years and four months with Venus. Her sweetness and sense of humor were easy to love. Though it was sometimes difficult to deal with, I admired her ferociousness. She possessed the power to control any situation at any time. She was the bravest dog I have ever known. I always felt safe with her. The sudden loss of my bodyguard was a jolt. Until I realized that because of Venus I had learned more than I ever wanted to know about bullies and harassment. Bullies come from all walks of life. They can be individuals, public officials, groups, or corporations. Whatever their disguise, bullies have an agenda and will stop at nothing to achieve it. It wasn't a lesson I wanted to learn. But it was the lesson I needed to learn. When confronted by a bully Venus stood her ground with bravery and, if necessary, ferociousness. She led me through the fire and I found the strength to push back against the bullies and reclaim my territory.

During her treatment and rehabilitation I had bought into the notion that Venus was a lucky dog. I believed she came to me because I was the only one who could help her. In my human condition, full of the selfish arrogance that afflicts us all in varying degrees, I saw myself as her savior. She needed me. We humans have a tendency to think we have everything figured out ahead of time.

With the passage of time I came to understand I was the lucky one. When I let her in, when I allowed myself to love her in spite of her flaws, she changed my life. Venus came to me because I needed her. Her strength, her bravery, and yes even her ferociousness, are now part of me.

"It is true that whenever a person loves a dog he derives great power from it." — Old Seneca Tribal Chief

http://www.crazy-bitch-book.com/

Acknowledgements

With thanks.

To the dogs who befriended Venus in life and followed her into spirit, with fondest memories: Moose, Yogi, Sheva, Scruffy, Fern.

To my family, Tod, Ema, Hailey and Bodi for loving Venus enough to be the dog she needed to be and allowed her to change their lives forever.

To Dr. Cheryl Pearce and Dr. Peter Langegger and everyone at Divide Creek Animal Hospital whose guidance and support gave me the courage to find a way to give Venus a normal life.

To Karen Johnson, Anthony Benham, and Seikh (Fern), who saw the big picture and believed in Venus, sometimes more than I did.

To friends who listened, offered advice and support, and ultimately trusted my ability tp test the limits of the canine psyche and the human experience and live to tell about it: Meg and Don Angelow, Lisa Bracken, John Carpenter and Ripley, Larry Dragon, Ann Ramsey and Honey, Bev Thompson.

To our Dogland friends who looked past the labels into the heart of a dog: Rebecca, Jerry, Samantha and Jessica Kidd (Yogi), Bill and Susan Harding and Olie and Sadie, Jodi Allbaugh and Hunter, George Doxey (Moose), Karen Sedilla and Sammy (Sheva), John and Polar, Kim and Whitney, Jim and Jobe (Scruffy).

To Natalie Collins and Garth McCarty for deliverance from evil.

About the Author

Peggy Tibbetts is the author of two middle grade novels, *Letters to Juniper* and *The Road to Weird;* two young adult novels, *PFC Liberty Stryker* and *Hurricane Katrina;* and a suspense novel for adults, *Rumors of War.* She has worked as a professional editor and is a fervent blogger.

Letters to Juniper was a finalist in the Colorado Book Awards.

She enjoys hiking, biking, skiing, and camping with her husband, Tod and beloved dogs, Zeus, Pepé, and Lupe Lu, in the mountains of western Colorado, where they live.

www.ingramcontent.com/pod-product-compliance
Lightning Source LLC
Chambersburg PA
CBHW060238050426
42448CB00009B/1494

* 9 7 8 1 9 4 0 0 1 6 0 1 6 *